How Policy Shapes Politics

STUDIES IN POSTWAR AMERICAN POLITICAL DEVELOPMENT
Steven Teles

Series Editor
Series Board Members
Paul Frymer Jennifer Hochschild Desmond King Sanford Levinson Taeku
Lee Shep Melnick Paul Pierson John Skrentny Adam Sheingate Reva Siegel
Thomas Sugrue

The Delegated Welfare State: Medicare, Markets, and the Governance of
Social Policy
Kimberly J. Morgan and Andrea Louise Campbell

Rule and Ruin: The Downfall of Moderation and the Destruction of the
Republican Party, From Eisenhower to the Tea Party
Geoffrey Kabaservice

Engines of Change: Party Factions in American Politics, 1868–2010
Daniel DiSalvo

Follow the Money: How Foundation Dollars Change Public School Politics
Sarah Reckhow

The Allure of Order: High Hopes, Dashed Expectations, and the Troubled
Quest to Remake American Schooling
Jal Mehta

Rich People's Movements: Grassroots Campaigns to Untax the One Percent
Isaac William Martin

The Outrage Industry: Political Opinion Media and the New Incivility
Jeffrey M. Berry and Sarah Sobieraj

Artists of the Possible: Governing Networks and American Policy since 1945
Matt Grossman

The First Civil Right: Race and the Rise of the Carceral State
Naomi Murakawa

How Policy Shapes Politics

Rights, Courts, Litigation, and the
Struggle Over Injury Compensation

JEB BARNES

AND THOMAS F. BURKE

OXFORD
UNIVERSITY PRESS

OXFORD
UNIVERSITY PRESS

Oxford University Press is a department of the University of Oxford.
It furthers the University's objective of excellence in research, scholarship,
and education by publishing worldwide.

Oxford   New York

Auckland   Cape Town   Dar es Salaam   Hong Kong   Karachi
Kuala Lumpur   Madrid   Melbourne   Mexico City   Nairobi
New Delhi   Shanghai   Taipei   Toronto

With offices in

Argentina   Austria   Brazil   Chile   Czech Republic   France   Greece
Guatemala   Hungary   Italy   Japan   Poland   Portugal   Singapore
South Korea   Switzerland   Thailand   Turkey   Ukraine   Vietnam

Published in the United States of America by
Oxford University Press
198 Madison Avenue, New York, NY 10016

Library of Congress Cataloging-in-Publication Data

Barnes, Jeb, author.
How policy shapes politics : rights, courts, litigation, and the struggle over injury
compensation / Jeb Barnes, Thomas F. Burke.
pages cm
ISBN 978–0–19–975611–7 (hardback : alk. paper)   1. Torts—United States.   2. Damages—United
States.   3. Compensation (Law)—United States.   4. Products liability—Asbestos—United States.
5. Vaccines—Government policy—United States.   6. Personal injuries—United States.   7. Disability
insurance—Law and legislation—United States.   I. Burke, Thomas Frederick, author.
II. Title.
KF1250.B37 2015
346.7303—dc23
2014009275

3 5 7 9 8 6 4 2
Printed in the United States of America
on acid-free paper

Contents

List of Figures and Tables

Figures

Tables

Acknowledgments

Not to be too dramatic about it, but fate, along with some common interests, seems to have brought us together. Although separated by a few years, we were both students of Bob Kagan and Nelson Polsby at UC Berkeley, and while at Berkeley we both became fascinated by the intersection of law and public policy. Then after graduation, again separated by a couple of years, we both did stints as Robert Wood Johnson Foundation Health Policy Scholars, at Berkeley's School of Public Health. (Jeb arrived just as Tom left, and literally took Tom's chair, from which both enjoyed a panoramic view of San Francisco Bay.) We share an interest in the politics of policymaking, but we also have been deeply influenced by law and society scholarship that seeks to study law as it exists outside of formal institutions. It is perhaps not surprising, then, that we are constantly working on parallel tracks, asking related questions from slightly different angles. Following our time as Robert Wood Johnson Scholars we found our intellectual paths had converged yet again. We had both spent several years studying the politics of policies that address injury and loss, and we began to think about what the development of these programs reveals about the influence of courts and litigation on politics. So, in addition to our other projects, we decided to join forces and write this book. Along the way, we have learned a lot from each other and have become good friends.

During our journey we have accumulated a number of debts of gratitude. It is our pleasure to acknowledge them here—as well as to absolve anyone who helped of any mistakes that remain in the final version of this work. For starters we would like to thank everyone at Oxford University Press. Special thanks are owed to Steven Teles and David McBride, who saw the promise of this project and exercised great patience in waiting for its completion. We would also like to thank the anonymous reviewers for their exceptional comments. A special debt is owed to Chuck Epp, Sean

Farhang, Keith Whittington, and Susan Silbey, whose wonderful comments pushed our thinking and made the manuscript much better. Both Jeb and Tom thank Parker Hevron and Kendell Bianchi for their research assistance.

Jeb would like to thank his colleagues at the University of Southern California, who offered him many opportunities to present his work and learn from their comments, including a very early presentation of the data at the inaugural meeting of the Raw Jell-O Group and several chances to present chapters in various graduate seminars. They include, in alphabetical order, Tony Bertelli, Ann Crigler, Christian Grose, Ange-Marie Hancock, Jane Junn, Jeff Sellers, and Nick Weller. Jeb also thanks Alison Gash and Steven Wasby for their insights.

Tom thanks his colleagues and students at the Political Science Department of Wellesley College, who provided a nourishing intellectual environment for both research and teaching. He specifically thanks Hahrie Han, Roxanne Euben, and Miya Woolfalk for helpful comments at a faculty seminar. Tom is grateful to participants in a seminar at Brigham Young University's Department of Political Science and the Boston Area Research Workshop on History, Institutions and Politics for helpful critical feedback at early stages in the development of the book, and to Anna Kirkland, at the University of Michigan, who shares Tom's fascination with vaccine injury politics and provided several helpful observations. He thanks his Boston comrades in the study of the politics of public policy, especially his friends Martin Levin and Shep Melnick. Tom is grateful to have had the friendship of Adrienne Asch, who through many long conversations over the years made him reconsider his approach to just about everything, including disability.

We also thank all of the people who agreed to be interviewed for this project. An office or library can be a dangerous place to view the world. It was always our pleasure to get out in the field and talk to people who are directly engaged in the ongoing battles over injury compensation policy. We cannot thank them enough for their generous willingness to share their time and insights.

We both thank our mutual mentor Bob Kagan. It is not an exaggeration to say this book would not have been possible without his ideas and his steady influence in our careers. We are proud to be students of Bob—"S.O.B.s."

Most of all, we are grateful to our families. Tom thanks his fantastic wife Ying, who came into his life midway through the making of this book and has enriched it ever since. Jeb thanks his loving wife, Annie, and two sons, Alexander and Ryan, whose unflagging support, kindness, and patience continues to amaze and delight him. It is to our families that we dedicate this book.

I

Introduction

The Question

Litigation is everywhere in American society, casting its long shadow over businesses, schools, public spaces, private lives, and nearly every aspect of government and policymaking. In recent memory, litigation has transformed how Americans finance election campaigns, how they buy health insurance, whom they can marry; it has even decided a presidential election. It has been central to struggles over civil rights, abortion, regulating tobacco, drawing electoral districts, cleaning up the environment, reforming the criminal justice system, making society more accessible to people with disabilities, and foreign policy matters such as the detention of "enemy combatants." Not every political question in the United States becomes a judicial question, as Alexis de Tocqueville claimed about 1830s America, but a remarkable share does (Silverstein 2009; Derthick 2005; Sabel and Simon 2004; Sandler and Schoenbrod 2003; Kagan 2001; Feeley and Rubin 1998; Melnick 1983, 1994; Barnes and Burke 2006, 2012). According to scholars, the United States has become a "litigation state" (Farhang 2010) in which "juridification" (Silverstein 2009), "litigious policies" (Burke 2002), "adversarial legalism" (Kagan 2001), "legalization" (Sutton et al. 1994), and "legalized accountability" (Epp 2009) proliferate.

However you label it—and we will discuss our preferred label below— the expansion of legal rights and litigation evokes deep ambivalence. In the United States, the mythic qualities of law, associated with heroic lawyers such as Thurgood Marshall and Perry Mason, landmark cases such as *Brown v. Board of Education*, and cultural touchstones such as *To Kill a Mockingbird*, are a familiar aspect of the popular culture. In this view, law is majestic and godlike, transcending the pettiness of everyday life and the partisanship of politics (Ewick and Silbey 1998). In the words of Judith Shklar (1964: 111), law "aims at justice, while politics only looks to expediency. The former is neutral and objective, the latter the uncontrolled child of competing interests and ideologies. Justice is thus not only the policy of legalism, it is a policy superior to and unlike any other." Steeped in this view, lawyers and legal scholars often celebrate litigation as a mechanism for vindicating and expanding individual rights, imposing accountability for the negligence and heedlessness of corporations and governmental agencies, and checking private influence on governmental rule-makers (Crohley 2008; Barnes 2009; Bogus 2001; Mather 1998).

Yet the deployment of courts, rights, and litigation to address social problems also generates powerful criticisms. Some see litigation and the invocation of rights as a rupture of community order, a sign of social breakdown (Engel 1984). For them, increasing reliance on courts, rights, and litigation is an indication of the decline of American civilization. The "common good," they contend, has been eclipsed by the litigious society (Howard 1995); Americans have lapsed into a "culture of complaint" (Hughes 1994) in which the virtues of stoicism and grit have been replaced by the entitled whines of victims (Cole 2007). Policy analysts and political scientists, less enamored with the rhetoric of moral decline, have sought to document the more tangible downsides of litigation. They warn that it is far less efficient and predictable than other modes of policymaking, such as social insurance programs (e.g., Carroll et al. 2005; Kagan 2001; Rabkin 1989; Schuck 1986; Melnick 1983; Bardach and Kagan 1982; Horowitz 1977), and that it often leaves those harmed by violations of law to "lump" it (Abel 1987; Bumiller 1988; Haltom and McCann 2004). Litigation in this view fails both ordinary citizens, who cannot afford to use it, and organizations, which cannot efficiently plan for it.

The claims most often made about the rising prominence of courts, rights and litigation, then, tend to concern its potential cultural, administrative and economic downsides. In this book, however, we do not seek to weigh the economic costs and benefits of litigation, or its relationship to various cultural vices or virtues. Instead this book probes the *political* effects of what some have called the judicialization of public policy. To put it more precisely, we assess how the design of public policy—around courts and litigation on one hand, or through agency implementation on the other—shapes politics. We ask questions like these: *Do "judicialized" and "non-judicialized" policies differ in the interests they mobilize? The coalitions they generate? The way problems are framed? What kinds of issues do they highlight? What issues do they obscure?*

Although these questions may not be as prominent as the moral and economic concerns that are frequently voiced in popular debates about law, they also tap into deep-seated concerns about using courts, rights, and litigation to make social policy. Some worry that the appeal of litigation will divert interest groups and social movements with limited time and resources from purportedly more consequential and legitimate modes of political advocacy, such as grassroots mobilizing, coalition building, and lobbying (Rosenberg 1991). Moreover, reliance on litigation and the pursuit of legal rights is said to be self-reinforcing because it creates a template for political action that frames grievances in legalistic terms (Silverstein 2009: 69; see generally Pierson 2004). This can choke off the pursuit of comprehensive social programs, even when litigation has produced mixed policy results, as legal doctrine and individual rights displace alternative approaches to social problems. From this vantage, litigation is not only ineffective as a policy matter—a "hollow hope"—but also politically counter-productive, acting either as "flypaper" that traps groups in the courts or as a lightning rod that attracts powerful backlash and hardens opposition (Rosenberg 1991; Klarman 1994, 2004; see also Forbath 1991). Litigation and the pursuit of individual rights, it also is claimed, privatizes social problems, framing them as discrete conflicts between individuals, thus obscuring the communal dimensions of social life. The individualization inherent in litigation creates a more fragmented, less communal polity that can fail to realize common interests (e.g., Tushnet 1984; Glendon 1987, 1991; Haltom and McCann 2004; Barnes 2011).

Concerns about the expansion of law seem particularly urgent at the moment in which we write, the early twenty-first century. In the United States, we live in an era when Congress has become increasingly dysfunctional (e.g., Mann and Ornstein 2012), making "Law's Allure" (the title of Gordon Silverstein's recent book on the risks of juridification) ever more alluring. The combination of tight budgetary constraints, party polarization, narrow majorities in Congress, and divided government create a policy vacuum that court-enforced rights can fill. Disgruntled interests may feel that litigation is their only viable option for pursuing their policy agendas; elected officials may be glad to have intractable political disputes resolved elsewhere and at the expense of private litigants (Farhang 2010; Silverstein 2009; Lovell 2003; Burke 2001; Kagan 2001; Barnes 1997; Graber 1993).

Beyond the United States, the growing significance of rights, courts, and litigation is even more apparent. Over the last two decades, a bevy of comparativists and international relations scholars have been document- ing rising levels of "judicialization" (Kapiszewski, Silverstein, and Kagan 2013; Ginsburg 2003; Hirschl 2004, 2008; Sweet 1999, 2000; Shapiro and Sweet 2002; Tate and Vallinder 1995), various types of "legalism" (Kelemen 2006, 2011; Bignami 2011; Kagan 1997, 2007), and "legalization" (Goldstein

et. al 2001) in other nations and at the international level. The judicialization of politics, Ran Hirschl claims, "is arguably one of the most significant
phenomena of late twentieth and early twenty-first century government"
(Hirschl 2008: 69). The global rise of judicial power reflects a variety of
possible factors, including the growth of transnational associations like the
European Union (Alter 2001; Kelemen 2009) and the expansion of international human rights institutions and organizations (Sikkink 2011; Goodale
and Merry 2007; see also Epp 1998). Whatever its causes, the rising prominence of rights, courts, and litigation in politics worldwide suggests that
scholars and commentators will be increasingly drawn to studying the questions raised in this book.

Our Approach

The prominence of rights, courts, and litigation in social life makes its political effects a subject of great interest, but also a challenge to study. If law is "all
over," as one particularly influential article in sociolegal studies put it (Sarat
1990),[1] how do researchers figure out what law is doing? To date, those who
have been most interested in understanding what law does to politics have
focused mainly on a small number of dramatic cases in which courts took
center stage, usually through a ruling on the constitutionality of some statute
or executive action (e.g., Rosenberg 1991; Silverstein 2009). This approach
has yielded important insights into the potential political risks of relying on
rights, courts, and litigation, but it can be misleading for two reasons. First,
the literature's focus on high-profile constitutional cases may provide a distorted lens for viewing the effects of judicialization, which can take many
forms and arise in a variety of contexts. Second, by definition, claims about
the political effects of judicialization/juridification/legalization necessarily
imply that politics would have been different if rights, courts, and litigation
had not intervened or had intervened to a lesser degree. By not focusing more
explicitly on what social scientists call the "counter-factual"—what would
have happened in the absence of judicialization—the existing literature on
the political risks of litigation may overstate its actual impact.

Accordingly, we start with the assumption that the best way to understand
the political effects of judicialization/juridification/legalization, whether in
the United States or elsewhere, is through comparison, and so in this book we
compare the politics of policies that are structured around rights, courts, and
litigation with policies that do not have this structure. We focus on the field
of injury compensation, which, like many realms of American public policy
includes a vast array of policies of diverse design, some based on litigation,

others on regulation and social insurance. We first make our comparisons using a quantitative study of patterns of participation in congressional hearings on injury compensation policies, and then with three in-depth case studies.

What do we find? There are some twists and turns along the way, but we come to two fundamental conclusions. First, at least for the cases we study, many claims about the use of rights, courts, and litigation in politics seem overblown. We see, for example, little evidence that the allure of law traps activists in its spell, or that law-focused public policies are any more difficult to reform than their bureaucratic alternatives. In many respects, then, the politics of rights and litigation does not look much different from other forms of politics.

But secondly, we find support for some of the long-standing criticisms of rights, courts, and litigation voiced by theorists, commentators, and social scientists. By organizing social issues as disputes between parties, the use of litigation does seem to individualize politics in some of the ways they have suggested. Litigation assigns fault to specific entities, and creates a complex array of winners and losers on the ground. That over time creates a distinctively fractious politics, in which interest groups associated with plaintiffs and defendants fight not only each other but among themselves as well. This pattern is particularly pronounced when we compare it to the political trajectory of social insurance policies that compensate for injuries, especially our main comparison case, Social Security Disability Insurance. There we see moments of great contention, but long periods of relative peace, and greater solidarity among interests. The bottom line, we think, is that some of the critics of judicialization/juridification/legalization are onto something when they claim that the effect of litigation is to individualize conflict over social issues, and so generate a more divisive, fractious politics.

In attempting to uncover the political effects of rights, courts, and litigation, we encountered a series of conceptual obstacles, and alas, we must begin by describing those obstacles and what we have tried to do to get around them. Discussions of concepts can be dry and technical, but to understand how we frame the rest of the book, you must first understand the reasoning behind our conceptual choices. After addressing these conceptual issues, the remainder of the chapter explains our case selection, summarizes our findings in greater detail, and outlines the chapters that follow.

Key Concepts and Comparisons

Our first assumption is that the central question of this book—what are the political consequences of relying on rights, courts, and litigation to address social problems?—implies a comparison between the politics of "judicialization" and "non-judicialization," or to put it more simply, between "law" and "non-law." Defining "non-judicialization" or "non-law," however, is more difficult than you might think. In *Law's Allure*, Silverstein argues that "law is different," but different from what? What is the thing that "judicialization" "juridification," "legalization," and "legal rights" are being compared to?[2] One possibility is that a "judicialized" policy could be compared to some kind of "non-judicialized" one, but which kind? Is the normal baseline of politics legislative? Executive? Electoral? Social movement mobilization? Some combination? Or is the baseline no policy at all?[3] So we need to know: Different from what?

There is yet another problem here, one that points to the profusion of terms used in this literature. We worry that these terms—judicialization, juridification, legalization and so on—can obscure rather than sharpen our understanding of the relationship of law and politics. When scholars argue that "law is different," they undoubtedly mean something like: courts are different from agencies or legislatures. But of course agencies and legislatures also produce law, and agency decision-making is often highly litigious. Indeed, it is hard to imagine anything in American public policy that is not connected to law and the potential threat of litigation in some way. Perhaps this point is so simple that scholars assume their readers could understand that when they write "law" they mean the kind of law produced by courts, but they rarely define the boundary of their concepts, and this creates difficulties (Burke and Barnes 2009). For example, if "law" is made up of the doctrines that appellate courts propound, what do we do with trial court decisions, or even more importantly, the vast majority of legal claims that are disposed of or settled prior to trial? What about the ideas people have about legal rights, which may or may not have much to do with decisions that courts make? Are all these things part of what's different? Some conceptual openness about the scope of "juridification" or "judicialization" is probably inevitable given the complexity (and contested nature) of scholarly accounts of law and rights, and the decentralized processes through which they are given meaning, but we also want to have some sense of the boundaries of these terms.

To cut through this conceptual morass, from this point forward we generally avoid formulations in this book such as "judicialization," "juridification," and "legalization." We are just not confident about how these terms should be defined. Instead, we start from the assumption that courts, like legislatures and executive branch agencies, are policymakers, and so we reject the law/politics distinction that underlies so much commentary on litigation and rights. We operate within the tradition of "political jurisprudence" pioneered by Martin Shapiro (Shapiro 1964a, 1964b, 1966, 1968; see generally Gillman 2004), in which courts are considered comparable to other political institutions, but with their own tilts and tendencies,[4] and we heartily concur with Stuart Scheingold's insistence that *The Politics of Rights* (Scheingold 2004) be analyzed as a species of politics rather than a different kind of animal entirely. This leads us to use concepts that are comparative, but not based on static assumptions about essential features of law or courts.

Although originally designed to describe cross-national differences, we think Robert Kagan's typology of policymaking processes (1991, 2001) offers a productive response to the conceptual problems we have posed for studying within-country variation, both because it is reasonably well-defined and because it is explicitly comparative. (An added benefit of using Kagan's typology is avoiding the introduction of yet another set of terms to the already confusing lexicon of judicialization/juridification/legalization.) The typology of policymaking is set forth in Table 1.1. Each cell in the box represents an ideal-type of policymaking regime, which connotes a distinct form of authority for creating and implementing policy—in this book, injury compensation policy.

The horizontal axis is the level of *formality* in defining and determining the underlying claim, meaning the degree to which decision-makers use preexisting rules in resolving disputes. The use of rules in dispute resolution involves all the paraphernalia of legal processes: precedents, records, documents, and written procedures. Informal processes, for example the use of expert administrative judgment by the Federal Reserve Board to adjust interest rates, are not closely constrained by preexisting substantive rules; the underlying policy decisions are made based on the professional judgment of its members and staff.

Table 1.1 Four Modes of Policymaking (Kagan 2001)

Organization of Decision-Making Authority	Decision-Making Style	
	Informal	Formal
Hierarchical	Expert or political judgment	Bureaucratic legalism
Participatory	Negotiation/mediation	Adversarial legalism

On the *formal* side of the horizontal axis are *adversarial legalism* and *bureaucratic legalism*. Adversarial legalism involves formal but participatory structures, meaning that the parties to the underlying dispute drive the decision-making process. In adversarial legalism, parties dominate policy construction from the bottom up: they make policy by arguing over the meaning of substantive standards and procedural rules, the application of those rules to the decision at hand, and even the fairness of the relevant rules and procedures. In the formulation and implementation of policy under adversarial legal regimes everything is a matter of dispute, and all those affected by a decision are free to participate in the disputing process. There is an official decision-maker, but the decision-maker acts as a referee and so does not dominate the proceedings. Bureaucratic legalism, by contrast, is formal and hierarchical. It connotes a Weberian bureaucracy that centers on civil servants implementing formal rules from the top down, as in the case of social insurance programs in which government officials determine compensation according to preexisting medical criteria and payment schedules.

The structural differences between adversarial legalism and bureaucratic legalism correspond to different emphases in decision-making. In adversarial legalism, the decision-makers (judges and juries in the American civil litigation system) are not tightly bound to a centralized higher authority and so a premium is placed on particularized justice, tailoring decisions to specific circumstances. In the bureaucratic model, civil servants are bound to a centralized authority, so that emphasis is placed in the uniform application of rule across cases. As a result of these different emphases, adversarial legalism is likely to be more unpredictable and administratively costly, though also more flexible, than bureaucratic legalism (Kagan 2001).

On the *informal* side of the horizontal axis are processes in which no preexisting rules are used to resolve disputes or make policy decisions. The hierarchical version is *expert or political judgment*; the decentralized party-centered version is *negotiation/mediation*. In expert or political judgment, the expertise can be purely scientific, as when a government commission like the National Transportation Safety Board investigates the causes of an accident, or it can mix expertise with political prudence, as when the Securities and Exchange Commission decides whether to use its authority to create a rule governing some market practice. Negotiation/mediation, the bottom/left quadrant, fits any situation in which decisions must be made among roughly equal parties. Although legislatures can be highly hierarchical, many would roughly fit this cell, as each elected legislator has the right to bargain over and vote on legislation.

The cells in Kagan's table offer a way to address the "Law is Different" problem. Adversarial legalism is a capacious term that we believe gets at many of the qualities that writers are referring to when they decry or praise the use of courts, litigation, and legal rights to address social problems. Further, we think negotiation/mediation, bureaucratic legalism, and expert judgment are the points of comparison implicit in criticisms of courts as defective (or commendations of them as heroic) in policymaking and implementation. Negotiation/mediation is considered the "normal" way in which policies are created through legislative deliberation, and bureaucratic legalism and expert judgment are considered the "normal" ways in which those policies are implemented by executive agencies. The combination roughly comports with textbook versions of federal policymaking in which elected lawmakers—the President and members of Congress—negotiate fundamental policy decisions, whereas issues of implementation are delegated to executive branch agencies. Commentaries about judicialization/juridification/ legalization are, we think, reacting to a view that adversarial legalism is reaching into areas normally left to other less court-based modes of policymaking and dispute resolution.

Sharp-eyed readers, though, will see immediately that adversarial legalism does not mean "courts," that negotiation/mediation does not mean "legislatures" and that bureaucratic legalism does not mean "agencies"—in fact all institutions can vary in the extent they reflect these ideal-types. For example, American courts are more adversarial than European courts because they are less hierarchical, making American litigation more party-centered (Atiyah and Summers 1987; Damaska 1986). American legislatures also better fit the negotiation/mediation ideal better than typical parliaments because of their relative decentralization. Executive agencies too vary in their degree of bureaucratic legalism because they vary in the extent to which hierarchical rules structure behavior. An agency that, for example, responds to complaints, and that does not provide street-level officials much guidance in resolving those complaints, has moved away from the Weberian ideal and more toward the pole of party-centered adversarial legalism. It is important to remember that our terms represent ideal-types, which imply characteristic divisions of labor among the branches, but that in the real world, policies and institutions typically fall on a spectrum between them, not at the ends.

In fact, we believe this is another strength of the typology, particularly for studying American politics, because in the separation-of-powers, checks-and-balances American system it is hard to find pure examples of anything, be it judicial, executive, or legislative, state or federal. Policymaking and implementation in such a system, we believe, is best thought of as a dialogue among the federal branches of government and with the states (Barnes and Miller 2004; Barnes 2007a, 2013). In this context, separating out the influence of rights, courts, and litigation on American politics is particularly difficult, because it requires analysts to weigh the influence of each line in the dialogue, to try to measure how a court ruling influenced a legislature that in turn influenced an agency which in turn may have influenced the judiciary. Two of the most prominent books in the literature on the effects of law on politics, Silverstein's *Law's Allure* and Rosenberg's *Hollow Hope,* which try to isolate the effects of particular decisions such as *Brown v. Board of Education* or *Buckley v. Valeo,* wrestle particularly hard with this problem. Kagan's typology leads us instead to make more holistic characterizations. Instead of trying to parse the effect of a single decision in a complex, ongoing dialogue among multiple branches and levels of government, we code the design of policies as being more or less adversarial or bureaucratic, and trace how the politics within an issue area develop in the shadow of these institutional arrangements.

Our approach, then, is fundamentally comparative, but it is also multi-method, mixing quantitative and qualitative data, and developmental, analyzing change over time. We start with a quantitative analysis of 40 years of congressional hearing data on adversarial and bureaucratic injury compensation policies. These data provide a useful starting place for probing the threshold question of whether the politics of adversarial and bureaucratic legalism differ by providing a common vantage to view a key point in the ongoing policy dialogue in multiple cases. We find important cross-sectional differences between the politics of the two types of policies, which raise questions about whether (and how) these differences play out beyond congressional hearings and over time.

To explore these questions, our case studies pick up where the hearings data leave off, tracing the politics of adversarial and bureaucratic policies as they mature from creation to expansion and retrenchment, and in some instances as they become more bureaucratic or adversarial. These case studies allow us not only to explore how the politics of policies evolve over time and across multiple political institutions, but also, where appropriate, to compare the politics of different structures, adversarial and bureaucratic, within the same policy field. In adding this developmental dimension to our analysis, we build on the work of Paul Pierson (1994), who famously argues that the politics of program retrenchment differs from the politics of program creation. Pierson leaves open whether the shifting politics of policy development differs across policy types. By contrast, we explore whether "policy feedbacks"—the ways in which institutional features of policies shape politics (see generally Campbell 2006, 2012; Mettler and Soss 2004; Pierson 1993)—not only vary across different stages of development, but also vary across different types of policy designs within the same issue area. The result is a comparative developmental approach to understanding the political consequences of adversarial legalism versus bureaucratic legalism.

Case Selection

If you think about it, the critical claims made about the effects of rights, courts, and litigation—that they tend to crowd out other forms of political participation, polarize and create backlashes, get a polity stuck in unproductive policy arguments, and undermine social solidarity—are really claims about propensities, not regularities. It is easy to think of cases that support each of the claims, but also easy to think of counter-examples. *Roe v. Wade* and *Brown v. Board of Education* clearly created a political backlash, but *Loving v. Virginia*, the anti-miscegenation case, seemed to have no such effect. Similarly, gay marriage has generated considerable political contention, while the right of gay couples to adopt children has mostly slipped under the political radar (Gash 2013). Victories in litigation can create polarizing backlashes, but they can also consolidate support for legislative reform, as when states joined parents for expansion of federal special education programs, in part because they feared courts would impose unfunded judicial mandates on them (Melnick 1994). The language of rights and the use of litigation may frame social life in individualistic ways, but rights claims can be used by activists to raise consciousness about common concerns and build coalitions that bring groups together (McCann 1994; Epp 2009). So part of the problem of assessing the political effects of adversarial legalism is the familiar one of sampling. It is easy to pick cases that support your claims and easy to find cases that go against them, but not so easy to come up with a strategy for picking cases that help you generalize beyond them to get a sense of overall tilts and tendencies.

Our primary strategy for addressing this problem is comparison. We want to compare policies that are closely related and similar in important respects, but that differ in their structure, with some falling on the adversarial side of the spectrum and others on the bureaucratic side. To do this we need to sample from a policy field that has a mix of adversarial and bureaucratic policy designs. The structure of the U.S. state makes this relatively easy, because it is remarkably fragmented and layered, built through the accretion of overlapping public and private programs, benefits and rights (Orren and Skowronek 2004; Hacker 2002; Berkowitz 1987). The resulting patchwork of programs and policies means that, in many areas of U.S. public policy—for example, the environment, health care, civil rights, safety regulation, and consumer protection—adversarial and bureaucratic designs operate side by side. This offers many opportunities for comparing the political consequences of different policy designs.

One such opportunity lies in the field of injury compensation, which features a vast array of overlapping public programs and private remedies, some adversarial, others bureaucratic, and still others hybrids. The overlap of many programs makes them confusing to navigate. Imagine, for example, that you fell off a ladder at work and broke your leg. You might bring any or all of the following claims: a tort lawsuit against the manufacturer of the ladder for poor design, a workers' compensation claim at either the federal or state level (depending on your job), a claim against your health insurer, and a claim for private and/or public disability insurance benefits (depending on the severity of your injury). In 1991, the Rand Institute of Civil Justice published a landmark study of this mélange of injury compensation programs, audacious because it tried to estimate both the cost of all injuries in the United States and all sources of compensation. The study concluded that accident injury costs $175 billion per year—more than $300 billion in today's dollars—consisting of roughly $100 billion in direct costs and $75 billion in lost earnings (Hensler et al. 1991, Table 4.21, 103). The study found that roughly 23 million people received $110 billion dollars in injury compensation each year, almost 4% of GNP at the time (102). A central finding of the study—and crucial for our purposes—was that compensation for accidents came from a variety of sources, including private insurance, employer benefits, public programs, and lawsuits (Table 4.22, 108). Given the array of policies that compensate for injury and the ways they are used, injury compensation provides promising cases for our study.

Indeed, injury compensation is almost too good, providing so many candidates for analysis that we cannot possibly cover them all. We can, however, take advantage of the institutional variation in these policies by targeting policies that feature different levels of adversarial and bureaucratic legalism. As summarized in Table 1.2, we have selected three sets of cases. All of these cases are included in our quantitative analysis of congressional hearings and a subset of these cases involving SSDI, asbestos, and childhood vaccines are subject to in-depth case analysis.

The first set of cases includes examples of adversarial legalism: litigation over product liability, medical malpractice, and securities fraud. You may be surprised to see these forms of litigation labeled as "policies" comparable to more conventionally legislated programs like Social Security or workers' compensation. Traditionally, these forms of litigation were considered "private law" because they governed disputes between individuals and so were not thought to raise the same kinds of political or policy concerns as public law fields such as constitutional law. Today, however, what is usually labeled "tort law" is a matter of great political conflict and ferment, and public policies governing tort are regularly debated at both the state and national level. (We will see in the following chapter how often Congress has held hearings to consider changes to the tort system over the past 40 years.) As with all injury compensation policies, disputes over tort center on issues of who decides, who gets what, from whom, and how much. These forms of litigation differ from each other in interesting ways. Product liability affects a broad array of manufacturers; medical malpractice targets a group of well-organized professionals. Securities fraud litigation is an unusual case for our study because it compensates financial losses and not physical or mental injuries.

The second set of cases are characterized primarily by bureaucratic legalism: SSDI, the Black Lung Disability Trust Fund (the black lung program), and the Longshore and Harbor Workers' Compensation Act (the longshore workers' program). While all share common bureaucratic institutional features, there are some important differences. SSDI is funded from a payroll tax on workers and employers and covers disabled workers and their families. Like SSDI, the

Table 1.2 Three Sets of Cases

Type of Case	Policy
Adversarial Legalism	Product liability, medical malpractice, and securities fraud
Bureaucratic Legalism	SSDI, the Black Lung Disability Trust Fund, and the Longshore and Harbor Workers' Compensation Act
Shifting Regimes	Vaccine injury compensation (adversarial legalism to bureaucratic legalism), asbestos litigation (bureaucratic legalism to adversarial legalism to a layered system)

longshore workers' program is funded by a payroll tax, but unlike SSDI, only covers injured workers from a specific industry. The black lung program targets a specific category of injuries, and it is funded differently from the other programs, through a tax on products. The size of SSDI dwarfs the other programs in our sample. In 2010 alone, the SSDI trust fund paid out over $124 billion in benefits; by contrast, the longshore workers' and black lung programs paid only about $26.6 and $208 million in benefits in 2010, respectively. Finally, these policies differ on federalism: SSDI is a federal program that is partly administered by the states while the other programs are federally administered.

The final set of cases is especially theoretically interesting for our study: injury compensation fields in which the structure of the policy shifted over time. The case of vaccine injury compensation is particularly valuable for our project because it involves an adversarial policy that was largely replaced by a bureaucratic policy, allowing for before-and-after comparisons of the politics of policies dealing with the same set of injuries. The asbestos case illustrates a more subtle pattern of development in which different types of polices are layered, so that adversarial legalism remains the dominant policy response but some bureaucratic sub-policies remain alongside tort law. If adversarial policies generate a politics different from bureaucratic policies, then we should observe changes in the politics of these fields that coincides with their change in structure. In the vaccine case, we should see a shift after bureaucratic legalism replaces adversarial legalism. In the asbestos case, we should observe a difference in the politics when activity centers on its adversarial as opposed to bureaucratic sub-policies.

Our historical case studies allow us to trace the politics of SSDI, asbestos, and vaccine policy through different stages of development, from creation through expansion and (attempted) retrenchment. They also give us the second major way we probe our questions, through within-case comparisons. Comparisons across cases are always vulnerable to the charge that what's driving differences in outcomes among the cases is not the factor that the researcher is interested in but some other unconsidered variable. Injury compensation policies have some common features, but there are many differences, say, between the history of product injury law and SSDI, and it would be problematic to assume that those differences can all be attributed to the fact that tort law is primarily adversarial and SSDI bureaucratic. By tracing developments within cases, however, we can make comparisons inside the case that are not so vulnerable to this problem. In two of our cases, covering vaccine and asbestos injury compensation, the structure of public policy shifts over time, and we take advantage of this variation by analyzing how this is related to changes in the politics of these two areas. Within the SSDI case, we compare the politics of an adversarial policy, the Americans with Disabilities Act, which addresses some of the same issues. We cannot replicate the ideal situation in social science—randomly assigning bureaucratic designs to some public policies and adversarial designs to others—but we can, by combining within-case and across-case studies, reduce some of the limitations of inductive, non-experimental research.

Our cases are not intended to be representative of the universe of injury compensation regimes within the United States, much less the universe of adversarial and bureaucratic policies. We have, for example, focused entirely on the national politics of federal programs and tort law. The vaccine case, moreover, is highly unusual in that reformers were able to replace adversarial legalism with bureaucratic legalism. We chose these examples because they provide clear examples of adversarial and bureaucratic policies in the area of injury compensation, and because they vary in several important respects: size, scope of targeted injuries, funding sources, and setting. Thus comparing patterns of politics within and across these cases should offer insight into the central question of what, if any, are the key differences between the politics of adversarial and bureaucratic legalism. We will save for our conclusion our thoughts about the possible limits on the generalizability of our cases, and the ways in which they connect to the vast literature on judicialization/juridification/legalization.[5]

Summary of Findings

We consider four serious charges against adversarial legalism: (1) it crowds out other forms of political action, especially lobbying for legislative change, (2) it is particularly "sticky" and path-dependent, potentially locking governments into bad policies, (3) it creates polarizing backlashes, and (4) it individualizes interests, thus undermining social solidarity. We find the first three counts are overstated, at least in our cases. Adversarial legalism is either not guilty or no more prone to these tendencies than bureaucratic legalism. On the fourth count, however, we find evidence to support the charge.

Crowd out and "flypaper courts"

Gerald Rosenberg's *The Hollow Hope* is perhaps the most prominent critique of the use of courts to make policy within political science and law. Rosenberg's argument is largely focused on the constraints on courts as policymakers, maintaining that courts can make social policy effectively only under very narrow circumstances. There must be precedent for the court's action; the elected branches must support the court's decisions; there must be some public support for the court's decisions and at least one of the following must be present: (1) incentives for compliance, (2) costs for non-compliance, (3) supporting market incentives, or (4) support from local officials. Unless these conditions are met, Rosenberg argues, relying on law and courts to make policy is a "hollow hope."

Reviewers have often commented about the seeming disjunction between Rosenberg's social science approach, in which he develops the theory of the "constrained court" and lists the variables that he thinks affect its performance, and the anguished rhetoric about the pitfalls of seeking social change through law that erupts in some passages of his book and is reflected in the title. It is one thing to find that courts are constrained, but why then are they "Hollow Hopes"? Congress cannot unilaterally dictate broad social change either; to translate its formal commands into social practice, it too needs help from the other branches and levels of government and some local support, but no one would suggest that seeking legislation is an empty exercise. The answer is that Rosenberg assumes that the use of courts inevitably crowd outs other presumably more effective (and legitimate) modes of political advocacy, such as grassroots mobilization, lobbying, and coalition building. From this perspective, courts are not only a hollow hope but also "political flypaper," trapping interest groups in an expensive form of advocacy that is unlikely to yield results.

Rosenberg is certainly not alone in his concerns about the turn to adversarial legalism. In his analysis of the labor movement, William Forbath makes a parallel argument, that unions diverted resources to litigation at the expense of the broader political movement (Forbath 1991). You can compare this to the most familiar claim about the diversion of political activity from the elected branches, that it is "undemocratic," a criticism voiced both inside and outside the academy. Take for example Justice Scalia's scathing dissent in *United States v. Windsor,* the divided Supreme Court decision that struck down the Defense of Marriage Act.[6] Scalia argues that judicial policymaking in the area of same-sex marriage diverted the debate from the elected branches and so tarnished the victory for advocates of gay and lesbian rights. Scalia's reasoning is that litigation channels activity away from the hard work of lobbying elected officials and members in the executive and persuading "the People."[7] For him the problem is that the judiciary is too powerful, sweeping away democratically-decided outcomes; for Rosenberg and Forbath, who clearly sympathize with the movements they are writing about, the worry is the courts and litigation are too weak. In either case, though, the critics are concerned that the turn to adversarial legalism is a turn away from other modes of politics.

In our study, however, we find no evidence that adversarial legalism "kills" politics, fixing social movements and interest groups on the pursuit of individual rights at the expense of other goals or means. Indeed, adversarial legalism seemed to fuel group mobilization, creating a more fragmented, pluralistic politics featuring more diverse interests with competing viewpoints. The high costs of litigation provided a stimulus for legislative campaigns for alternatives to litigation. The converse was also true: bureaucratic legalism did not kill *litigation*. We found a number of striking examples of interest groups using the courts to challenge the status quo within bureaucratic policies. The interest groups in our study seemed adept at moving from one institution to another, looking for levers wherever they could find them.

In part because interest groups were able to move across branches and levels of government, policymaking was shared among the branches and levels of government in our cases.[8] Elected officials often created policy designs that empowered litigants and judges, deferred to courts that developed adversarial policies, or at least invited judicial interpretation of vague or open-ended phrases (and then codified these judicially developed interpretations). Whatever the mix of adversarial and bureaucratic legalism in each case, interest groups found ways to try to influence policy. In the American system of overlapping, diversely representative forums, policymaking takes place in many forums, often at once, and American interest groups in our cases were adapted to this context, routinely combining litigation with lobbying.

Path dependence and framing effects

A related charge is that adversarial legalism is particularly prone to "path dependence," so that bad or outdated policies are stuck in place, and frame political debate in ways that are problematic. The concept of path dependence has proven to be a bit like an inkblot in a Rorschach test; it means different things to different scholars. In some writings, path dependence seems merely to note that events in the past have an effect going forward, that "history matters." We prefer Paul Pierson's formulation, which defines path-dependent processes as those involving "increasing returns," meaning that with each step it gets more and more costly to get off whatever path one is on (Pierson 2004).

Life seems filled with *decreasing* returns. Your first mouthful of ice cream is much more pleasurable than the last. As more businesses move into a city, it becomes more affluent, real estate prices increase and wages rise, increasing the costs of business and reducing the appeal of the location for new ventures. A product that satisfies a lot of consumers leads rival manufacturers to develop an alternative that is even more attractive. But sometimes we see *increasing* returns, cases in which every bite of ice cream, strangely enough, tastes better and better. Silicon Valley grows richer and richer, but also more and more the place for certain companies to locate, whatever the cost. The QWERTY keyboard may or may not be the best arrangement of the keys, but as more people learn to use it, it becomes harder to sell a different design, especially if the design becomes embedded in other technologies (Pierson 2004).

Litigation is arguably somewhat like the fabled ice cream cone that gets tastier with each bite. This is certainly true for some litigants. "Repeat players" with each iteration theoretically gain over "one-shotters," as Marc Galanter posited in his classic "Why the Haves Come out Ahead" (Galanter 1974; Kritzer and Silbey 2003). Lawyers and the organizations they work for accrue expertise in how to litigate and attract new clients. They learn how best to make litigation pay, both in terms of their long-term goals but also in a more crude material sense. As the expected returns of litigation increase, interest groups may eschew other modes of advocacy, such as lobbying for new legislation, which is almost always a long shot in the lawmaking obstacle course on Capitol Hill. In contrast to the crowd out argument, in which the costs of litigation divert groups with limited resources from other modes of advocacy, the path dependence argument implies that groups come to *prefer* litigation to other modes of advocacy given its increasing returns, even when they can afford to fight in other forums.

Particular legal doctrines can also, at least theoretically, become like the ice cream cone you just cannot stop eating. Or to put it more like Gordon Silverstein (2009) would, when a public policy is juridified, the resulting accretion of precedents narrows the scope of political debate, not just in court but also in the larger political system. The idea is that legal precedents do not merely shape legal discourse but also the terms of policy debates outside the courts. As legal precedents become "givens," reform proposals that are inconsistent with them are deemed out of bounds, which limits policy options. Affirmative action becomes a matter of weighing "diversity"; abortion is framed around a woman's right to privacy. Silverstein uses campaign finance to illustrate his contention. He argues that the claim that "money is speech"—a point that was controversial at the time *Buckley v. Valeo* was decided—has become taken for granted in the politics of campaign finance, sharply delimiting the scope of reforms that are seriously considered. Silverstein explains his claim:

> When policy bounces from Congress to courts, to the administration, and back again,…the influences [of legal precedents] become more complex and often more constraining. We might think of a game of *Scrabble,* a game in which players often end up where none had originally planned or imagined. In a game of *Scrabble,* players start with a blank board, and the first player can head off in any direction he or she chooses. But slowly, over the course of the game, the players often end in one corner of the board, whereas another part of the board is totally empty.…In theory, it is still possible to move the game off in a radically different direction, but it becomes increasingly difficult (and unlikely) for that to happen (2009: 66).

Juridification, according to this claim, can lead to a highly constrained politics in which public policy debate looks like the end of a Scrabble game rather the beginning.

Silverstein's case studies focus on constitutional issues, where the institutional barriers to reversing judicial doctrines are the highest. It may be that path dependence is not so much a function of "juridification," or to use our preferred term, adversarial legalism, but merely the one form of it, American federal judicial review, in which it is hardest to reverse course once a ruling has been made. Constitutional rulings are particularly "sticky" because, as Charles Evans Hughes once said, the U.S. Constitution is what the judges say it is[9]—it is rare for a ruling to be reversed through constitutional amendment, and so difficult to recast the political debate over campaign finance or abortion in ways that would conflict with Court rulings. That said, there are reasons to believe that, U.S. constitutional law aside, adversarial legalism in all its forms should be resistant to change. The underlying dynamics of path dependence that Silverstein and Pierson identify—framing effects and increasing returns—are not wholly dependent on the existence of institutional barriers to formal revision. These dynamics are largely generated by the litigation process itself, and so apply to other forms of litigation, including common law and statutory interpretation decisions, where judicial decisions can be overridden through the passage of ordinary legislation (which itself is no mean feat).

In our study, adversarial policies were in fact prone to some degree of path dependence. The law in our cases is mostly common law, which is much easier to change than constitutional law, but still hard to reverse entirely. As a formal matter, once a legal doctrine was established, it became difficult to reform. But in our study, path dependence was hardly a unique property of adversarial legalism. Bureaucratic legal policies in our cases exhibited the same tendency: once created, agency-based programs proved hard to retrench or reform. The fact that adversarial and bureaucratic legal regimes are both formally sticky should come as no surprise. The influence of pre-existing institutional arrangements in public policymaking and administration was sketched out at least as far back as Herbert Simon's *Administrative Behavior* (1947). As John Kingdon (2011: 79) once observed, policymakers of all stripes tend to "take what they are doing as given, and make small, incremental, and marginal adjustments" (see also Epp 2010). In fact, when we looked beyond the formal structures of programs and examined how the details of policies were adapted through practice over time—what Erkulwater (2006) calls "microlevel" as opposed to "macrolevel" changes— bureaucratic programs and agencies often proved *less* flexible than legal doctrines and courts, failing to adjust existing rules to new policy circumstances and political demands, and forcing stakeholders to turn to the courts, which proved remarkably adept at adjusting administrative regulations and legal doctrines to new circumstances.

Similarly, it is true, as Silverstein (2009) persuasively argues, that adversarial legalism can have powerful framing effects that preclude the consideration of various types of claims, but bureaucratic legalism also has framing effects that bound debate and cut off consideration of alternatives. As our case study of the politics of SSDI describes, attempts to change people's understanding of the problem of disability have run up against the powerful framing that bureaucratic policies have reinforced. So, leaving aside the special case of U.S. judicial review, we found little evidence that adversarial legalism was any *more* path-dependent than bureaucratic legalism; indeed it seemed less so at the microlevel.

Backlash

Critics charge that adversarial legalism engenders strong reactions from powerful interests that lose in courts, in part because policymaking by unelected judges is seen as illegitimate, a form of judicial encroachment on the prerogatives of elected officials' turf. This argument has been made perhaps most

prominently by Michael Klarman in his account of the civil rights movement. Klarman's analysis of backlash is subtle. On one hand, he argues *Brown
v. Board of Education* set back the struggle for civil rights by catalyzing resistance by even relatively moderate Southern states. Litigation, in effect, eliminated the moderate middle. On the other hand, violent resistance by Southern
extremists was instrumental in setting the stage for a counter-backlash at the
national level. Klarman's (2012) more recent account of the fight for marriage
equality is also subtle, arguing that early cases recognizing civil unions and
gay marriage, like the Massachusetts litigation, engendered backlash, but the
risk of backlash has ebbed as public opinion continues to swing in favor of
gay marriage.

Rosenberg (1991), by contrast, makes stronger claims in connection with *Roe
v. Wade*, arguing that the decision resulted in an organized counter-movement
by social conservatives that has stigmatized abortion and limited access to it.
In a similar vein, Mary Ann Glendon has argued that *Roe* polarized the politics of abortion, thus helping to explain why the United States continues to
have such a fervent pro-choice/pro-life politics even as other nations (even
largely Catholic ones) have largely resolved the issue (Glendon 1987).

Although we tend to think of the backlash argument in connection
with high-profile constitutional rights, others have noted the catalytic
effect of more mundane types of litigation in mobilizing opposition.
A good example of this is William Haltom and Michael McCann's study
of conservative and business counter-mobilization against tort law, which
documents a sustained effort to shift public discourse on personal injury
litigation by emphasizing one-sided and sometime false anecdotes about
"frivolous lawsuits" and bogus claiming practices (Haltom and McCann
2004). Backlashes are problematic in this account partly because they
divert attention from the underlying substantive issues to the propriety
of judicialization itself, but also because they polarize interests and hinder compromise. The backlash argument takes many forms, but a common
thread is that reliance on adversarial legalism has a potentially polarizing
effect on politics.

In our cases we found lots of examples of the counter-mobilizing tendencies of adversarial legalism. Lawsuits against manufacturers for injuries
purportedly caused by their products eventually stimulated massive mobilization, as one would expect. But this counter-mobilization was far more
complex and variegated than is implied by the backlash literature. The targets of litigation, for example, often internally divided based on the degree
of their exposure to litigation. Moreover, in some cases, by raising important

issues, bringing all the parties to the table, and stimulating the building of coalitions across the plaintiff/defendant divide, litigation set the stage not for backlash but political resolution. In our cases, adversarial legalism engendered counter-mobilization but not necessary a polarizing backlash.

Individualization of political interests
(and undermining of social solidarity)

A final charge is that adversarial legalism makes it harder to resolve social problems because it frames them as individual disputes and so divides interests from one another. Unlike the backlash argument, the concern is not that adversarial legalism will engender *unified* opposition but that it will Balkanize interests or internally fragment them, making the finding of common ground difficult even among groups that we might expect to be allies.

This charge takes many forms and has deep theoretical roots. A long line of political theorists, starting with Edmund Burke and Karl Marx, have critically examined how legal rights structure people's grievances and understanding of social obligations (Waldron 1987). Burke criticized the espousal of the leaders of the French Revolution of the "rights of man" as abstract, extreme, ahistorical, and so removed from the practicalities of governance. Government, he insisted, "is a contrivance of human wisdom to provide for human *wants*," and attempting to govern through abstract rights ignores the complexity of social arrangements and the intricacies of human nature (Burke 1987: 52). Marx contended that "the rights of man" are merely the rights of "egoistic man, of man separated from other men and from the community." The struggle for these political rights, Marx argued, are a symptom of the individualism and lack of social connectedness that plagues capitalist societies (Marx 1978: 43). These are very different diagnoses—and Burke and Marx were radically different thinkers—but both point to the gap between the magisterial promise of universal rights and the practical, material consequences of framing social issues as matters of rights, which they argued neglect the communal aspect of human life.

One can see echoes of these Burkean and Marxian themes in the critiques of rights that sprung up in the 1970s and 1980s, a period when the luster of social change through law began to fade in the United States. Communitarian political thinkers such as Alasdair MacIntyre, and Critical Legal Studies scholars on the left, such as Mark Tushnet and Duncan Kennedy, for all their differences, shared a basic premise: framing political conflicts as matters of legal rights (and thus channeling them through the courts and litigation process) individualizes politics, undermines social solidarity, and reinforces a narrowed and flattened view of social life (Tushnet 1984; Gabel and Kennedy 1984; Freeman 1978; MacIntyre 1981; Taylor 1998). Critics such as Wendy Brown, on similar grounds, argue that rather than emancipating citizens, rights are liable to reinscribe the very power relations they are meant to challenge (Brown 1995; Baynes 2000).

Although they start from quite different premises, we do not think it is too much of a stretch to link these legal and political theorists' commentaries to critical accounts of judicial policymaking in law and political science. The judicial policymaking literature is typically grounded in Pluralism, the interest group–focused approach to politics, rather than Marxian or Burkean themes, and so would be anathema to many radical critics of rights, but it too concerns the way in which litigation narrows and individualizes the framing of social problems. Litigation, this literature suggests, requires multi-faceted problems with many dimensions to be reduced to discrete legal disputes between individual claimants. The legalistic framing of social problems, it is contended, precludes consideration of broader concerns, and excludes some stakeholders from the deliberative process, as not all relevant parties will necessarily participate in precedent-setting lawsuits (or their settlement) (e.g., Fuller 1978; Horowitz 1977; Katzmann 1986; Melnick 1983; Derthick 2005). The process undermines the Pluralist ideal of bargaining among all affected interests.

It is admittedly a long distance from Marx to Melnick, but the common element we see is a concern about the divisive, fragmenting effects of the way in which adversarial legalism addresses social issues. And this is the concern that seems vindicated by the data in our study, which not only show a correspondence between adversarial legalism and a fractious brand of politics, but also illustrate the mechanisms that connect policy and politics.[10]

Our findings on the connection between legal policies and their politics dovetail nicely with the enormous literature on "policy feedbacks," which tend to focus on how traditional welfare programs shape politics (e.g., Schattschneider 1935; Lowi 1964; Wilson 1973; Walker 1991; Skocpol 1992; Pierson 1993, 1994, 2004; Thelen 1999; Pierson and Skocpol 2002; Mettler and Soss 2004; Mettler 2011; Campbell 2003, 2012). This literature illustrates how policies "define, arouse, or pacify constituencies" by creating incentives for political actors and by influencing beliefs about what is "possible, desirable, and normal" (Soss and Schram 2007: 113). In a widely cited review of this literature, Paul Pierson (1993) identified two general categories of policy feedbacks, resource or incentive effects (now often simply referred to as resource effects), and interpretive effects. Policies in this view provide material resources to actors that affect the way they engage in politics, but policies also frame the way social problems and actors are conceived.

We find both types of feedback mechanisms arising from the injury compensation policies in our study (Figure 1.1). First, injury policies create distinctive *distributional effects,* patterns of payout and compensation for injury that affect the material interests of the stakeholders. These distributional effects shape the stakes of interest groups in preserving or reforming the policy; this in turn affects how groups mobilize and build coalitions. Second, injury policies shape the *assignment of blame,* the framing of fault for injury. Blame assignment, in turn, affects how policymakers argue about the appropriate scheme for compensating injury.

In our cases, adversarial legalism and bureaucratic legalism created distinctive patterns of distributional and blame effects, and these effects result in distinctive political trajectories, patterns of politics over time. The distributional and blame effects of adversarial policies initially *limit* the scope of political conflict. Because adversarial legalism organizes injury compensation claims into discrete, private lawsuits, at an early stage it tends to have a privatizing effect. When there are just a few lawsuits against, say, a particular manufacturer who uses asbestos, or a particular vaccine producer, the cost and the blame for injury falls on just a few individual actors. At this stage members of Congress are disinclined to get involved, and quite willing to defer to judges who act in their traditional role as adjudicators of individual lawsuits. Even other companies in the affected industry or field fail to mobilize. They may calculate that the problem is limited to the named defendants. But as litigation expands, more and more companies and stakeholder groups become

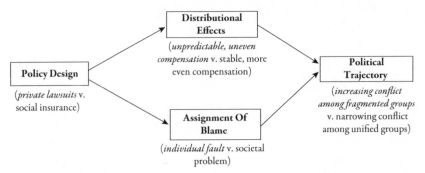

FIGURE 1.1 How policy shapes politics: injury compensation policy (*adversarial legalism* versus bureaucratic legalism)

involved, and the stakes increase. At this stage, the distributional effects of adversarial legalism are powerful: as some plaintiffs and defendants win while others lose, the uneven pattern of costs and benefits generates cross-cutting interests within and across key stakeholder groups. Those most affected by litigation on the defendant side run to Congress to try to make the pain go away. Those with lower risk, even in the same field, stay on the sidelines or even fight to preserve the adversarial legal system. The distributional effects of litigation then, reduce political conflict at an early stage, but increase factionalization at a later stage.

The other mechanism, blame assignment, also shapes injury politics in a powerful way: it forces those who seek reform to reframe responsibility for injury. Where individual lawsuits frame the problem as the culpability of individual entities, would-be reformers have to recast the issue as a social problem so as to make the sins of individual actors less relevant. This is a difficult political task. The combined effect of distribution effects and blame assignment associated with adversarial legalism is to create a political trajectory of increasing intensity and factionalization.

The distributional effects and blame assignment generated by bureaucratic legalism create a strikingly different political trajectory. Here the intensity and scope of conflict diminishes over time. Our cases of bureaucratic legalism all involve social insurance in which some kind of tax is created to fund an injury compensation scheme. At creation, there is a bitter and familiar conflict over the assignment of blame: business groups and their conservative allies argue against the tax as unfair and unwarranted. If there are injuries, they contend, it is not their problem. Liberals and their allies, on the other side, argue that it is a social responsibility to provide for suffering individuals. This is a fundamental political conflict, and in two of our cases, Social Security Disability Insurance and vaccine injury compensation, it is ferocious. But once the compensation scheme in those cases is enacted, the distinctive distributional effect of bureaucratic legalism kicks in: costs are spread so widely and evenly that the incentive to mobilize against the programs dissipates. Business groups largely demobilize, and conflict over the maintenance and expansion of the programs is reduced. Moments of conflict occasionally redevelop, but they are narrower in scope and less fragmented than in our cases of adversarial legalism. Again, there is a central irony here: the same aspect of policy design that increases conflict at the outset—the socialization of the costs of injury—over time seems to reduce conflict.

In sum, from a comparative developmental perspective, adversarial legalism and bureaucratic legalism have political trajectories that are mirror opposites. The politics of adversarial legalism commences in a decentralized fashion but becomes more pluralistic and fractious. The politics of bureaucratic legalism, by contrast, is highly polarized at the outset but over time becomes more consensual, coinciding with bureaucratic legalism's more even and predictable spreading of costs and benefits, and with the acceptance of its underlying principle of social responsibility for injury.

Road Map for the Following Chapters

We provide the grounds for our conclusions in the following five chapters. Chapter 2 is a quantitative analysis of patterns of congressional testimony from 1971 to 2011 on a range of adversarial and bureaucratic injury compensation policies. The data in this chapter suggest that adversarial legalism and bureaucratic legalism generate radically different types of congressional oversight. Hearings on adversarial policies, as compared to bureaucratic policies, feature more diverse types of interests, more conflicting testimony, and relatively high levels of participation by business interests. The fragmented patterns of participation and greater degree of conflict seem consistent with the concern that adversarial legalism individualizes conflict and fragments interests.

These cross-sectional findings are suggestive but only a start because they rely on the narrow prism of congressional hearings. Relatively quiet politics in Congress might mask high levels of conflict in other venues, particularly the other branches of government. Accordingly, chapters 3 through 5 feature three historical case studies of the politics of injury compensation policies. We begin with Social Security Disability Insurance, a bureaucratic policy that provides a baseline for comparison with the adversarial cases. We then turn to the asbestos case, tracing its evolving politics in several steps, first as claimants established a right to recovery, then as business interests attempted to contain their liability, resulting in a layered response to the problem of asbestos injury compensation. We end with the vaccine injury compensation case, in which an adversarial design was largely replaced by a bureaucratic design. Consistent with our quantitative analyses, these case studies suggest that the politics of adversarial legalism and bureaucratic legalism differ, but the case studies demonstrate that the differences are developmental: they lie in how patterns of conflict develop over time, with adversarial policies generating an increasing scope of conflict and bureaucratic policies tending to narrow conflict. In the concluding chapter, we summarize our findings and their limitations, and put our study in the broader context of research on law and public policy.

2

Congressional Hearings
and the Politics of Adversarial
and Bureaucratic Legalism

Congressional hearings data are a logical place to begin probing the differences between the politics of adversarial and bureaucratic legalism. Congress routinely holds diverse types of hearings on injury compensation programs and tort law, including hearings on all of the policies in our sample. Sometimes these hearings center on reform bills. Other times Congress gathers information on agency and court practices or engages in routine policy maintenance. So, just as a geologist takes core samples to get a sense of a terrain, we can use congressional hearings as common points of reference for observing interest group politics over a relatively long period of time in injury compensation policy. These observations, in turn, can provide clues to the broader political landscape of injury compensation policy that can be explored using the case studies.

Our data, which draw on observations from 40 years of congressional hearings from 1971 to 2011, reveal stark differences in patterns of interest group participation and testimony in the policy areas of our sample. Overall, hearings on adversarial policies featured significantly more witnesses and greater diversity of types of groups than hearings on bureaucratic policies. Along with the greater diversity of participants at hearings on adversarial policies there were also much higher levels of conflict; the participants were much more apt to disagree about the core issues in injury compensation politics of who pays, how much, to whom and by what mechanism. These patterns held regardless of how we sliced the data, including analyses of participation rates in individual hearings, participation rates within the population of group appearances across all of our hearings, and participation rates over time, across specific issue areas, and within issue areas that featured different types of policies. These patterns are consistent with the argument that adversarial legalism individualizes politics, generating more diverse participation and interest group conflict in Congress than bureaucratic legalism.

The Data

We collected observations on witnesses and testimony in congressional hearings from 1971 to 2011 on the injury compensation policies in our sample using the Congressional Information Service (CIS) hearing abstracts.[1] (Appendix I discusses these data and their collection further, including how we tested their reliability.) The abstracts provide a list of witnesses and a brief summary of the testimony along with various pieces of background information about the hearing, such as the committee, the hearing date, and whether the hearing focuses on a particular reform proposal or bill. We used the abstracts' witness lists—in combination with Google searches about each organization and witness and, when needed, an analysis of their actual testimony—to ascertain (a) the total number of witnesses and (b) whether witnesses fell into the following general categories of stakeholder interests and specific types of groups, which are summarized in Table 2.1:

1. *Business interests*, consisting of business groups, individual businesses, insurance companies, and defense counsel;
2. *Claimant interests*, consisting of claimant groups (where claimants represent themselves), unions on behalf of claimants, pro-claimant consumer groups, and claimant counsel;
3. *Government officials,* consisting of federal, state, and local officials, and Democratic and Republican members of Congress;
4. *Experts,* consisting of legal (typically law professors) and medical experts (doctors or public health experts); and
5. *Others,* a miscellaneous category that accounted for less than 5% of all group type appearances and included, among others, pro-tort reform public interest groups, taxpayer groups, and government employee unions.

To develop this list, we began with stakeholder interests and types of groups that have been identified in the literature on the politics of various injury compensation programs and tort law (e.g., Derthick 1979; Kagan 1994; Erkulwater 2006; Burke 2002; Barnes 1997, 2011). As we coded the hearing

Table 2.1 List of Stakeholder Interests and Group Types

Stakeholder Interest	Group Type
Business Interests	Business Group
	Individual Business
	Insurance Companies
	Defense Counsel
Claimant Interests	Claimant Groups (claimants representing themselves)
	Unions for Claimants
	Pro-Claimant Consumer Groups
	Claimant Counsel
Governmental Officials	Federal Officials
	State Officials
	Local Officials
	Democratic Members of Congress
	Republican Members of Congress
Experts	Legal Experts
	Medical Experts
Others	E.g., Pro-Tort Reform Interest Groups, Public Employee Unions

abstracts, we assigned specific witnesses to these categories and group types, making some minor adjustments to the lists of group types as we learned more about the contending interests in our sample. For example, we distinguished consumer groups for claimant interests that generally favor the tort system (such as Public Citizen), which were treated as claimant interests from conservative public interest groups that favor tort reform (such as ATRA), which were included as one of our miscellaneous groups.[2]

The coding of the hearings and related measures are discussed more fully below and in the Appendices that appear at the end of the book, but a brief example of how we coded participation is worth considering at the outset so you will have a better sense of the data. On January 11, 2005, the Senate Judiciary Committee held a hearing on the Fairness in Asbestos Injury Resolution Act (CIS No. 2007-S521-18). The following witnesses testified: Judge Edward Becker of the Third Circuit, a leading jurist in asbestos litigation who helped draft the bill under consideration and summarized some of its technical provisions; John Engler, President and CEO of National Association of

Manufacturers (NAM), representing the Asbestos Alliance (a group of large manufacturers who supported asbestos litigation reform); Craig Barrington, Senior Vice President and General Counsel for the American Insurance Association (AIA); Margaret M. Seminario, Director, Safety and Health, AFL-CIO; Michael Forscey, plaintiff lawyer representing the Association of Trial Lawyers of America (ATLA); Mary Lou Kenner, daughter of a victim of asbestos-related diseases; Billie Speicher, a victim of asbestos-related disease; and Jeffrey Robinson, defense counsel. In coding the participation in this hearing, we counted the total number of witnesses and then assigned them to stakeholder categories and group types. In this case, there were eight witnesses total, representing three categories of stakeholder interests: business interests, claimant interests and experts. Seven group types, specific groups that fall within different categories of stakeholder interests, appeared: business groups (NAM), insurance (AIA), defense counsel (Robinson), unions (AFL-CIO), claimant counsel (ATLA), claimants for themselves (Kenner and Speicher), and a legal expert (Judge Becker).[3]

In addition to coding witnesses, we used the CIS Abstracts' summaries of testimony to code for "conflict," meaning whether the abstracts did or did not report opposing viewpoints among the witnesses (o for no conflict, 1 for opposing views). To gain some confidence that the CIS abstracts were accurate in this regard, we took a random sample of them and checked their coding against actual testimony. We found that the CIS abstracts were accurate about the existence of conflicting viewpoints in the hearing transcripts, although sometimes vague with respect to the specific content of those disagreements.[4] In many cases, the coding was straightforward because the CIS Abstract explicitly reported "opposing viewpoints" or "differing views." For example, on the January 11, 2005 hearing, the CIS Abstract stated that the testimony presented "views on issues related to the draft bill" and "perspectives on problems with the proposed trust fund," so it was coded as involving conflict. Our coding resulted in an original dataset spanning four decades and 414 hearings (291 hearings on bureaucratic policies and 123 on adversarial ones), and featuring 4,003 witnesses, including 1,689 appearances by different group types (839 in bureaucratic policy hearings and 850 in adversarial policy hearings) representing all five categories of stakeholder interests.

Several points bear emphasis. First, in assessing patterns of interest group participation in hearings, we are looking for relative differences across hearing types. There are no absolute threshold amounts for "high" or "low" levels of diversity or conflict. At this stage, we are only interested in whether significant differences exist in levels of diversity and conflict in hearings on

adversarial injury compensation policies as compared to hearings on bureaucratic policies. We develop a more nuanced and textured understanding of
the differences in our case studies.

Second, it is not unusual for hearings to feature multiple witnesses for the
same organization or redundant witnesses who represent a single set of interests and concerns, as when multiple victims testify to their injuries and the
need for Congress to act, or when multiple business groups line up to testify
against the need for a new program or the expansion of existing ones. From
the perspective of the diversity of interest group participation, a litany of similarly situated witnesses with similar policy concerns represents a single type
of interest, not a diversity of group types. Accordingly, although we report
the average number of witnesses in hearings on adversarial versus bureaucratic
injury compensation policies, we concentrate on the types of interests represented at the hearings as the better measure of the diversity of stakeholder
participation.

Finally, in exploring patterns of conflict in the hearings, we focus on whether
witnesses offer competing views on core issues related to injury compensation.
Here, the central task is to assess whether witnesses disagree, regardless of their
group membership. This is important because diversity of formal group representation will not necessarily correlate with a diversity of viewpoints. If hearings are a kind of show to promote committee members' policy preferences,
they might invite a wide range of groups who unanimously endorse the favored
policy to create an impression of broad support and consensus. Alternatively,
elected officials might ask a small number of competing interests to express their
differences on the public record to create an appearance of vigorous debate. As
a result, to the extent that the CIS Abstract data allow it, we assess the breadth
of participation and the amount of conflict in the hearings separately, if only
to gain some confidence that greater diversity in formal representation corresponds to higher levels of conflict in hearing testimony. (We will consider further limitations of our data in the discussion section below.)

Patterns of Participation

Levels of Diversity

As seen in Table 2.2, we found that the average hearing on adversarial legalism featured significantly more witnesses than hearings on bureaucratic programs (13.96 to 7.86), and, more importantly, these witnesses represented
over twice as many group types (6.79 to 2.82). Looking beyond the aggregate

Table 2.2 Patterns of Participation in Congressional Hearings on Adversarial versus Bureaucratic Injury Compensation Policies: 1971 to 2011 (n=414)

Type of Hearing	Hearings on Bureaucratic Policies	Hearings on Adversarial Policies	Difference in Means (t-value)
Total Number of Hearings	291	123	—
Mean # of Witnesses (standard error)	7.86 (.65)	13.96 (.86)	−6.10 (−5.64)***
Mean # of Group Types (standard error)	2.82(.13)	6.79(.23)	−3.97 (−14.04)***

Hypothesis: (BL Mean) (AL Mean)≥ 0 *p<t ≤.05; ** p<t ≤.01; *** p<t ≤.001.

T-tests were run assuming unequal variances using Welch's formula.

differences reported in the table, we see the same patterns emerge across specific policy areas and within the cases of asbestos and vaccine that have a mix of adversarial and bureaucratic policies, although the numbers for these within case comparisons are rather small. So, an average of 7.38, 6.22, and 7 types of groups respectively participated in hearings on the adversarial policies, product liability, medical malpractice and securities fraud litigation, and an average of 1.84, 2.33 and 3.92 types of groups participated in hearings on the bureaucratic policies, Black Lung, longshore, and SSDI. In the vaccine case, where Congress replaced an adversarial policy with a bureaucratic policy, an average of about 5.5 group types participated in hearings during the period in which the adversarial policy was in force, while only about 2.6 types of groups typically appeared in hearings during the time of the bureaucratic policy. In the asbestos case, where adversarial and bureaucratic injury compensation policies co-exist side-by-side, an average of about 6.8 types of groups participated in hearings on the adversarial policies, whereas an average of about 4.5 types of groups participated in hearings on relatively more bureaucratic policies such as state workers' compensation programs.

Across the dataset, the differences in the diversity of participation between adversarial and bureaucratic policies have been fairly stable over the past 40 years. Figure 2.1 plots the average number of group types that appeared in the two types of hearings in our sample from 1971 to 2011, charting the results from the Nixon/Ford Administrations to the Obama Administration.[5] Consistent with

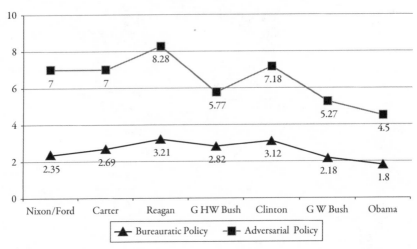

FIGURE 2.1 Average number of group types testifying in congressional hearings on adversarial versus bureaucratic injury compensation policies: 1971 to 2011 (n=414)

the aggregate cross-sectional comparisons, hearings on adversarial policies consistently involved about twice the number of group types as compared to bureaucratic policy hearings, despite the wide ideological and congressional differences across these administrations. So, the general patterns of participation are consistent over a variety of types of comparisons: (a) across policy types and issue areas, (b) within policy types (despite the differences between them, such as the differences between the adversarial policies of product liability and securities fraud and the bureaucratic policies of black lung program and SSDI) and cases with diverse policy types, *and* (c) over time.

Of course, factors other than the type of policy might affect patterns of participation in committee hearings and we need to control for them to ensure that these differences are, in fact, significant. (For a full discussion of our model, including our measures, see Appendix II.) For example, congressional hearings focus on different types of subject matter that may affect interest group participation. On one end of the continuum, Congress holds hearings on specific reform proposals that inevitably involve some policy trade-offs ("referral hearings"), which we might expect to generate high levels of participation, as one of the few regularities in politics is that people will be more energetic about preserving rights and benefits that they already have than seeking new ones.[6] On the other end of the continuum, Congress holds yearly budgetary reviews and appropriation hearings on federally funded programs, which might not generate as much interest because referral hearings on specific reform measures seem more likely to upset the status quo and engender conflict than hearings on routine appropriations and policy maintenance ("budgetary hearings") (see generally Pierson 1994).[7] Between these extremes, Congress regularly holds hearings to gather information about problems related to court and agency practices ("oversight hearings"). Common topics of oversight hearings include the reasons for delays in processing lawsuits or claims or the unintended policy consequences of the rising costs of claim adjudication.[8]

Similarly, the committee's institutional setting may make a difference. Congressional scholars have long-recognized that the Senate and House are very different institutions and we might expect them to conduct different types of hearings (Polsby 1986; Fenno 1982). Committee-level attributes might also plausibly influence who is invited to participate. There is a literature on court-Congress relations that suggests committees that deal with the budgeting and appropriation processes (so called "money" committees), such as the Appropriations Committees, have a very different relationship to the courts than other types of committees, such as "policy" committees like the Judiciary Committees (Melnick 1994; see also Miller 1992; Barnes 2004).[9]

Attributes of the committee chair might also influence the type of groups invited to participate. It is possible that chairs who have served for a considerable period of time might change their practices, as they grow more familiar with the subject matter (and stakeholders). For instance, they may become less reliant on outside sources of information and call fewer witnesses.[10] Conservative and liberal chairs also might tend to call different types of witnesses, just as chairs who believe their party is vulnerable in the next election might call different witnesses compared to chairs who are more secure. Moreover, a committee chair whose legislative preferences are out of step with pivotal players in the legislative process, such as the median voter and majority party leaders in their respective chambers as well as the president, might call different types of witnesses than a chair whose preferences are in line with key players and thus whose proposals have a better chance of passage. Similarly, committees featuring a large ideological gulf between the chair and ranking member of the opposing political party might behave differently than a committee that is less ideologically polarized. Finally, any analysis would need to control for time by (among other things) accounting for each congressional session in our sample, both as a general control for idiosyncratic features of particular Congress and as a way for controlling for hidden maturation effects, such as the possibility that conflict in a policy area naturally diminishes over time. (See Table 2.3 for a summary of the main controls and measures.)

When we account for all these complexities, however, we still find sizeable differences between hearings on adversarial and bureaucratic policies. Table 2.4 reports the findings of an analysis that probes the relationship

Table 2.3 List of Variables and Measures

Name	Measure
Adversarial Policy	0 if the hearing is on a bureaucratic injury compensation policy; 1 if the hearing is on an adversarial injury compensation policy
Referral	0 if the hearing does not consider a specific bill or reform proposal concerning who pays, how much, to whom or who decides; 1 if it does
Oversight	0 if the hearing considers a specific bill or is a routine budget hearing; 1 if the hearing focuses on gathering information about court or agency practices related to injury compensation policy, such as issues related to the cost of resolving claims, delays in claim processing, problems in administration
House Committee	0 if Senate committee; 1 if House committee
Money Committee	0 if the oversight committee is not a money committee (e.g., House and Senate Judiciary Committees); 1 if the oversight committee is a money committee (e.g., House and Senate Appropriations Committees)
Chair Risk of Loss	Gains or losses as a proportion of total seats in the next election by the majority party in the relevant chamber
Chair Seniority	Cumulative number of years served as chair for a specific committee
Chair Ideology	Common Space NOMINATE first dimension score for the committee chair from the Poole and Rosenthal dataset (accessed July 25, 2011)
Chair-Ranking Member Distance	Absolute value of the distance between the Common Space NOMINATE first dimension scores of committee chair and ranking member from the opposing political party
Chair-Chamber Median Voter Distance	Absolute value of the distance between the Common Space NOMINATE first dimension scores of committee chair and median voter of the relevant chamber
Chair-Chamber Majority Leader Distance	Absolute value of the distance between the Common Space NOMINATE first dimension scores of committee chair and leader of relevant chamber in Congress
Chair-President Distance	Absolute value of the distance between the Common Space NOMINATE first dimension scores of committee chair and president
Congressional Session	Dummy variable for each session of Congress in the sample

Note: Appendix II discusses these measures and alternative measures more fully.

Table 2.4 Group Type Participation (Poisson Regression)

Variable Name	Coefficient (Standard Error)	Incidence Rate Ratio
Adversarial Policy	.46 (.07)***	1.59
Controls		
Referral	1.54 (.12)***	4.67
Oversight	1.26 (.12)***	3.52
House Committee	−.10 (.07)	.91
Money Committee	.02 (.07)	1.02
Chair Risk of Loss	2.28 (1.18)*	9.74
Chair Seniority	.01 (.01)	1.01
Chair Ideology	.23 (.21)	1.25
Chair-Ranking Member Distance	−.11 (.13)	.89
Chair-Chamber Median Voter Distance	.46 (.28)	1.58
Chair-Chamber Majority Leader Distance	−.20 (.30)	.82
Chair-President Distance	.38 (.21)	1.47

Controls for each session of Congress, 92nd through 110th.

*p<.05; **p<.01; ***p<.001.

Goodness-of-fit chi2 = 282.2684; prob>chi2(382)=1.0.

between adversarial injury compensation policies and the total number of group types that appeared in the hearings, controlling for the variables listed in Table 2.3.[11] The incidence rate ratios reported in Table 2.4 offer a measure of the magnitude of the effect of the different variables.[12] Using that measure, we see that hearings on adversarial legal policies are expected to have a rate of 1.59 times more group types participating than their bureaucratic counterparts, while holding all control variables constant. This suggests that, all things being equal, hearings on adversarial policies are about 60% more diverse than their bureaucratic counterparts. These results were statistically significant and robust across a range of models and types of statistical analyses (see Table 2.5). Adversarial legalism seems correlated with more diverse hearings than bureaucratic legalism in our sample.

Identity of Participants

We are concerned not simply with the *number* of group types that participate but also the *identity* of those groups, the "who" of injury compensation

Table 2.5 Robustness of Findings: Alternative Models

Variable	Model 1 (Poisson)	Model 2 (Poisson)	Model 3 (Poisson)	Model 4 (Poisson)	Model 5 (OLS)
Adversarial policy	1.59*** (.11)	1.60*** (.10)	1.55*** (.11)	1.56*** (.13)	2.45*** (.28)
Controls included					
Referral	Yes	Yes	Yes	Yes	Yes
Oversight	Yes	Yes	Yes	Yes	Yes
House Committee	Yes	Yes	Yes	No	Yes
Money Committee	Yes	Yes	Yes	No	Yes
Chair Risk of Loss	Yes	Yes	Yes	No	Yes
Chair Seniority	Yes	Yes	Yes	No	Yes
Chair Ideology	Yes	Yes	Yes	No	Yes
Chair-Ranking Member Distance	Yes	Yes	Yes	No	Yes
Chair-Median Voter Distance	Yes	Yes	Yes	No	Yes
Chair-Chamber Majority Leader Distance	Yes	Yes	Yes	No	Yes
Chair-President Distance	Yes	Yes	Yes	No	Yes
Congressional Session	Yes	No	No	No	Yes
Session Number	No	Yes	No	Yes	No
Session Number Squared	No	Yes	No	Yes	No
Session Number Cubed	No	Yes	No	Yes	No
Year	No	No	Yes	No	No
Committee Name	No	No	No	Yes	No

Dependent variable is number of types of groups testifying in the hearing.

Cell entries for adversarial policies are incidence rate ratios with standard errors in parentheses. *p≤.05; **p≤.01; ***p≤.001. Because the likelihood-ratio chi-square test for the dispersion parameter alpha was small and thus p≥.05, we used Poisson regression. However, we ran each of these models as a negative binomial regression and the results were nearly identical. Note also that the variance inflation factor (VIF) in the OLS model did not exceed 10 for any variable, although the mean VIF was around 5.

politics. Here too the data on hearings on adversarial policies are generally consistent with an individualized politics in which diverse interests participate in the policymaking process. Figure 2.2 summarizes the overall participation rates of each type of group that underlies the various stakeholder interests. It is a radar graph in which each spoke represents the participation rate of each type of group in the hearings. A score of 100% indicates that at least one representative of the relevant group type participated in all the hearings. (Note that the group types within stakeholder interests are adjacent in the figure, so, for example, all business interests appear in the upper right-hand quadrant of the graph and claimant interests appear immediately below.)

The differing shapes in the radar graph tell the story. The graph representing hearings on adversarial policies is much rounder, reflecting high levels of participation among a wide range of stakeholder interests. Three types of interests were highly active (business groups (78%), individual businesses (70%), and legal experts (68%)); three groups participated in about 50 to 60% of the hearings (claimant lawyers (60%), defense counsel (55%), and federal officials (49%)); three groups participated in 40 to 50% of the

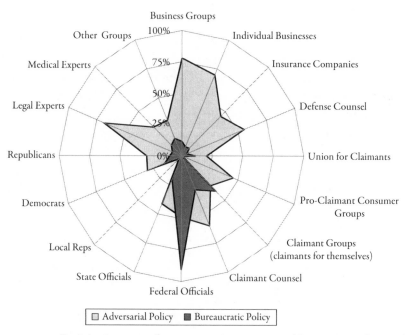

FIGURE 2.2 Participation rates of group types in congressional hearings on adversarial versus bureaucratic injury compensation policies: 1971 to 2011 (n=414) (compiled by authors from CIS hearing abstracts)

hearings (consumer groups (46%), insurance companies (45%), and state officials (42%)); four groups appeared in about 30 to 40% of the hearings (claimant groups (in which claimants represent themselves) (33%), medical experts (33%), Democrats (30%), and Republicans (28%)); and unions on behalf of claimants appeared in 20% of the hearings.

The graph for bureaucratic policies differs starkly. It is sharp and pointy because there is such a big gap between the participation of federal officials and everyone else. Federal officials appeared in 91% of the hearings; the next closest were claimant groups (40%) and state officials (20%). Experts were also less visible, with medical experts appearing in about 12% of the hearings and legal experts appearing in 8%, a huge difference from adversarial legalism where legal experts appeared in nearly 70% of the hearings. Hearings on bureaucratic programs were clearly dominated by federal officials, with regular input from claimants but relatively little participation by business interests, consumer groups, or experts.

Some worry that claimant groups are likely to be outgunned in the politics of adversarial legalism because they are less likely to have the resources to both litigate and lobby. Marc Galanter's classic article "Why the Haves Come Out Ahead" argues that "one-shotters" are likely to be dominated by repeat players in litigation because their relationship to the legal system is so fleeting. As a result, they are not likely to pursue their interest strategically over the long haul or organize to shape the rules governing future litigation (Galanter 1974). In contrast, bureaucratic legalism, because it often involves an ongoing relationship with a government program, should energize claimant groups and engage their interest over time. As seen in Table 2.6, however, claimant interests are equally, if not more active in adversarial legalism hearings. So, with respect to overall hearing participation, at least one claimant interest testified in 67% of all the hearings in adversarial legalism, whereas at least one claimant interest testified in only 40% of the bureaucratic legalism hearings. The composition of claimant representation also varied: claimant groups testified at a statistically equivalent rate in both types of hearings, while unions, pro-claimant consumer groups, and claimant counsel all participated at higher rates in adversarial legalism hearings.

These differences persisted regardless of whether we look at participation rates at individual hearings or at the aggregate level of participation among all group types.[13] Figures 2.3 and 2.4 tell this story. Specifically, whereas Figure 2.2 presents participation rates of groups types in specific hearings, Figure 2.3 presents participation rates of categories of stakeholder interests as a percentage of all group type appearances—a 20% score indicates that

Table 2.6 Participation Rates of Claimant Groups in Congressional Hearings on Adversarial versus Bureaucratic Injury Compensation Policies: A Closer Look (n=414) (compiled by authors from CIS hearing abstracts)

Type of Hearing	Hearings on Bureaucratic Policies	Hearings on Adversarial Policies	Difference in Means (t-value)
Total Number of Hearings	291	123	—
Participation Rate by Any Claimant Group (standard error)	.40 (.03)	.67 (.04)	−.27 (−5.32)***
Participation Rate by Victim Group (standard error)	.40 (.03)	.33 (.04)	.07 (1.20)
Participation Rate by Claimant Union (standard error)	.11 (.02)	.20 (.04)	−.09* (−2.20)
Participation Rate by Pro-Claimant Consumer Group (standard error)	.01 (.004)	.46 (.05)	−.45 (−9.89)***
Participation Rate by Claimant Lawyer (standard error)	.29 (.03)	.60 (.04)	−.31 (−5.98)

Hypothesis: (BL Mean) (AL Mean)≥ 0 *p<t ≤.05; ** p<t ≤.01; *** p<t ≤.001.

T-tests were run assuming unequal variances using Welch's formula.

member groups of a stakeholder interest accounts for one-fifth of all group type appearances across all hearings in our sample.[14] (See Table 2.1 for a list of stakeholder interests and the related group types.) Again, the key differences lie in the patterns of the graphs. Participation on the adversarial policy side, represented by the right-hand column, is more evenly distributed. No single category of stakeholder dominated the testimony: business stakeholders accounted for about 36% of all group appearances, governmental

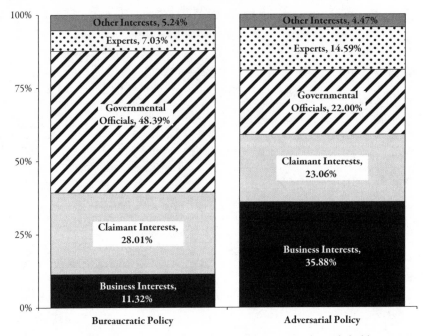

FIGURE 2.3 Distribution of congressional hearing appearances by stakeholder interest type: 1971 to 2011 (n=1,639; 839 BL hearings, 850 AL hearings)

officials and claimant interests each accounted for about 22 and 23% of the group appearances, respectively; and experts accounted for about 15% of all appearances, with the remaining 5% falling into the miscellaneous "other" category. By contrast, government officials made nearly 50% of all group type appearances in hearings on bureaucratic policies, with claimant groups at about 28%. Perhaps most surprisingly, despite the fact that businesses are well-organized and might be expected to be a consistent voice in programs that tax the salaries they pay and the products they produce, they made up only about 11% of all group type appearances in bureaucratic legalism hearings, less than one-third of their rate of appearance in adversarial policy hearings. Using a common measure of market share concentration, stakeholder interest participation in bureaucratic policy hearings was over 30% more concentrated than in adversarial policy hearings.[15]

Figure 2.4 takes a more granular look at these aggregated data, presenting participation rates at the level of specific group types (as opposed to the level of stakeholder interests) vis-à-vis all group appearances. The relative diversity of participation in hearings on adversarial policies again stands out. As seen in the gray horizontal bars in the graph, no single group type accounted for more than 12% of all appearances in the adversarial legalism hearings.

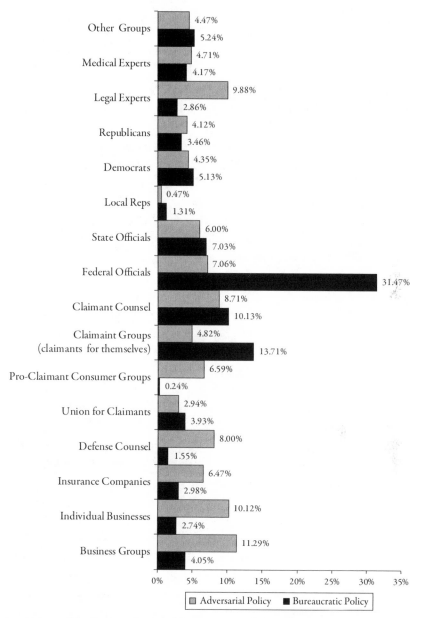

FIGURE 2.4 Distribution of stakeholder appearances by specific group type: 1971 to 2011 (n=1,689; 839 BL hearings, 850 AL hearings)

Participation in hearings on bureaucratic legalism, represented in the black horizontal bars, is spikier, as federal officials comprised more than 30% of all appearances in bureaucratic legalism hearings, more than double the next most active group.

There was not only more diversity across all group types in adversarial policy hearings, but also more diversity *within* active categories of stakeholder interests. So, three sets of stakeholder interests made up 20% or more of all group type appearances in adversarial policy hearings: business interests (36%), claimant interests (23%), and governmental officials (22%). Participation in each of these blocks of interests was spread among different group types. Business interest participation was distributed as follows: business groups, like the National Association of Manufacturers, accounted for 31% of all business interest appearances; individual businesses accounted for 28% of these appearances; defense counsel accounted for 22% of these appearances; and insurance companies made up 18% of these appearances.[16] The same can be said of claimant stakeholder interests, whose participation was divvied up among claimant counsel (38% of all claimant interest appearances), consumer groups (29% of all claimant interest appearances), claimant groups (where claimants represent themselves) (21% of these appearances) and unions (13% of these appearances). Government officials reflect the same dispersed pattern, as participation was divided among federal officials (32%), state officials (27%), congressional Democrats (20%) and Republicans (19%), with local representatives accounting for the small remaining amount.

Bureaucratic policy hearings reflected far less within-category diversity in the only two stakeholder interests that topped the 20% mark: government officials (48%) and claimant interests (28%). Whereas adversarial policy hearings involved a mix of federal, state, and elected officials, federal officials accounted for nearly two-thirds of governmental official appearances in bureaucratic policy hearings (65%), which was more than four times the next-most prevalent group of governmental officials (state officials (15%)). Claimant interests were also less diverse in bureaucratic policy hearings as compared to adversarial policy hearings. In hearings on adversarial policies, claimant interests were represented by a range of groups, including unions, consumer groups, claimant counsel, and claimants speaking for themselves. In bureaucratic policy hearings, claimants were much more likely to represent themselves. They made up about half (49%) of all claimant interest appearances, while claimant counsel accounted for about 36% and unions accounted for 14%. In a sharp contrast with adversarial legalism, consumer groups were largely absent from hearings on bureaucratic legalism.

Testimony Conflict

The diversity in formal representation translated into the expression of competing viewpoints in the legislative process. As seen in Table 2.7, the modal hearing on adversarial policies featured conflict, whereas the modal hearing on bureaucratic policies did not. The rate of conflict also significantly differed, as 88% of all hearings on adversarial policies featured differing viewpoints versus 42% for bureaucratic policies. Moreover, these differences were reasonably stable over the four decades in our sample, as the rates of conflict on hearings on adversarial policies were consistently much higher than rates on hearings on bureaucratic policies, despite the differences in administrations and congresses during this period (see Figure 2.5).[17]

Again, a wide range of other factors might account for these differences. Table 2.8 reports the results of a logit analysis that probes the relationship between policy design and conflict in hearings testimony, controlling for the variables listed in Table 2.3. We find that hearings on adversarial policies are more than twice as likely to feature conflicting viewpoints than hearings of bureaucratic policies.[18] This finding complements the findings on the diversity of participation, suggesting that the different groups not only represent different interests in a formal sense but also appear to represent substantively different points of view. (This also suggests that, at least in our sample, members of Congress did not systematically pack hearings with groups that ostensibly represented different interests but shared the same views.)

To summarize, hearings on adversarial policies in our sample feature more witnesses, more types of groups, and more conflict than hearings on bureaucratic policies. Moreover, whereas participation in bureaucratic policy hearings was dominated by federal officials with regular input from claimants, hearings on adversarial policies featured significant participation across

Table 2.7 **Testimony Conflict in Hearings of Adversarial versus Bureaucratic Injury Compensation Policies: 1971 to 2011 (n=414)**

Type of Hearing	Hearings on Bureaucratic Policies	Hearings on Adversarial Policies	Difference in Means(t-value)
Total Number of Hearings	291	123	—
Modal Level of Conflict	0	1	—
Rate of Conflict	.42	.88	$-.46 \ (11.16)^{***}$

Hypothesis: (BL Mean) (AL Mean) < 0 *p<t ≤.05; ** p<t ≤.01; *** p<t ≤.001.

T-tests were run assuming unequal variances using Welch's formula.

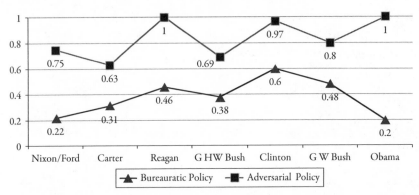

FIGURE 2.5 Rates of conflict in congressional hearing testimony on adversarial versus bureaucratic injury compensation policies: 1971 to 2011 (n=414)

various stakeholder interests and group types. Not surprisingly, businesses, governmental interests, and professional experts were all active in policies on adversarial policies, but claimant groups were active as well. The activity of claimant groups is notable; they tend to have fewer resources and, because they are the actors bringing the lawsuits, they might be expected to become diverted from legislative struggles. Yet two-thirds of all adversarial policy hearings featured testimony from at least one claimant interest, and participation rates by claimants, pro-claimant consumer groups and unions, and claimant counsel were either statistically the same or significantly higher in adversarial policy hearings. This diversity translated into higher levels of conflict, as nearly 90% of adversarial policy hearings featured opposing viewpoints. These general patterns hold regardless of whether we look at participation rates in individual hearings, aggregate participation rates, participation rates across policy types and issue areas, and participation within issue areas that feature different types of policies.

Discussion

When compared to hearings on bureaucratic policies, hearings on adversarial policies are a melee, in which a wide range of groups descend on Washington, representing a mix of business, claimants, consumer groups, legal experts, and lawyers from both sides of the payer/payee divide. To the extent the hearing summaries allowed us to delve into substance, adversarial policy hearings feature disagreements about basic issues such as the actual rate of injury litigation, the science related to the underlying claims, and the costs to payees

Table 2.8 Conflicting Testimony (Logit Regression)

Variable Name	Coefficient (Standard Error)	Odds Ratio
Adversarial Policy	.87(.45)*	2.38*
Controls		
Referral	6.82(.87)***	911.93***
Oversight	4.54(.78)***	93.76***
House Committee	−.60(.46)	.55
Money Committee	1.07(.45)*	2.93*
Chair Risk of Loss	−2.36(9.31)	.09
Chair Seniority	.01(.05)	1.01
Chair Ideology	2.09(1.57)	8.12
Chair-Ranking Member Distance	.40(.90)	1.49
Chair-Chamber Median Voter Distance	3.38(1.97)	28.16
Chair-Chamber Majority Leader Distance	.60(2.04)	1.82
Chair-President Distance	.68(1.60)	1.97
Constant	−4.91(1.50)**	—

Controlling for each congressional session from 92nd to 110th.

84.06% Correctly Predicted; *p<.05; **p<.01; ***p<.001.

of adversarial legalism. Hearings on bureaucratic programs are much more sedate, and tilt to the side of the beneficiaries, with federal officials dominating the proceedings and claimant groups appearing regularly. Other groups, most notably business interests, are largely absent. This less diverse pattern of participation coincided with much less conflict in the testimony, and a narrower range of issues.

The contrast between the two sets of hearings looks a lot like the distinction congressional scholars have made between "fire alarm" and "police patrol" oversight (McCubbins and Schwartz 1984; Lupin and McCubbins 1994). In fire alarm oversight, it is left to interest groups to sound warnings about ongoing problems. In the hearings on adversarial policies, business interests often fulfill this role, but they are opposed by competing interests that disagree on nearly every aspect of the issues being raised, including whether there is a problem at all. By contrast, hearings on bureaucratic injury compensation policies typically resembled "police patrol" oversight in which federal officials monitor policies from the top-down, with some input from claimants but relatively little participation by other groups. Here, testimony did not typically feature opposing views.

Our finding that there is an association between the shape of public policy and the politics it generates may seem to many political scientists a dog-bites-man story, just another confirmation of the now not-so-new neo-institutionalism in the discipline. Injury compensation, however, is a field that offers a particularly tough test of the claim that policy shapes politics, for many reasons. First, as Lowi argued, the underlying material basis of an issue should shape its politics (Lowi 1964, 1972). From this perspective, injury compensation politics is bound to be highly contentious because it is inherently redistributive: injury compensation policies always involve transfers of wealth, and redistribution should create conflict whether it handled by courts or agencies. A second reason injury politics, at least in the United States, offers a tough test of the policy-shapes-politics claim is the extent to which American individualism makes demands for compensation, whatever their form, inherently suspect and thus subject to attack by conservative groups and business interests (Haltom & McCann 2004). This culture-based perspective suggests that however they are designed, injury compensation policies will create sharp political conflict because they violate a basic norm in an individualistic society, that people should take care of themselves.

Even scholars in the policy-shapes-politics tradition recognize that the effects of policy design may be blunted in some contexts. Consider James Q. Wilson's classic analysis of the politics of regulation (Wilson 1989). In general, consistent with standard neo-institutionalist and contemporary policy feedback arguments, Wilson hypothesized that policies with diffuse costs or diffuse benefits should not mobilize interests, because individuals with small stakes in policy outcomes are likely to face a collective action problem: the costs of mobilizing outweighs the expected return at the individual level, even if the collective stakes justifies action at the group level (see also Olson 1965). From this perspective, one might expect that policy design would shape group mobilization, and that court-based public policies such as tort should make the collective action problem particularly acute for claimants, who have only a one-time encounter with the tort system. What is often missed, however, is that Wilson stressed the importance of context, arguing that the collective action problem would not greatly affect politics if "watchdog" or "public interest" groups have already organized in the policy area or policy entrepreneurs were ready to act on behalf of neglected interests (1989:396). In the area of injury compensation, key stakeholders have already organized, including business groups, lawyers (both claimant and defense counsel), unions, consumer groups, liberals and conservatives (Burke 2002; see generally Berry 1999; Skocpol 2003).[19] Moreover, there is no shortage of policy entrepreneurs dedicated to challenging and protecting adversarial legalism, ranging from the Chamber of Commerce and Freedom Works on the right to Ralph Nader and the American Association of Justice (formerly the American Trial Lawyers Association (ATLA)) on the left. Under these circumstances, even if it seems likely that a policy's distribution of costs and benefits might shape its politics as a general matter, injury compensation issues are a less likely case for those effects because there is no collective action problem on either side of the cost-benefit equation, especially given the explosion of interest groups in the past 40 years and the high-stakes nature of policies in our sample. Nevertheless, despite all of the theoretical reasons to suspect that policy design will not greatly affect the politics of injury compensation, we observe stark differences in patterns of participation in hearings on adversarial and bureaucratic policies.

What are the implications of these observed differences for the standard political critiques of adversarial legalism? While it is important not to overstate these findings—and we will discuss some of their key limitations below—these data offer some tantalizing clues about the alleged political costs of adversarial legalism. On one hand, they are inconsistent with the concern that the cost of litigation prevents groups from lobbying. If this were the case, we would expect to see less claimant group participation in congressional hearings on adversarial policies than bureaucratic policies. We did not. Our data suggest claimant groups participated at statistically equivalent levels in hearings on adversarial policies as compared to hearings on bureaucratic policies—and that other types of claimant interests, including unions, claimant counsel and consumer groups, participated at higher levels in hearings on adversarial policies. Indeed, instead of undermining the pluralist ideal of vigorous interest group participation, hearings on adversarial policies seems to embody it, at least as compared to hearings on bureaucratic policies.

On the other hand, these findings are broadly consistent with the idea that adversarial legalism individualizes politics by factionalizing interests. The contention is that the distributional effects of adversarial legalism fragment stakeholder groups. Uneven distribution increases tension among businesses, some of whom bear heavy litigation costs that others escape, and among claimants, some of whom win large recoveries while others get nothing. Adversarial legalism's assignment of blame reinforces this fragmentation by identifying some businesses as villains while ignoring others. This contrasts sharply with the distributional effects and assignment of blame of bureaucratic injury compensation programs. These programs socialize compensation, making costs and benefits relatively smooth and predictable, and so reduce conflict among interests. The even distribution of costs and risks may also facilitate the organization of claimants to protect their benefits and seek higher levels of compensation. On the business side, the smoothing of costs and risks may allow them to pass costs onto employees or consumers, and so reduce the incentive of business interests to mobilize. Issues of individual fault recede as the principle of social responsibility for compensating claimants becomes accepted. Here, all groups, business and claimant included, share an interest in improving the efficiency of program administration.

While the hearing abstracts offered only a limited window into the content of hearings, that window reveals a type of debate that also seems consistent with the individualization argument. While hearings on bureaucratic policies often focused on improving the efficiency of program administration, hearings on adversarial policies seemed a free-for-all. When there was conflict in the bureaucratic hearings, it centered on whether the agency's efforts at improving operations were adequate or not, with government officials defending their efforts and claimant groups demanding better program administration. The legitimacy of the program itself was not a subject of concern.

These findings open several avenues of inquiry that are well suited for case analysis.[20] One task for the case studies, already alluded to, is to explore the *content* of political conflict, not just the lineup of participants. Probing into the details of the interest group politics and policy debates will lend insight into a host of questions that are simply beyond the scope of the congressional hearing abstracts but relevant to assessing the alleged political costs of adversarial legalism: crowd out, path dependence, backlash, and individualization. These questions include: Do groups focus narrowly on litigation once adversarial legalism is established or do they seek a variety of remedies in multiple forums? In the ongoing discourse over policy reform, does adversarial legalism become a "given" once litigation takes hold, preventing consideration of alternatives? Does litigation produce unified opposition or a more fluid, internally-divided pattern of counter-mobilization? Does adversarial legalism hinder coalition-building, or does its fragmentation of interests provide opportunities for temporary, cross-stakeholder alliances?

The case studies also allow us to look beyond congressional oversight, which is obviously just one aspect of politics. This is critical because, in the American system of overlapping policymaking forums, a relatively quiet and consensual politics in Congress might mask a highly contentious brand of politics in executive agencies and the courts (Barnes 2011; Lovell 2003; Powe 2000; Graber 1993). Indeed, in our system of overlapping and diversely representative policymaking forums, there is every reason to suspect that agency and judicial activity will flow where congressional activity and attention has ebbed (Barnes 2011; Erkulwater 2006; Hacker 2004; Melnick 1994).

In a similar vein, the case studies add a developmental perspective to our quantitative comparisons of the politics of adversarial and bureaucratic legalism. By comparing the politics of adversarial and bureaucratic policies as they develop from creation, expansion, and (attempted) retrenchment, we can plot the sequence of events that connect shifts in policy structures to changes in interest group politics. Plotting these sequences, in turn, should help identify the mechanisms that link policy design to politics. To return to the geology metaphor with which we began the chapter, our core samples suggest a potentially diverse political terrain lying between adversarial and bureaucratic legalism. The time has come to map that terrain in greater detail, exploring whether the patterns of conflict revealed in the hearings data also emerge within the case studies.

3

Social Security Disability Insurance: The Politics of Bureaucratic Legalism

In a book about the political effects of adversarial legalism, of public policies that resolve social issues through legal disputing, our first case concerns a public policy that works quite differently. Social Security Disability Insurance (SSDI) is a program that provides a monthly check to workers with disabilities and their families. To qualify for SSDI benefits, an individual has to show that he or she is disabled enough to be unable to work and must have a qualifying work history.[1] There are two major aspects of SSDI that make it, in our terms, an example of bureaucratic legalism. First, the determination of whether a person is disabled is made according to hierarchically determined rules. There are disputes over whether people are really disabled according to the Social Security Administration's (SSA) criteria, and even court cases about the meaning of those rules, but SSA's authority to propagate those rules is not up for dispute. Those who feel they are eligible for SSDI apply to the agency for benefits; they do not begin a struggle over whether SSA's criteria are just or proper or efficient, as they might under adversarial legalism. Second, the funding for SSDI comes from a trust fund that is financed by a tax on work-related income currently set at 1.8%.[2] Thus, where funding of adversarial legalism is usually privatized, the funding of SSDI is socialized across all workers and employers.

If this is a confusing point, think about it this way: People end up on SSDI for all kinds of reasons, but many of those reasons might have led them into court suing another party for some kind of compensation. If you were to become disabled because of an accident, for example, you might sue those you consider responsible, as in the case of those injured by asbestos, the topic of the next chapter. (You might also be unable to get a job and become convinced that a prospective employer is discriminating against you because of your impairments. In that case you might sue under disability discrimination laws such as the Americans with Disabilities Act (ADA).) So if we define the problem SSDI addresses as "being unable to work because of an impairment" then one can imagine many ways a polity might address the issue. SSDI is a bureaucratic policy in that it is implemented primarily through a top-down agency process and the cost of paying for it is socialized.

SSDI is our "control" policy, the comparison point for our later chapters on asbestos injury compensation, in which the policy was predominantly adversarial, and vaccine injury compensation, where the policy shifts from adversarial legalism to (mostly) bureaucratic legalism. The purpose of our case study, then, is to understand in broad terms the political trajectory of SSDI. We do not attempt in this chapter to provide a comprehensive political history of SSDI. That would fill several volumes, as indeed it has (e.g., Derthick 1979, 1990; Berkowitz 1987; Erkulwater 2006; see also Stone 1984). We are fortunate to be able to draw on these accounts in our analysis, which begins with a brief overview of SSDI and its politics. We proceed thematically and focus on several key periods in the history of the program: (1) its creation in the 1950s, (2) its expansion from the late 1950s to the 1970s, (3) an attempted retrenchment under the Carter and Reagan Administrations, and (4) its subsequent growth and modest modifications. By tracing the politics of SSDI during key points of its development, we hope to observe how the politics of bureaucratic legalism plays out across different branches of government and over time, as the policy matures and experiences both expansion and retrenchment. We end with a brief digression on the politics of the ADA, which provides a window into the politics of a federally created, anti-discrimination disability policy that is largely adversarial. Although this policy centers on issues of discrimination and not injury compensation, and thus is not strictly comparable to our cases, the ADA offers an interesting contrast to the politics of SSDI, as well as a transition to the analysis of adversarial injury compensation policies in the later chapters.

Overview

SSDI is huge and growing, by far the biggest injury compensation policy in the United States, and one of the nation's biggest welfare programs.[3] As of 2012, SSDI had more than 12 million beneficiaries, including nearly 5% of all adults between 18 and 64 years of age.[4] In 2010 they received a total of nearly $140 billion per year, an average of about $1,100 per month for each beneficiary, about $13,500 per year. Recipients of SSDI are automatically insured by Medicare at an additional cost of around $60 billion, making the total cost of the program in 2010 around $185 billion per year, or roughly $1,500 for every household in the United States (Autor 2011). The increase in beneficiaries over the past few years has not coincided with an increase in receipts for the Disability Insurance Trust Fund. The program ran a $31 billion dollar deficit in 2012, reducing the Fund to $122 billion, and leading the Social Security Trustees to project the Fund would be depleted by 2016 if no changes are made.[5]

As one might expect, the creation of this program generated intense political conflict, as labor and its allies in Congress fought to provide a federal response to the broad problem of worker disability over the objection of business interests and their allies. Once created, however, conflict has generally subsided, and business has largely stepped aside, leaving the administration of the program to federal officials and a cadre of well-organized beneficiary groups. There have been moments of conflict over the program's cost overruns and attempts to rein the program in, yet in an era of polarized budget politics, in which "entitlements" are under renewed scrutiny, SSDI appears thus far largely immune from attack.[6] SSDI is a welfare program that seems to grow in the shadows of national politics. Aid to Families with Dependent Children (AFDC), the program that was for so many years at the center of the loud national debate on welfare, never reached more than a fraction of the size that SSDI (and SSI, its poorer cousin) has reached today: Back in 2006, SSDI already cost three times as much as AFDC did at its peak (Olsen and Flugstad 2009). This massive budget would seem to make SSDI politically vulnerable, as would its design, which is anachronistic, out of step with the social movement of people with disabilities, for whom a basic premise of the program—that "disabled" means "unable to work"—is pernicious. For both conservatives and disability activists, the continued rise in SSDI rolls, and the declining employment of people with disabilities, would seem to make the program a target of special scrutiny. Instead, after a moment of crisis in the 1980s, SSDI politics has been relatively quiet. As the program continues to expand, it remains obscure to all but a small number of stakeholders. To better understand this political trajectory, it is useful to look at its development in steps, beginning with the contentious politics of SSDI's creation.

The Contentious Politics of Creation: 1949 to 1956

The idea of governmental benefits to help families with disabled breadwinners has deep roots in the creation of modern administrative states, arguably reaching back to the beginnings of the wage economy. Deborah Stone argues that the "very notion of disability is fundamental to the architecture of the welfare state" (Stone 1984: 14). She traces the concept of disability to fourteenth-century England, and shows that it functioned as a marker for those legitimately exempt from the demands of wage employment. In the United States, Theda Skocpol has traced the politics of disability benefits to the nineteenth century, and particularly to the creation of veteran's benefits, a massive welfare program that belies the U.S. reputation as a welfare state laggard (Skocpol 1995).

While the idea of providing benefits to people with disabilities has a long history, our story focuses on SSDI, which traces its roots to the New Deal, when the idea of a federal disability insurance program began to percolate through various study groups and committees. In 1935, after President Roosevelt signed the Social Security Act into law, he appointed a committee, the Interdepartmental Committee to Coordinate Health and Welfare Activities, whose mandate included studying the possibility of federal action on disability compensation. But while this committee eventually recommended some movement toward a compensation program, even liberals in the SSA were wary. In 1938 the Social Security Board declined to recommend such a program, given the administrative difficulties and high costs involved (Stone 1984: 69). In its 1941 annual report, though, the Social Security Administration turned around and made its first formal recommendation for a compensation program, concluding that "[o]ne of the most serious aspects of existing social insurance measures... is the failure to provide protection against the major hazard of disability" (CQ Researcher 1956: 3). The Social Security Board predicted that workplace disability would gain greater urgency after World War II because many workers would not be able to continue working "after the strain of the war years" and there would be a need to open up jobs for soldiers returning home (ibid.). Calls for creating a federal disability insurance program gained momentum after the war, when President Harry Truman endorsed the idea, and SSA officials urged Congress to consider it. The Senate Finance Committee's own blue ribbon commission, the Advisory Council on Social Security, assessed a variety of proposals to expand Social Security, including its extension to workers with disabilities. By the late 1940s, the issue was firmly on Congress's agenda, even if it had not gained much public salience.

Splits within the Advisory Council foreshadowed the conflict that shaped the contentious battle over the creation of SSDI. In an attempt to gain consensus within the Council, Nelson Cruikshank, director of social security issues for the American Federation of Labor (AFL), reported that liberals and labor representatives "compromised and compromised" on a proposal in order to get conservatives and their business allies on board (Derthick 1979: 298). Among other things, they agreed to a narrow definition of disability, the exclusion of workers with temporary disabilities, a six-month waiting period for benefits, and offsets for benefits received from other programs. The report included the eligibility criterion that would eventually become so central to SSDI's operations: applicants would "have to be unable, by reason of a disability medically demonstrable by objective tests, to perform *any substantial gainful activity.*"[7][Emphasis added.] In presenting its recommendations to Congress, Sumner Slichter, associate chairman of the Advisory Council and economics professor at Harvard, stressed the cautious nature of its approach. The central problem, according to Slichter, was "one of providing insurance on such terms that it will not be abused."[8] To meet this challenge, Slichter emphasized the Council's concessions to conservatives, including its limiting of disability to conditions that are "medically demonstrable by objective tests. That rules out a lame back, lumbago, rheumatism, and so forth, if the symptoms are only subjective; it rules out some real disabilities, I am sorry to say, but it seemed necessary."[9] He concluded, "we think that the sound procedure is to start out with a rather modest plan, to give the Government agencies the best possible chance to make a success of administering it, to keep their problems which are going to be difficult in any event to a minimum."[10]

These concessions did not mollify conservative business members of the Council such as M. Albert Linton of the Provident Mutual Life Insurance Company and Marion Folsom of Eastman Kodak. In a dissent from the Council Report, Linton and Folsom argued that however carefully crafted at the outset, a program for disabled workers would be unwieldy and prone to expansion. This was in part because the concept of disability was inherently hard to define, but also because the program would create an entitlement that would reinforce demand, particularly during times of high unemployment. Linton and Folsom pointed to the experiences of private companies who offered disability insurance during the Great Depression. The dissenters predicted that beneficiaries would inevitably pressure Congress into expanding the program: "Once on the statute books, continuous efforts would be made to liberalize the eligibility rules and raise the benefit levels. The country would be well advised not to start on this seductive path in the first place."[11] Linton and Folsom advised that rather than creating a new federal bureaucracy, the national government should instead provide grants to support state disability programs.

But if conservatives like Folsom and Linton were unhappy with the Council recommendations, liberals were also dissatisfied. They sought a broader program, one with fewer work requirements, the provision of benefits to dependents, and, most controversially, the inclusion of workers suffering temporary disabilities. Expansion-minded SSA officials proposed a plan with all these features, though Derthick notes that the temporary disability provision was controversial even within the Administration, as some officials worried that it would prove difficult to administer (Derthick 1979: 298).

Interest groups were deeply divided. Labor sided with SSA and pushed for the creation of the broadest possible program, echoing SSA's stance that the lack of disability coverage presented a major gap in Social Security's safety net. The Chamber of Commerce and insurance companies, meanwhile, opposed the creation of federal disability insurance altogether. As Linton had argued, they suspected that any federal disability benefits program would be hard to contain. They preferred that the federal government channel aid through existing state programs for the disabled poor, a position that was anathema to the liberals in SSA who favored broad social insurance programs over state means-tested programs. The American Medical Association (AMA) was another major opponent. Although the House of Delegates for the AMA had voted to support the creation of a federal disability program before World War II, by the late 1940s it vigorously opposed any program for disabled workers. The AMA reasoned that assessing disability would require a medical diagnosis, which implied government doctors (or federally designated doctors) performing medical services for a large social benefits program at federally approved rates. It feared that an army of doctors making disability determinations would lay the foundation for "socialized medicine" (Berkowitz 1987: 69). Opposition to disability insurance was intense. Arthur Hess, an SSA official, said that business, medical, and insurance groups fought federal disability insurance "tooth and nail," a campaign even more ferocious than their later struggle against Medicare (Derthick 1979: 301).

Opponents won the initial battles. In 1950, advocates proposed both a federal disability insurance program and federal grants to states to supplement their means-tested programs. The liberal House Ways and Means Committee divided along party lines but eventually adopted both proposals. The Senate Finance Committee, much more conservative, voted both down. The conference committee, formed to reconcile the resulting House and Senate bills, split the difference, rejecting the creation of a federal program, but approving federal grants to state assistance programs, the preferred conservative solution.

After this initial setback, disability insurance proponents adopted an incremental approach. Their first step was to link coverage of disabled workers to Social Security by arguing that the retirement system was unfair to those with permanent disabilities. Social Security payments were based on a workers' wage history, so that workers who became permanently disabled and stopped working faced reduced retirement benefits, or no benefits at all. To rectify this injustice, SSA officials in 1952 proposed a "disability freeze" under which years of permanent disability would be excluded when calculating Social Security eligibility and benefits. That year, sympathetic Republican Senator Robert Kean (NJ) added the disability freeze to a package of technical amendments to a Social Security Act that was then approved by the House Ways and Means Committee. Although seemingly innocuous, the freeze proposal created sharp political divisions when it hit the House floor, as opponents of federal disability insurance correctly foresaw it as the first step in a campaign for a federal program. The ranking Republican member of the Ways and Means Committee, Daniel Reed, echoed AMA rhetoric about disability insurance, decrying the freeze as the "entering wedge" for "socialized medicine in this country."[12] As in earlier congressional battles on disability, the proposal passed the House but was rejected in the Senate. The conference committee struggled to reach a compromise. The retiring chair of the House Ways and Means Committee, the notoriously stubborn "Mulely" Doughton, was determined to leave a legacy on the issue, but there was equally determined opposition among Senate Finance Committee members. The conference committee came up with a bizarre provision that had no practical effect yet allowed Doughton to claim he had enacted the freeze: the disability freeze was adopted but set to expire on June 30, 1953, even as another provision precluded SSA from receiving any applications for the freeze until July 1, 1953, the day after. The freeze ended before it had begun.

It was another setback for disability insurance proponents. Nevertheless, in the course of designing the freeze proposal, they hit upon an idea that helped reduce opposition to a disability program: they decided to use state officials, not federal bureaucrats or doctors, to make disability determinations. This appealed to conservatives, who feared that SSA executives would have a vested interest in growing the program, and thus would not hold the line against questionable claims, and to the AMA, which opposed the plan in part because they did not want doctors to serve as program administrators or make final decisions on what constitutes disability. To further allay these concerns, SSA would only be given the power to reverse a finding of disability; it could not reverse a denial made by local officials. Limiting the power of SSA's oversight in this way seemed to promise that federal officials could only serve as a brake on enrollments into the program, never an accelerator, an arrangement that blunted fears of an expansionist federal bureaucracy.

The election of President Eisenhower in 1952 was pivotal in breaking the deadlock over the freeze. Somewhat surprisingly, the Eisenhower Administration sided with SSA and organized labor over the objections of many Republicans and business interests, who saw the disability freeze as a Trojan horse for creating a federal disability benefits program. Roswell Perkins, assistant Secretary of the Department of Health Education and Welfare (HEW), defended the Administration's position among GOP members of Congress by stressing its intent to emphasize the rehabilitation of workers in the program's administration, primarily through existing state programs. Vocational rehabilitation was a cornerstone of the Eisenhower administration's vision of a different kind of welfare state, one that addressed social welfare problems while still encouraging independence. The administration believed that the disability freeze would complement the administration's push for greater vocational rehabilitation funding; an individual considered disabled under the freeze would be a good candidate for the new rehab programs the administration supported (Berkowitz and McQuaid 1980). Congressional Republicans remained skeptical but fell into line. The disability freeze passed as part of the 1954 Amendments to the Social Security Act.

With the freeze in place, proponents of disability insurance promptly did exactly what GOP skeptics feared: they pushed for the next step, a federal program. To implement the freeze, SSA developed a disability determination process very much along the lines of one that would be required to run a disability insurance program, and proponents argued the operation of the freeze showed that worries about a federal disability program were overstated. The Eisenhower Administration balked. It insisted that the disability freeze was intended as a limited fix to the Social Security Act and not the first step toward a new form of social insurance. On March 22, 1956, Secretary of HEW for the Eisenhower Administration, Marion B. Folsom—the same Folsom who had dissented from the initial Advisory Council report—testified against the creation of a new program before the Senate Finance Committee. He advocated a wait-and-see approach: "I believe the wisest course at this time would be to gain further experience under the recent far-reaching amendments [establishing the freeze]...We all have sympathy with the special needs that may arise for some individuals... [but] we cannot provide every desirable benefit or cover every possible need without imposing a future tax burden on the people that might endanger public support for the system we are trying to uphold" (CQ Researcher 1956: 2).

SSA officials and their allies in organized labor decided to press ahead. The fight came to a head in the summer of 1956, just prior to the presidential election. The Senate, which had been the graveyard of earlier proposals, was the epicenter of the fight. In the congressional hearings, familiar battle lines were drawn between business and labor. A.D. Marshall, Chairman of the Chamber of Commerce's Committee on Economic Security, argued that "The proposal to pay disability benefits is not a new one. It was carefully considered and—we believe, wisely—rejected by the Senate Finance Committee in 1950."[13] In opposing the bill, the Chamber of Commerce reiterated its arguments that the bill would undermine incentives to work, prove costly and hard to administer, and unnecessarily impinge on state programs. Walter Reuther of the United Auto Workers rejoined that the "most serious omission in the original Social Security Act was its failure to provide income for employees suffering from long-term disabilities. We in labor have long urged that this omission be corrected by the incorporation of disability insurance in the Nation's social security system."[14]

The policy arguments were familiar, but the political ground had shifted. A Democratic majority had been elected to Congress in 1954, and with the 1956 presidential election looming, was spoiling for a fight with the Republicans. In addition, Wilbur Cohen, a powerful advocate, had left the Eisenhower Administration to become a professor at the University of Michigan, thereby freeing himself to lobby for disability insurance on the Hill. In the Senate, where the task was to unite Democrats, Lyndon Baines Johnson had become Majority Leader, while Harry Bird became chair of the Finance Committee, replacing the influential (and up to this point less pliant) former chair, Senator Walter F. George of Georgia, who had taken over as chair of the Foreign Relations Committee. Perhaps most importantly, Senator George, who had strongly opposed disability insurance as Chair of the Finance Committee, had a change of heart, becoming a leading supporter. Berkowitz (1987: 74–75) attributes George's flip to persuasive lobbying by organized labor, including a letter from AFL leader George Meany arguing that disability insurance would be a proud legacy of George's service in the Senate. Whatever the reason for his conversion, on the last day of the 84th Congress, George gave the final speech in the Senate in favor the bill, an hour-plus presentation that SSA official Alvin David believed helped turn the tide: "Nobody in the world could have done this except Senator George. He had the prestige and the ability [to] make these ideas come out and hit people, make an impact."[15] As George gave his speech, organized labor, Wilbur Cohen, and Majority Leader Lyndon Johnson did some joint arm-twisting, and the Senate passed the measure by the barest of margins, 47 to 45. It is not entirely clear why President Eisenhower, whose administration had opposed the legislation, nonetheless failed to veto it.[16] The strict limits put into the program, particularly its limitation to those aged 50 and over, may have played a role, as this was the group least likely to benefit from vocational rehabilitation, the administration's preferred approach to disability (Berkowitz and McQuaid 1980).

In summarizing the early politics of SSDI, Derthick emphasizes the role of interest groups: "The contest over disability insurance, though intense, was narrow. It involved organizations only: the coalition of SSA and organized labor on one side against the AMA, the insurance industry, and the Chamber of Commerce on the other" (1979: 303). It is worth adding that divisions were almost entirely across stakeholder groups, not within them. The AMA, business groups, and insurance groups united against the program, while labor and SSA staunchly supported it. These groups fought over nearly every aspect of the program, including who should be paid, how much, who should decide, and of course whether there should be a program at all. But though these were intense struggles in Congress, especially the Senate Finance Committee, they happened without a lot of public fanfare. Indeed, in the 1952 election, neither the Democratic nor Republican party platform even mentioned the issue—"a sign of both of the haphazard quality of the [political] parties' involvement in social security policy-making and of the limited public awareness of the issue" (Derthick 1979: 303).

The Bureaucratic Legal Structure of SSDI

The newly created SSDI program was housed in HEW and placed under the auspices of the Bureau of Old Age and Survivors Insurance of SSA, headquartered in Baltimore, Maryland. The program was financed by a .25% payroll tax both employers and employees, with self-employed workers chipping in 3/8ths of a percent of their earnings. From the start, SSA faced large backlogs, mainly because the disability freeze required it to assess applications involving disabilities reaching back to 1941. Nevertheless, SSA ramped up quickly. According to a 1960 report from the Subcommittee on the Administration of Social Security to the House Ways and Means Committee, within four years of its creation, 750,000 disabled persons and their dependents were benefiting from the program and the disability freeze, more than 1.3 million determinations of disability had been made, and disability determinations were continuing at a rate of 30,000 a month.[17]

As the result of the politics at the program's creation, SSDI was designed with a complex federal structure, and this structure continues to shape the way claims are handled. Cases are initially filed in district offices at the state level, which make the initial determinations and reconsiderations of eligibility. Cases can then be appealed to an administrative law judge and then, eventually, to the federal courts. In the first four years of the program, the vast majority of the cases—more than 95%—were determined at the earlier stages of the process, where state officials made the key decisions subject to oversight by the Bureau. Of the 1,450,500 total filings during this period, 312,700 (21.6%) were dismissed by the district office after the preliminary interview; 1,088,600 (75%) were determined by the state disability teams (about 70% during the first review, and 5% during reconsideration); 27,000 (1.8%) were decided by an ALJ after an administrative hearing; and 64 cases (less than .00005%) went to federal courts.[18] Only one case reached a federal appeals court, and that court affirmed the SSA's decision. Perhaps because of this limited role of courts, the process proceeded relatively quickly. In December 1959, the median time for a determination was between 73 and 119 days.[19]

Although no policy represents a pure example of bureaucratic or adversarial legalism, SSDI was, and continues to be, operated largely as a bureaucratic policy. It is *formal* in that decisions are made according to preexisting rules and procedures; it is *hierarchical* in that the administration of the policy is driven from the top down. Given the importance of the structure and operations of SSDI to our analysis, it is worth taking a closer look at the structure before exploring its politics. Most aspects of that structure remain in place today.

To be eligible for disability payments, claimants have to be "fully insured" under the program, which generally means that they have to have been employed and paying Social Security taxes for some proportion of their adult lives. This determination is made by officials at the initial screening of candidates using existing federal records. Determining whether a claimant is disabled is far less straightforward. To qualify as disabled under the statute, individuals have to be unable to "engage in any substantial gainful activity by reason of any medically determinable physical or mental impairment which can be expected to result in death or to be of long-continued and indefinite duration." Although this definition was intended to be narrow to facilitate administration, it leaves lots of room for interpretation, particularly in determining the scope of "substantial gainful activity" (or SGA).

The publicly available regulations and guidelines at the outset of the program did little to elaborate. SSA's formal regulations on the meaning of "disability" stated that "[w]hether or not the impairment in a particular case constitutes a disability is determined from all the facts of a case."[20] The regulations added that, in assessing whether the applicant is unable to engage in a SGA, "primary consideration is given to the severity of the impairment. Consideration was also given such other factors as the individual's education, training, and work experience."[21] HEW also published a booklet entitled "Disability and Social Security," which was intended to explain the process to the public, but its explanations were hardly illuminating. It stated that "earnings rate" would be a factor and that "[d]emonstration of capacity to work regularly and substantially by a self-employed person would rebut disability even though he operates at a loss." The booklet did provide a list of common medical conditions that resulted in a finding of disability. The listings were essentially a set of clinical descriptions of conditions under general headings, such as "musculoskeletal system," "special sense organs," and "cardiovascular system," as opposed to specific clinical benchmarks. So, for example, under "digestive system," the booklet defined "diseases and disorders of the digestive system" as conditions that "interfere with proper food intake, digestion or excretion [that] may prevent proper body nutrition." It added that, "In evaluating capacity to work in cases of applications involving impairment of the digestive system, the evaluation team considers the following: (a) Severity of anemia, malnutrition or loss of strength despite therapy, (b) Existence of ascites (fluid in abdominal cavity), bleeding from digestive system, or other sighs of advanced disease unrelieved by therapy; and (c) Residuals of surgical intervention (e.g., colostomy, ileostomy) and manageability of device."[22] Arthur Hess, a top SSA official, explained that the listings were not intended to be hard and fast rules, rather a means to separate easy cases from those that required more careful, individual assessment (Erkulwater 2006: 100).

Taken together, the publicly available rules and booklet left considerable room for the exercise of professional judgment, raising questions as to the degree of the program's formality, the extent to which preexisting rules shape decision-making according to the bureaucratic ideal. Indeed, SSA intentionally resisted the publication of detailed rules for fear that it would invite applicants to manipulate their applications to fit the stated criteria and avoid work.[23] However, the SSA developed a set of confidential guidelines that were used internally to decide cases. These internal guidelines were far more specific than the publicly available material. So, while the statute, regulations, and booklet helped identify "easy" cases and gave a general sense of the relevant factors governing the determination of SGAs in closer ones, the confidential manual provided an across-the-board rule of thumb: if applicants earned over $1,200 annually, they were engaged in a SGA in the absence of contrary evidence.[24] The 1960 Subcommittee Report on the operations of SSDI added that the "binding nature of this guide is shown by the fact that…a survey was undertaken which showed that no disability beneficiary was maintained on the rolls after he demonstrated an earning capacity of more than $1,200 a year in competitive nonsubsidized employment."[25] In short, while the early SSDI program lacked transparency and there was room for officials to use their judgment, program administration was governed by fairly detailed formal rules and presumptions that applied to all cases.

In structure, SSDI varies from an ideal type hierarchical program in one significant respect: the initial determination of eligibility is made not by SSA officials but by state agencies that contract with the federal government. This introduces a level of decentralization that is at odds with the hierarchical ideal of bureaucratic legalism. At the outset of the program, 56 state agencies contracted with the federal government to make the determination of eligibility using Bureau standards.[26] It was typically the state rehabilitation agencies that took on the task of assessing disability, although four states (New York, North Carolina, Oklahoma, and Washington) administered SSDI through public assistance programs. The decentralized design helped quell fears of an overweening federal bureaucracy, but threatened to create inconsistencies in the disability determination process across states. To try to limit these inconsistencies, the SSA has used its oversight over the state agencies and the claiming process to make the process more uniform, in line with the bureaucratic ideal. For example, although the law formally limited the power of the Bureau to reversing only positive findings at the state level, the Bureau reviewed all district office determinations in practice under a procedure known as "bounce back" or "write backs." Using this procedure, the central office would return any case that it believed was wrongly decided, including denials of benefits, to root out inconsistent application of the rules.[27] The tension between the bureaucratic ideal of consistency and the realities of a decentralized system of claim processing remains a source of distress in the program.

If an application was denied at the state or bureau level, the claimant had several opportunities to appeal the decision. Because appeals potentially increase the scope of discretion on the part of decision-makers and so make advocacy on behalf of the claimant more significant, they can inject adversarial legalism into an otherwise hierarchical process, but the SSDI appeals process was designed to curb this. The first appeal was to an Administrative Law Judge (ALJ) within SSA. The ALJ's could hold hearings, and claimants could bring attorneys to represent them in these hearings, but the ALJ process was designed as an administrative review, not a trial or judicial appeal: it was not an adversarial process because the SSA was not represented by counsel and did not participate as an opposing party. If the ALJ decision was negative, a claimant could turn next to the Appeals Council of the SSA, which could conduct an additional review of the decision. Finally the claimant could file an appeal with a U.S. federal district court, but the court's scope of review was designed to be deferential to SSA: the court reviewed the case based on the administrative record to determine if the decision was supported by "substantial evidence" and could not take new evidence on the case. The district court could also remand the case for further hearings or the taking of additional evidence. (A negative decision in the district court could of course be appealed up the federal hierarchy all the way to the Supreme Court.) The main objective of this multi-tiered system of appeals was to make decisions more uniform and enhance accountability of the district offices, in line with the bureaucratic ideal.

As we describe below, over time there have been changes in the appeals process, some of which have injected more adversarial legalism into the program. Today there is greater use of attorneys, of appeals, and of judicial review in the federal courts. That said, in its basic structure the claiming process and funding remains much as it was at the outset of the program, and so in most important respects the program has remained fundamentally bureaucratic in design, especially in comparison to the tort system, the subject of the next chapter.

The Quiet Politics of Program Expansion: Late 1950s to Late 1970s

SSDI was forged in a contentious political environment that yielded major compromises aimed at limiting the scope of the policy, preventing its growth, and facilitating its administration. These compromises included the following:

- Exclusion of dependents from the program;
- Provision of offsets for benefits received from other programs;
- Limitation of benefits to workers aged 50 to 65;
- Exclusion of temporary benefits;
- Requirement of a six-month waiting period;
- Narrow eligibility requirements based on participation in the workforce; and
- Limitation of SSA's power to reverse state determinations to cases of acceptance.

Almost immediately, and continuing over the next decade and a half, many of these concessions were removed, relaxed, or circumvented. In 1958, coverage of dependents was added and offsets for benefits from other programs were dropped. Two years later, the age limit of 50 was dropped and, in 1965, Congress replaced the "long continued and indefinite duration" requirement in the definition of disability with a 12-month duration requirement, which opened the door to coverage of some temporary disabilities. In 1972, the six-month waiting period was reduced to five months, and throughout this period—in 1958, 1960, 1965, 1967, and 1972—the eligibility requirements were liberalized (Derthick 1979). (See Table 3.1 for a summary.)

Other key concessions were reversed by administrative practice. A classic example concerned the law's limit on SSA's power to review state decisions. Recall that, under the statute, SSA could only reverse *positive* decisions accepting claims, not *negative* ones disallowing them—a crucial concession to conservatives who feared SSA would approve borderline claims to grow the program. However, the SSA instituted the practice of "bouncing back" decisions with which it disagreed, including decisions by state officials denying claims. Moreover, SSA made no secret of its intent to interpret the

Table 3.1 Legislative Expansions of SSDI's Eligibility: 1958 to 1972

Date	Legislation	Summary
1958	Social Security Amendments of 1958 (PL 85-840)	• Coverage of dependents added • Offsets for other programs dropped • Eligibility standards liberalized
1960	Social Security Amendments of 1960 (PL 86-778)	• Age limit of 50 years dropped • Eligibility standards liberalized
1965	Social Security Amendments of 1965 (PL 89-97)	• Opening coverage to some temporary disability by replacing "long continued and indefinite duration" requirement with 12-month duration requirement in the definition of disability • Eligibility standards liberalized
1967	Social Security Amendments of 1967 (PL 90-248)	• Eligibility standards liberalized
1972		• Six-month waiting period reduced to five months • Eligibility standards liberalized

program broadly. In 1957 congressional hearings, the head of SSA's Division of Disability Operations Robert Ball stated his belief that "[w]here there is a reasonable doubt in a close case, the disabled individual should be given the benefit of the doubt" (quoted in Derthick 1979: 310).

Given how hard the fight over the creation of SSDI had been, and given the suspicions by program opponents that the key compromises would be abandoned once the program began operations, one would think that any attempt to reverse these compromises would engender backlash. They did not. In summing up this period in the history of SSDI, Martha Derthick (1979: 311) writes:

> The remarkable thing about the post-1956 liberalization of the law was that it encountered so little resistance. As issue that had provoked intense conflict for much of a decade suddenly seemed to lose its political salience. Congressional committees that had labored to write suitably restrictive language could not recall that they had written it, or why, and instead began asking administrators why it took so long to adjudicate disability claims and why seemingly disabled claimants sometimes had their claims denied. This important change stemmed, first of all, from the changed behavior of the hostile pressure groups.

The sharp decline in overall business participation is all the more striking because there is little evidence that business had warmed to the idea of a federal program. In its 1957 policy statement, the Chamber of Commerce explicitly criticized the creation of the program, stating that voluntary and state programs for the disabled are "the appropriate means of providing for the disabled who need help. The recent enactment of a federal system of disability benefits...does not alter this fundamental concept" (quoted in Derthick 1979: 311). Moreover, the Chamber signaled its intention to hold SSA to the legislative bargain for a narrow program, calling for "rigorous screening of disability claims"—precisely contrary to Robert Ball's 1957 testimony that the program would give close cases the benefit of the doubt.

Just as opponents had warned, SSDI grew steadily from its inception. According to Annual Statistical Reports from SSA, the total number of SSDI beneficiaries grew from roughly 500,000 in 1960 to 1.2 million in 1965, 1.8 million in 1970, 2.9 million in 1975, and over 3.4 million in 1980. Total monthly payments to workers, whose benefits make up the lion's share of all benefits under the program, rose in parallel during this period from roughly 40 million dollars in 1960 to one billion in 1980.[28] The tax burden of the program also increased. Growing costs in SSDI can be financed by either expanding the taxable wage base of the whole Social Security program or increasing the portion of the Social Security tax devoted to Disability Insurance. From the 1950s to the 1970s Congress repeatedly did both. It raised the wage base from $4200 to $29,700 in 1981. (Figure 3.2 shows the wage base increase in 2011 dollars.) The part of the Social Security tax that funded SSDI was raised from .5% to 1.2%, shared equally by employees and employers. (See Figure 3.2.)

Despite this growth, business and other critics of SSDI's creation largely stayed on the sidelines. In the words of Derthick (1979: 369), program expansion occurred under the auspices of a small "subgovernment" of like-minded SSA executives, Social Security specialists in organized labor, members of the House Ways and Means and Senate Finance committees, and key members of the Advisory Council on Social Security—"not exactly a neat triangle, but nonetheless a very limited and stable set of actors with a high degree of autonomy and well-developed doctrines to guide their decisions." As a result, during this period, "[p]olicymaking came to resemble a prolonged symphony in which the movements were conceived by 'executive composers'" (Derthick 1979: 46), largely free from the normal veto points in the legislative process, as key committee proposals were approved without amendment.

A Struggle over Retrenchment

The growth of SSDI accelerated in the late 1960s and 1970s. Annual applications grew from 500,000 per year in 1965 to nearly 1.3 million in 1975; annual awards doubled from roughly 250,000 to 500,000 in the same period. The total number of awards per 1,000 insured jumped from 4.8 in 1970 to 7 in 1975, or more than 45% (see Figure 3.1). At the time, experts attributed the growth in SSDI to a number of causes. Some were structural, including the aging of the population, the souring of the economy, rising unemployment, the declining stigma associated with disability, and the growing generosity of benefits relative to wages (the "replacement ratio") (Erkulwater 2006; see also Autor and Duggin 2006; Lando and Krute 1976: 3–17).

Whatever its causes, this growth created problems for the program. Fiscally, although both the wage base (in 2011 inflation-adjusted dollars) and payroll tax rates were going up during this period (see Figure 3.2), they did not keep pace with growth in enrollments, resulting in the potential insolvency of the SSDI Trust. Administratively, SSA became swamped, especially in 1969 when Congress gave it an additional job, running the

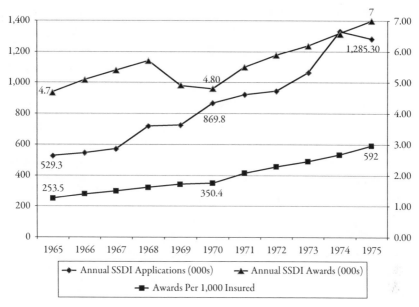

FIGURE 3.1 SSDI program growth 1965 to 1975: applications, awards, and awards per 1,000 insured (compiled by authors from Annual Statistical Report 2010)

FIGURE 3.2 Increases in combined employer and employee SSDI payroll tax and wage base: 1965 to 1975 (in 2011 inflation-adjusted dollars)

Black Lung Benefits program. SSA learned that it was going to implement the Black Lung Program a mere three weeks before it received a flood of applications. According to agency employees, applications stacked up in the hallways, as some district offices in coal mining states like Kentucky, West Virginia, and Pennsylvania received more claims for black lung benefits in two months than they did for all other claims combined for the last year (Erkulwater 2006).

In many ways Congress set SSA up for failure, first with the Black Lung Program, and then with the passage in 1972 of Supplemental Security Income (SSI), a needs-based program for disabled and aged people who did not qualify for SSDI or the Old Age Social Security benefit. Implementing SSI was a daunting task, even under the best of circumstances. It required SSA to, among other things, develop formal rules for administering the program, collect data on the millions of potential beneficiaries from over 1,000 state and local agencies, open hundreds of new offices, hire thousands of new staffers, publicize the program and develop the infrastructure—including software and computer systems—to process claims (Derthick 1990; Berkowitz and DeWitt 2013). In the months prior to the formal processing of claims on January 1, 1974, the office in Lima, Ohio, noted that "SSI could well be the program that ruins the reputation of the Social Security Administration," while others lamented that "we have serious doubt we'll have the time with which to do justice to the public we serve" (quoted in Derthick 1990: 160). After the Program officially began, the office in Lancaster, California, quipped that "By mid-February we tried 'Dial a Prayer' and by mid-March were negotiating for an exorcist" (ibid.) Problems with the Black Lung program and SSI inevitably resulted in a slew of constituent complaints and administrative reviews in which administrative law judges and the federal courts became increasingly willing to reverse SSA decisions (Erkulwater 2006).

These problems inevitably spilled over to the administration of SSDI. Increasing concerns in Congress and in the Carter Administration about the program's management and growth precipitated a major retrenchment. A combination of legislative and administrative actions sharply reduced the rate at which working-age people gained benefits. As seen in Figure 3.3, total SSDI applications fell more than 13%, from roughly 1.23 million in 1976 to 1.06 million in 1985. Annual awards dropped almost 25% from roughly 550,000 to about 416,000 during the same period. The number of awards per 1,000 insured plummeted from 6.4 to 3.9, a drop of nearly 40% (see Figure 3.3). A long era of quiet, unchecked growth had come to an end.

Welfare state retrenchment is often associated with the Reagan Administration, but the process of retrenching SSDI began under the Carter Administration. President Carter's Secretary of HEW, Joseph Califano, was characteristically blunt in assessing SSDI, calling it a "caricature of bureaucratic complexity" and in need of "fundamental reassessment and overhaul" (Berkowitz

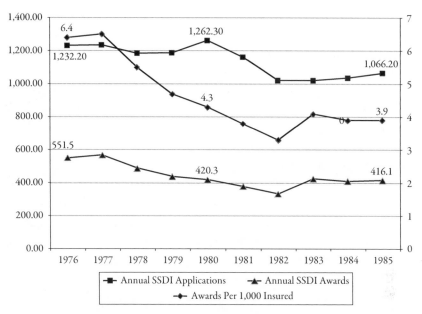

FIGURE 3.3 SSDI program retrenchment 1975 to 1985: applications, awards, and awards per 1,000 insured (compiled by authors from Annual Statistical Report 2010)

1987: 106). The Carter Administration worked on a variety of proposals to shore up the whole Social Security system. For SSDI the culmination of these efforts was the enactment of the Disability Benefits Reform Act of 1980.

The Act was intended as a compromise. On one hand, it cut payments to future beneficiaries, limiting the amount of family benefits and reducing the wage base used to calculate the benefit, especially for younger workers. On the other hand, it included several provisions designed to make it easier for existing beneficiaries to return to work. The Act allowed beneficiaries to deduct the cost of personal attendants from their earnings so that they could work and not lose benefits, it extended Medicare coverage for the first four years after the return to work, and it lengthened the trial work period during which beneficiaries could immediately return to the rolls if they could not continue in their jobs. It also made some administrative changes aimed at reducing inconsistencies across states, thus reinforcing the hierarchical structure of the program. The Act formally required state offices to make determination of disability according to federal regulations, as opposed to agreements negotiated between the federal government and the states that had traditionally governed the program, and it required SSA, beginning in 1982, to review at least 65% of all state decisions awarding benefits. Finally, the bill mandated that SSA review every beneficiary who was not permanently disabled and assess his or her eligibility.

In describing the bill, Stanford Ross, the Commissioner of SSA, stressed the need to bring the program back into balance by placing a higher priority on getting people back to work and creating greater uniformity of standards. Ross testified that the bill incentivized work not only by cutting benefits, especially for young people, but also by eliminating barriers to those who wanted to work. When asked whether cutting benefits was punitive by Senator Heinz, Ross argued that it was not:

> You really have two cross-cutting concepts built into this program. It is a social insurance program. Social insurance principles are important in disability programs. Somehow when the amount of benefits one can get by going on the rolls gets too high, you break too far away from the insurance concept. The other concept is the social adequacy concept. Yes, you do attempt to provide more adequate benefits when there is a family than there is a single worker. But you have to balance the two concepts. We feel that it is out of balance because you can receive more money by being on the rolls than off the rolls.[29]

Business groups and insurance companies agreed. Michael Romig, representing the Chamber of Commerce, stated that "We believe passage of this legislation would signal to the American public that Congress is able and willing to make some of the rough decisions that lie ahead of it on social security."[30] Gerald Parker, on behalf of the Health Insurance Association of America, added that, "You will hear many emotional assertions, and probably have already heard some, that the disabled are too crippled, too sick, too old, too poor to return to work. Most of them are, but we are not talking about rehabilitating 50 percent, or even 10 percent. What we hope to do, and what we think this bill might do, is to raise the recovery rate from around 1.5 percent to about 3.5 percent."[31] The National Association of Manufacturers echoed these arguments in its written statement.

While advocates for beneficiaries applauded efforts to expand Medicaid payments and make it easier for beneficiaries to return to work, they fought any cuts in benefits on a number of grounds. Some questioned whether the SSDI Trust was in fact in trouble. Representative Claude Pepper, a Democrat from Florida and staunch advocate for the elderly, testified that contrary to the naysayers, the SSDI Trust was "expected to grow from 31 percent of outlays in fiscal 1979 to 56 percent in fiscal 1984."[32] More important, from Pepper's perspective, the beneficiaries in the program had been found to have serious disabilities, so that the idea that cutting their benefits would create an incentive for them to work made little sense. Wilbur Cohen, former head of the SSA and president of SOS Coalition to Save our Social Security, also weighed in against any cuts, stating that "all of the disabled and blind groups are vigorously opposed to ... the 150 percent cap, the 80 percent lifetime earnings, and the reduction in benefits for younger workers."[33] They were joined in their opposition by a host of advocacy groups for beneficiaries, including the National Multiple Sclerosis Society, Paralyzed Veterans of American, Veterans of Foreign Wars of the United States, the American Council for the Blind, and the Association for Retarded Citizens. Unions, including the International Association of Firefighters and the AFL-CIO, also spoke out against the cuts in benefits. Groups representing claimants remained unified in their opposition, even though the proposed cuts would fall hardest on younger and future beneficiaries. Ironically, there was little testimony on the provision that would become the most controversial under the Reagan Administration, the medical reviews of those receiving benefits. Indeed, Wilbur Cohen, the program's longstanding proponent, strongly supported them, stating that, if Congress funded extra staff, he would encourage reviews every year instead of every three years as the bill envisaged.[34]

While Congress was wrestling over statutory changes to SSDI, SSA was quietly tightening its practices in determining disability, placing greater emphasis on standardized, "objective" factors. SSA adopted a two-stage approach to assessing disability. Initially, examiners would assess an applicant's condition with SSA's Listing of Medical Impairments. If an applicant failed to satisfy these criteria, examiners would proceed to a more individualized assessment based on the applicant's functional and vocational abilities (Erkulwater 2006: 99). In the late 1970s, SSA officials sought to tighten disability standards by using objective standards that could be verified with medical examinations and laboratory tests. So, for example, it was not enough for claimants to assert that they were experiencing pain; they had to have clinical symptoms of a medical disease or condition that was known to cause pain. Particular emphasis was placed on standardizing the assessment of mental disorders. To replace holistic assessment of the claimant's condition, SSA developed a complex rating scale based on specific system. In disability reviews, the SSA would assess whether the beneficiary met the new standards, not whether the individual's impairments had improved.

According to Erkulwater, these subterranean changes at the administrative level, while gaining notice of program officials on the frontlines, did not generate a strong political reaction among beneficiaries at first and, indeed, may "have continued indefinitely, without anyone noticing, had President Reagan not launched a very visible and very controversial assault on Disability Insurance in 1981" (2006: 115). Reagan came into office determined to cut taxes and increase defense spending while trimming the federal budget, in part by restricting eligibility for federal benefits. Initially, the Reagan proposed to limit access to SSDI by moving toward a stricter medical definition of disability. When Congress refused, Reagan turned to an administrative strategy, which would use his executive authority to rid the rolls of those who were not "truly" disabled—a strategy he employed as governor of California under the banner of "purifying" (Erkulwater 2006; Berkowitz 1987).

SSDI was an attractive target for the Reagan Administration for several reasons. First, the program was ripe for reform. SSA's own studies suggested as many as 20 to 26% of beneficiaries did not satisfy the program's eligibility standards. The Government Accounting Office used these numbers to estimate that 584,000 ineligible claimants were receiving checks, costing taxpayers $2 billion annually (Berkowitz 1987: 126). Second, in passing the Benefits Reform Act, Congress had created the legal framework for some belt-tightening, including mandated triennial reviews of every beneficiary who was not permanently disabled beginning in 1982. Moreover, the need for such reviews did not appear controversial; after all, even some advocates of beneficiaries, such as Wilbur Cohen, endorsed them.

The Reagan Administration wasted no time and began the reviews in March 1981, a year before they were required by the Benefits Reform Act. What had been intended as a bureaucratic procedure for carefully sifting through files by professionals to ensure the integrity of the program was turned into a mechanism for purging the rolls, retrenching the program, and cutting a projected $3.4 billion from the federal budget (Erkulwater 2006: 108). From the start, the process was a debacle for the Administration. As a practical matter, SSA was overwhelmed with the reviews, as their number leaped from about 100,000 in 1980 to more than 435,000 in 1984, while the SSA had no time to increase its staffing. Reviews were made quickly without interviewing recipients, much less thoughtful deliberation. By the time the reviews were ended in 1984, more than 1.1 million beneficiaries had been reviewed, and more than half had been dropped from the rolls.

While the Administration bulldozed through the process, the media picked up horror stories of beneficiaries who were kicked off SSDI. A Vietnam War veteran who had been given the Congressional Medal of Honor by Ronald Reagan for an incident in which he was beaten and shot multiple times was declared able to work by the Administration even though he was still considered disabled by the Veterans Administration. When an administrative law judge overturned the decision, the story made front-page news ("War Hero Regains Disability Benefit" 1983). A 53-year-old former waitress with arthritis and severe depression committed suicide by shooting herself in the head after being cut off from SSDI benefits, one of several stories that circulated in the press about suicides by those cut off by SSA ("Work or Die" 1983). The reviews resulted in a surge of appeals, and the courts that heard these appeals abandoned their traditional deference to the SSA, reversing terminations in 41% of the cases and a whopping 91% in cases involving mental impairments (Erkulwater 2006: 109–110). Tension between the courts and SSA increased, as SSA refused to apply appellate court rulings beyond individual cases causing some courts to issue contempt citations. By 1984, several states were operating under court-imposed rules while 28 others simply refused to implement continuing disability reviews (Fessler 1984: 1253).

The continuing disability reviews galvanized beneficiaries who mobilized to liberalize the administration of disability claims. Erkulwater (2006) details their three-part strategy. First, they sought to frame their political claims for more liberal treatment as being consistent with the existing law. SSA had sought to use a series of clinical tests and observable symptoms to determine eligibility, harkening back to a long tradition of trying to limit the program to those with "objective" conditions. Advocates countered that SSA relied too heavily on clinical tests. They urged greater reliance on functional tests that turned on more holistic assessments of an individual's behavior, ability to cope in a work environment, and capacity to find a job. The advocates maintained that this was consistent with the legal definition of disability, which centered on the inability to engage in substantial gainful activity, a standard that could only be assessed in a modern economy in relation to a claimant's age, education, and work experience.

Second, advocates created a coalition with medical experts to argue that the functional approach was consistent with leading medical opinion. They joined forces with professional organizations such as the American Psychiatric Association (APA) in order to link their policy arguments with best practices within the medical community. A critical ally in this endeavor was an APA committee on disability reviews chaired by Arthur Meyerson, a New York psychiatrist who was concerned about the effect of deinstitutionalization on patients. Under Meyerson's leadership, the APA joined beneficiary groups in arguing that the review process was too narrow, and that a functional approach that encompasses both medical and social factors was more in line with doctors' understanding of disability. Where the AMA had once opposed the creation of SSDI on the grounds that disability could not be reduced to a series of objective medical test, the APA pushed for the expansion of the program on similar grounds, maintaining that over-reliance on clinical factors failed to capture the nature of disability.

Third, advocates combined litigation with lobbying in their campaign. Given their experience with patients' rights, advocates realized that winning victories over benefit cutoffs in court was only a first step. Court victories had to be parlayed into changes in administrative rules and ultimately codified in statutes. In Congress advocates had allies such as Senators William Cohen (R-ME) and Carl Levin (D-MI) whose committees lacked formal power over the disability program, but who nonetheless held hearings on the disability reviews. The hearings, and the attendant horror stories, forced congressional leaders to act, though there was considerable disagreement over what exactly to do.

For the next three years Congress wrestled over a series of legislative reform bills. The Reagan Administration, trying to stave off reform legislation, introduced an array of administrative reforms, including a June 1983 moratorium on disability reviews for claimants with mental disabilities. Congressional critics, however, were not appeased, and on September 19, 1984, just four years after its previous foray into SSDI reform, Congress enacted a new set of guidelines for the program, The Disability Benefit Reform Act of 1984. The new law provided that the HHS Secretary could terminate benefits only if there was substantial evidence that a recipient's medical condition has improved and cut benefits only if (a) the recipient had benefited from vocational therapy or there had been advances in medical or vocational therapies or technology that made the individual capable of substantial gainful activity; (b) an individual's impairments were not as severe as originally thought based on improved diagnostic techniques; (c) the original decision was made in error or fraudulently obtained; and (d) the individual was unlawfully working, could not be located, or failed to cooperate in the review process. The law also allowed beneficiaries who appealed to continue to collect benefits provided they repaid if they lost their case. To try to resolve the problem of mental disabilities, the law created a moratorium on reviews until new standards for evaluating such disabilities were developed.

In the aftermath of the acrimonious review process and the legislative back-and-forth, SSA struck a conciliatory note. Patricia Owens, who took the reins of the Office of Disability toward the end of the reviews, decided to reach out to advocates: "I had the opportunity to fix the disability program,

which was a mess. I decided to go to the people most critical of us and lis-
ten to their concerns and communicate the agency's constraints" (Erkulwater
2006: 175). Gwendolyn King, George H. W. Bush's head of SSA, followed
suit, allowing local SSA offices to contract their outreach work to advocacy
groups that are already working to sign up people for their programs. She also
created the SSI Modernization Project, which solicited recommendations for
reforms from disability groups.

Erkulwater (2006) observes that these changes were reflected in a shift
within the agency. Under Reagan, officials that favored a strict medical
approach had the upper hand. After the reviews debacle and outreach by SSA,
the in-house medical staff played a less prominent role. So, for example, over
the objections of SSA medical experts, the Office of Disability agreed with
outside groups and decided that evidence from non-medical sources should
be included in disability examinations. More importantly, a more liberal con-
ception of disability was written into the new rules for determining mental
disabilities by (a) expanding the number of mental disorders consistent with
new professional standards embedded in the latest diagnostic and statistical
manual (DSM-III); (b) lowering the threshold from complete inability to
perform the tasks of daily life to the suffering of two or three marked limitations in activities of daily life, social functioning, or concentration, persis-
tence or ability to perform tasks in a timely manner; and (c) requiring much
more thorough collecting of evidence.

Although these changes did not go as far as disability groups may have
wanted, their effects were dramatic. As seen in Figure 3.4, SSDI grew rapidly
after the Reagan years. Moreover, the composition of beneficiaries changed. In
1983, before the changes, 30% of beneficiaries had either mental disorders or
musculoskeletal disorders such as back pain; in 2003 this group was a majority
(52%) of all beneficiaries. The rate of disability in the insured population from
these disorders tripled between 1983 and 2003, but crept up only slightly for
the other disorders (Autor and Duggan 2006: Table 1, 79). SSDI expanded for
many reasons, including growth in the population, especially aging baby boom-
ers, but a good share of the growth was clearly driven by the change in standards.

The ADA and the Politics of SSDI

As the rolls began to grow again after the passage of the 1984 legislation,
the increasing prominence of the disability rights movement brought a new
perspective to the politics of SSDI. For years, disability activists and scholars
had criticized the welfare system as paternalistic and dependency-inducing.[35]

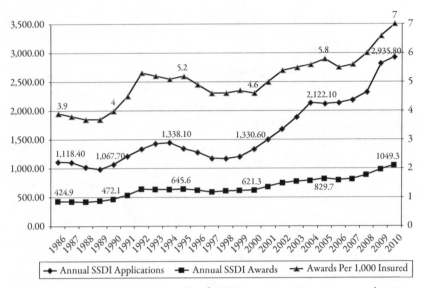

FIGURE 3.4 Post-retrenchment growth of SSDI program 1986 to 2010: applications, awards, and awards per 1,000 insured (compiled by authors from Annual Statistical Report 2010)

For them, the idea that people with disabilities were unable to work—the very definition of disability built into SSDI and SSI—was deeply flawed. They argued that people with disabilities were excluded from work not because they could not be productive, but because they faced social and physical barriers to their full participation in the workplace. This argument reflected a radical critique of the premises both of disability benefit and rehabilitation programs, which scholars called the "medical model" of disability. Under the medical model, disability is seen as an illness and people with disabilities are seen as patients. As patients, people with disabilities are excused from the normal social responsibilities of ordinary citizens and told that they will be taken care of. In exchange, they are expected to defer to the experts, follow the guidance of their caretakers, and be grateful for their care. Rehabilitation in this model is aimed at helping people with disabilities to become more "normal" so that they can take back some of their responsibilities as citizens (Charlton 1998; Funk 1987; Bowe 1978; Hahn 1985; DeJong 1979).

Advocates for disability rights flatly rejected this model. In its place, they pushed for a "social model" of disability. Instead of asking people with disabilities to fit in and overcome their disabilities, government from this perspective should act to eradicate discrimination and other barriers that forced people with disabilities into a subservient role, so that people with disabilities could control their own lives as much as possible. This call for rights and greater independence resonated with both political parties, culminating in the passage of the ADA in 1990 (Burke 2002). At the center of the ADA was a definition of disability sharply at odds with the one embedded in SSDI and SSI. Instead of tying disability to earning potential, the statute defines disability as "a physical or mental impairment that substantially limits one or more major life activities" of an individual.[36] The ambiguities of this definition—what exactly is a "major life activity," for example?—generated litigation, and as described below, further legislation, but those who drafted the ADA clearly envisioned people with disabilities as a much larger group than SSDI and SSI beneficiaries. The preamble of the ADA proclaimed that "some 43 million Americans have one or more major physical or mental disabilities, and this number is increasing as the population as a whole is growing older."[37] Further, the statute all but names the disability welfare programs as evidence of the problem the ADA is meant to solve:

> the continuing existence of unfair and unnecessary discrimination and prejudice denies people with disabilities the opportunity to compete on an equal basis and to pursue those opportunities for which our free society is justifiably famous, and costs the United States billions of dollars in unnecessary expenses resulting from dependency and nonproductivity.[38]

Of course, disability rights advocates were aware of the need for social and health care benefits, and advocated changes in SSDI that would help recipients get back to work. The advocates favored reforming the program, not defunding it. The campaign for the ADA, though, framed the issues in terms of equality of opportunity and independence, in part to broaden the appeal of disability rights to conservatives. Indeed, as the preamble to the ADA suggests, disability rights were often touted by groups like the National Council on the Handicapped and the Commission on Civil Rights as a way to significantly reduce social spending, as the elimination of socially constructed barriers to the workplace, it was argued, would translate into fewer people on the rolls (Bagenstos 2003, 2009; Burke 2001).

Over time, the rise of the disability rights movement and growth of the SSI and SSDI created cross-cutting pressures in disability policy. On one hand, SSDI and SSI had greatly expanded in part because of a more expansive definition of disability that stressed the functional limitations of those with a wide range of impairments. On the other hand, disability advocates insisted that their community was entitled to work and that government programs often created obstacles to this goal (Bagenstos 2009; Erkulwater, forthcoming). These pressures inspired reform proposals from right and left. On the right, conservatives questioned the expansion of the program generally and particularly to categories of recipients seen as undeserving. On the left, disability activists argued for expanding benefits and forms of assistance to enable beneficiaries to return to work.

Meanwhile, by 1994, SSDI was in the middle of a fiscal crisis. Thanks in part to an unexpectedly big increase in beneficiaries in the early 1990s, the Trust Fund was quickly running out of money. In 1992, the Trustees of the program warned that an infusion of cash was needed, and when Congress failed to act, the Trustees declared in their April 1994 annual report that "It is imperative that legislative action be taken as soon as later this year."[39] In October 1994, Congress acceded to the Trustee's wishes by passing legislation that reallocated roughly .6% of the Social Security tax from the retirement program to fund the disability program.[40] This represented a 50% increase in the disability insurance wage tax, from 1.2% to 1.8%, a huge increase in revenue for the program, but outside the small world of disability policy it seemed to pass unnoticed. The reallocation was tucked into the "Nanny Tax" bill, a measure that increased the minimum annual wage at which the Social Security tax kicked in. The "Nanny Tax" bill, or as it was officially titled, the "Social Security Domestic Employment Reform Act of 1994," had been prompted by a series of scandals involving President Clinton's executive branch nominees, most prominently Attorney General nominee Zoe Baird, who failed to pay Social Security taxes on domestic workers they had employed. The Nanny Tax bill, after some wrangling in committees over the amount of the minimum ($1,000 eventually was chosen), sailed through Congress, passing unanimously in both the House and Senate (CQ Almanac 1994). In the publicity over the nanny scandal the reallocation was ignored. Newspapers such as the *Washington Post* and the *New York Times* that covered the passage of the Nanny Tax failed to mention the reallocation.

Thus the financing problem of SSDI was resolved just a month before the transformational election of 1994, when Republicans swept into power in the House of Representatives for the first time since the Eisenhower Administration. The election, and the rising costs of both SSI and SSDI, seemed to open a political window for reform of the disability insurance programs. The costs of SSDI had doubled from $19 billion to nearly $38 billion from 1985 to 1994, but SSI had grown even faster, from $7 billion to $19 billion over the same period in 1994 dollars. Combined, the two programs by 1994 served nearly ten million recipients, up from seven million just 10 years before.[41] Analysts attributed the speedy growth in the disability programs to an array of factors—the liberalized disability standards that stemmed from the backlash over the Reagan retrenchment, particularly for mental impairments, greater outreach by SSA and by states to eligible claimants, a decrease in the rate at which recipients left the program, greater use of the program by immigrants, and the downturn in the economy in the early 1990s.[42] SSI was particularly affected by *Sullivan v. Zebley*, a 1990 Supreme Court ruling that the SSA's eligibility criteria for children with mental impairments were more stringent than Congress had commanded when it had included benefits for children with disabilities in the SSI statute. The resulting liberalization of standards corresponded with a big jump in children receiving SSI, from nearly 300,000 in 1985 to roughly 900,000 in 1994.[43]

As in the 1970s, the difficulties of administering SSI and SSDI compounded the fiscal problems in the two programs. SSA struggled with cuts in staff and funding just as it was enduring soaring workloads from judicial and congressional reforms, aggressive outreach programs, and broadened definitions of disability. Backlogs of new application swelled. Stretched thin by the onslaught of new claims, administrators dedicated fewer resources to eligibility reviews of existing beneficiaries, so that the number of people found to have recovered or no longer disabled dropped to record lows. The review backlog stretched to 1.8 million by 1995.[44]

Allegations of fraud and abuse proliferated. Immigrants, drug addicts, and the children's program were the primary targets of criticism. Republican Senator William Cohen, who had fought against the Reagan Administration's continuing disability reviews, crusaded to restrict SSDI and SSI payments to active alcoholics and drug addicts, arguing that besides being wasteful they were bad for the addicts themselves.[45] Disability advocates pushed back, contending that cutting benefits for addicts was cruel and counterproductive. The defenders were, however, unable to block a 1994 law endorsed by Cohen that limited SSI (but not SSDI) payments to drug addicts to three years.[46]

To many of the Republicans who took power after the 1994 election, though, the three-year cutoff was just a first step; they sought further curbs, and not just on benefits for drug addicts (Berkowitz and DeWitt 2013). If the ascendant Republicans had been so inclined, it might have been a good moment politically to attempt a fundamental restructuring of the disability programs. But disability was just one small part of a much broader politics of welfare reform in the 1990s, and attention was mostly focused elsewhere.

When Bill Clinton promised to end welfare as we know it, his target was not SSI or SSDI; it was AFDC, the welfare program for needy families. The Contract for America, the platform on which the House Republicans ran in 1994, called for a transformation of nearly every component of the welfare state, from food stamps and child care programs to Medicaid and school lunches. The proposals for the disability programs that House Republicans introduced in Congress in 1995 were, by contrast, relatively modest. The most radical proposal was to cap SSI spending, adjusting it for inflation and population growth. The main goal, though, was to restrict eligibility for the programs' most controversial recipients: non-citizen immigrants, drug addicts and alcoholics, and children with less serious impairments who had gained access to SSI after the *Zebley* decision. These reforms touched SSDI only indirectly, as only a small percentage of addicts, alcoholics, and non-citizens had the work history that made them eligible for the more generous SSDI benefits. The focus on SSI was understandable given that funding for that program came from general revenues rather than SSDI's trust fund, so that cutting SSI had a direct effect on the federal budget deficit. Perhaps there would have been more attention paid to SSDI if it had not had its own finances straightened out a mere month before the November 1994 elections.

For two years, Clinton and the GOP battled over welfare reform, finally coming to agreement in the summer of 1996. The law that resulted was most famous for ending AFDC as an entitlement; henceforth states would have much greater flexibility in deciding who would receive TANF (Temporary Assistance to Needy Families), the successor program. On SSI and SSDI there was compromise. The welfare reform law overturned the *Zebley* decision and tightened eligibility standards for children, but not as much as congressional Republicans had wanted. Caps on SSI spending were rejected. Drug addiction and alcoholism were eliminated as compensable impairments, and most non-citizens were rendered ineligible for SSI benefits.

These measures fell well short of the major structural reforms some conservatives had envisioned. As Erkulwater concluded, "Rather than overhaul DI and SSI, lawmakers merely picked off the most controversial and vulnerable parts of the programs" (2006: 213). Indeed, many of the initial cuts were eventually reversed, so that by 1998, Congress had repealed many of the cuts to benefits for immigrants, warned SSA to proceed cautiously with its review of children's benefits, and extended health coverage to many children. Meanwhile, those suffering from addiction were often able to re-apply for benefits under other impairments. No wonder conservatives during this period lamented that fundamentally reforming the American welfare state was like "trying to sweep a sidewalk during a blizzard" (Payne 1997: 38).

The Politics of "Ticket to Work"

A more comprehensive reform of the disability programs would have likely required an alliance between the disability movement and conservatives. There was some basis for such an alliance. Both sides, after all, saw the existing benefits program as fostering dependency, and both sides shared an interest in getting people with disabilities back to work. This was the shared vision that resulted in the creation and enactment of the ADA during two Republican administrations, Reagan and Bush. Disability movement scholars and activists had long imagined reforms to the disability welfare system that would provide supports and incentives to enable employment.

The limited potential of this left-right alliance was exposed in the one major attempt to reform SSDI and SSI to make them more pro-work, "The Ticket to Work and Work Incentives Improvement Act of 1999." The main feature of this legislation was a voucher (or "ticket") that beneficiaries could take to either state or private rehabilitation services; if the beneficiary returned to work, the services would get bonuses tied to the reduction in benefits paid by SSA. In addition, proponents wanted to eliminate disincentives that stopped SSI and SSDI recipients from going back to work, for example by extending medical and other benefits to those who exceeded SSI and SSDI income limits. The politics of Ticket to Work can be understood on two separate levels. On the level of interest group politics, the passage of the bill featured a remarkably unified and well-organized cadre of disability groups that, with the help from policy entrepreneurs from both sides of the aisle, built a broad, bipartisan coalition in Congress in favor of the bill, which included members as ideologically diverse as Paul Wellstone (D-MN) on the left to Jesse Helms (R-NC) on the right. This coalition ultimately produced lopsided votes in the House and Senate, and garnered the Clinton Administration's support. On the level of congressional politics, though, the bill was caught up in the broader, ideological fight between the Clinton Administration and congressional Republicans over balancing the budget. Although Republican leaders avowed support for the principles of Ticket to Work, they were even more committed to limiting budget deficits, and so there was a hard-fought struggle over the scope of the bill, resulting in relatively modest reforms.

The origins of Ticket to Work can be traced to hearings organized in 1997 by Republican House Representative Jim Bunning, Chair of the Ways and Means Subcommittee on Social Security. The hearings featured a report on work and disability insurance by an expert panel of the National Academy of Social Insurance, a think tank devoted to social insurance programs (Mashaw and Reno 1996). During the welfare reform debate of 1995 and 1996, discussion had focused on benefit cuts, tightened eligibility standards, and fraud and abuse. The panel offered a very different perspective on the disability programs, concluding that in comparison to similar schemes in the Western European democracies, SSDI and SSI were relatively "strict and frugal," with narrower definitions of disability, longer waiting periods, and less generous compensation. Rather than fraud and abuse, the panel focused instead on disincentives in the program for returning to work, particularly the loss of Medicare. The panel proposed to modify those disincentives and to create "a radical new approach" to providing rehabilitation services. Instead of relying on state rehabilitation agencies, SSDI beneficiaries would receive a "return to work ticket" that they could use to shop among private or public rehab services. If the beneficiary found a job, the rehab provider could redeem the ticket and collect a portion of the savings that this return to work generated for the SSA. The "ticket to work" then in theory gave beneficiaries more control over rehabilitation services and created strong incentives for the rehab provider to get the beneficiary off benefits.[47] The Panel's approach captured a central theme in the politics of Ticket to Work: advocates framed their proposals as embodying both the empowerment ideals of the disability movement and the conservative concerns with getting people off welfare and into jobs. The proposals combined an expansion of Medicare and Medicaid services with a conservative policy idea, the voucher system that partially privatized rehabilitation services, in order to create a broad, bipartisan coalition for reform. Bunning followed this path in developing his bill, which included the ticket proposal and a two-year extension of Medicare benefits for SSDI recipients who returned to work. He joined forces with Barbara Kennelly (D-CT), and together they built a coalition from an array of disability and business groups in support of the bill. Dubbed "Ticket to Work," the bill passed the House overwhelmingly on a 410-1 vote (Kirchhoff 1999b: 2762).

After that point, however, Ticket to Work got stuck in a series of disputes over its scale and cost. The first dispute arose because Senator Edward Kennedy (D-MA), who had been working on his own, more generous plan to extend health care benefits to disability program beneficiaries with Senator Jim Jeffords (R-VT), prevented the House bill from being referred to the Senate Finance Committee, apparently because he was afraid the Committee would approve the House bill instead of his own measure (ibid.). But the Kennedy-Jeffords bill stalled out in the Senate, and following the 1998 election, the two senators scaled back their bill, incorporating many aspects of the Bunning measure. The revamped bill attracted bipartisan sponsorship in the House, and received overwhelming support in committee votes in both the Senate and House. During the House Conference Committee vote, one of the bill's co-sponsors, Rick Lazio (R-NY), summarized the goal of Ticket to Work: "We're here today to remove people from the cycle of dependency" (CQ Almanac 1999). The committee room burst into applause, and some supporters reportedly wept (ibid.).

But the House and Senate bills also aroused skepticism from powerful members of Congress who raised questions about the cost of extending benefits. Senate Majority Leader Trent Lott (R-MS) was concerned about a provision that allowed states to provide Medicaid to people with degenerative conditions who did not yet qualify for disability benefits. "Why should you get insurance before you're disabled?" Lott asked at one point. "You could have people playing professional basketball or walking the halls of Congress that could get this" (Kirchhoff 1999a: 1270). Lott was particularly upset that HIV–positive non-disabled individuals would receive Medicaid coverage (ibid.). Bill Archer (R-TX), Ways and Means Committee Chair, objected to the House bill, which added new spending without including an "offset," a tax or budget cut that would make the legislation budget-neutral. The Senate bill had offsets in the form of an increased tax on foreign business, and that also stimulated opposition. Senators John Kyl (R-AZ) and Phil Gramm (R-TX) put holds on the bill, stopping it from reaching the Senate floor.

In the face of these obstacles, Ticket to Work advocates ramped up the pressure on the key veto players. They convinced President Clinton to appear at a press conference in which he strongly endorsed the bill. The president linked Ticket to Work to the emancipatory goals of the disability movement: "The full promise of the Americans with Disabilities Act will never be realized until we pass this legislation" (Kirchhoff 1999a: 1271). Disability groups mobilized people with disabilities from around the country to lobby Congress. Lott was a special target. Protesters picketed Lott's Mississippi and

Capitol Hill offices, but the most celebrated campaign against him was the duck protest. Lott had aroused the ire of the disability groups when he added to a massive spending bill a provision extending the duck-hunting season in his home state of Mississippi. Frustrated that Ticket to Work, an apparently lower priority, had been left out of the spending bill, disability advocates sent out an angry e-mail entitled "Dead Ducks and Disability." GOP lawmakers were soon barraged by phone calls consisting entirely of quacks. According to an account by *Congressional Quarterly* journalist Sue Kirchhoff, who closely followed the path of Ticket to Work through Congress, "The effort did not clinch passage, but it did make a point: This was no polite, inside-the-Beltway policy discussion. It was a crusade" (Kirchhoff 1999b: 2762).

Congressional supporters of Ticket to Work made compromises to move their bills forward. The sponsors of the Senate bill jettisoned the tax provisions that had stimulated Gramm's opposition; after this, the bill reached the floor, where it passed on a unanimous vote. In the House, advocates pared back some of the benefits in their bill, and accepted a package of several offsets added by the House Ways and Means Committee to fund it, including a surcharge on attorney fees in SSDI benefit cases, a rebate for low-income people with federal mortgage insurance, and a change in the interest rate for student loans. The resulting legislation eventually passed 412-9.

When the House and Senate bills reached conference committee, the biggest issue remained financing. The Clinton Administration and congressional liberals such as Edward Kennedy strenuously opposed the package of offsets that had been added by the Ways and Means Committee. The disability groups split over the House offsets (Kirchhoff 1999c: 1460). With Kennedy's support, some groups sent a letter to President Clinton urging him to veto any bill with the offsets. Other groups were willing to take the deal. This included The Arc, a group that represents people with intellectual and developmental disabilities. "We didn't have the same problems with the pay-fors as some other organizations," said Marty Ford, assistant director of The Arc. "There's a difference of opinion" (CQ Almanac 1999). The Consortium on Citizens with Disabilities, a broad coalition group, also accepted the offsets. The Clinton Administration, though, suggested a different package of offsets that included savings from cuts in the federal school lunch program and from changing rules regarding payments for foster children as part of the earned income tax credit. This substitute package was accepted by the conference committee, and on November 18, 1999, the House adopted the conference report 418-2; the Senate cleared the bill 95-1 on the following day. On December 17, 1999, President Clinton signed Ticket to Work into law.

As enacted, Ticket to Work was considerably scaled down from the bill Kennedy had originally proposed (CQ Almanac 1999). Kennedy's original bill would have spent more than $5 billion; the law as signed was closer to $500 million. The legislation did, however, retain the core elements of the original Bunning proposal, including the measure creating a "ticket" for job services that gave the law its name. Previously Medicare coverage for SSDI beneficiaries who found employment ended after 4 years; the law extended this to 8.5 years. Ticket to Work also allowed states to provide Medicaid to people with disabilities whose incomes disqualified them for SSI, and to workers with disabilities whose conditions had improved. A $20 million grant program encouraged states to provide personal attendant care and other services to people with disabilities. The provision Senator Lott had objected to, which allowed some individuals with degenerative conditions to get medical benefits before they met the statutory definition of disability, was retained as a pilot project in which $20 million in grants would be provided to states who tried it. Another small pilot program provided reduced benefits to some SSDI beneficiaries who returned to work, rather than cutting the beneficiaries off entirely.

The struggle over Ticket to Work illustrates two significant aspects of SSDI politics. First, disability groups by this time had become effective advocates. The journalist Sue Kirchhoff concluded that "The bill's survival was due, foremost, to the determination of the disability community, with its united Washington coalition and grass-roots presence" (Kirchhoff 1999b: 2762). If not for the efforts of well-organized disability groups, Ticket to Work likely would have languished in the difficult political environment of the late 1990s. But second, the episode illustrates the extent to which fiscal considerations have limited the scope of reform of both SSI and SSDI. Scholars and activists have urged much more sweeping reforms to bring and SSI and SSDI more in line with the principles of the ADA. Ticket to Work represented at most a small move in this direction. Ticket to Work's extension of Medicare benefits to people who leave SSDI is useful, but limited, disability policy advocates argue, because it does not include funding for devices or personal assistants, supports that might be used to enable a return to work. Further, they contend that medical care, personal assistance, and assistive devices should be provided to people with disabilities *before* they endure an unemployment spell necessary to qualify for SSDI (Bagenstos 2009: 140–141; O'Day and Berkowitz 2001: 636). Aside from a couple of pilot projects, Ticket to Work was built around the premises of the current system, targeting those already receiving benefits.[48]

The most radical reform of SSI and SSDI would be to eliminate inability to work as a standard for compensation, and instead assume that people with all but the most severe impairments are able to work. Instead of the disability programs' "cliff," in which beneficiaries are entirely cut off from payments once they reach a certain level of income, a more graduated reduction would provide incentives for beneficiaries to engage in part-time or temporary work.[49] According to Stapleton et al. (2006), "a growing portion of people with disabilities can work at some level but still need some type of assistance so they can attain or maintain a reasonable standard of living. Yet the Social Security Act contains the notion of a narrow, medically determinable line between those who can work above the SGA and those who cannot." Ticket to Work offered only a pilot program to experiment with a graduated reduction in SSDI benefits.

To go further and embrace the more sweeping proposals of disability advocates and their academic supporters would require substantial investment with uncertain returns. Compared to these reforms, Ticket to Work was a humble plan. The avowed goal of proponents to Ticket to Work was to double the rate, .5%, or 5 in a thousand, at which beneficiaries returned to work and so left the program. This might seem like a modest target, but research thus far has failed to demonstrate that Ticket to Work has had any effect on the rate at which beneficiaries leave SSDI.[50] The big fight over Ticket to Work suggests that there has been no political window for the more extensive reforms envisioned by disability advocates, just as there has proven to be limited support for the major retrenchments sometimes advocated by conservatives. Judged from the perspective of disability activists and scholars, the reforms in Ticket to Work were inadequate (Stapleton 2006), but the costs of more far-reaching reforms made them politically unavailable.

The lack of major reform in both SSDI and SSI can be tied in part to the patterns of participation in the politics of the programs. In her thoughtful account, Erkulwater (2006: 221–222) sums up the politics of the disability welfare programs in dualistic terms. At the "macrolevel," there have been some high-profile congressional battles, especially during the Reagan era, over the scope of the program. But these moments of high struggle have been rare. In their absence, policymaking has mainly occurred at the "microlevel," in which courts and agencies have made smaller changes and sought to shape the meaning of disability. Erkulwater (2006: 221–222) argues that this complex story of SSDI's politics post-enactment defies the standard account of redistributive politics, which predicts broad and intense political conflict over these programs. Instead, the "subterranean and technical nature" of SSDI "limited the number of political actors involved, and allowed advocacy groups to exert a great deal of influence on policy outcomes despite their limited popular base. Policymaking essentially became a dialogue limited to a small circle of political actors who were conversant in the many technical intricacies of disability" (2006: 222).

The Claims Process Today

The intricacies of the disability programs arise in large part from the complex bureaucratic process by which claims are decided. SSDI has grown tremendously over its five decades. The SSA in 2012 considered roughly three million SSDI applications and awarded roughly one million claims.[51] But while the proportions of the program have swollen, in many respects it operates just as it did at its outset. Claimants today still apply first to the Social Security Administration, though now most apply through the Internet rather than a district office. The work history requirement is still assessed by SSA based on its record, and the question of whether a person is unable to engage in substantial gainful activity is still made by a contracting state agency. But while the basic criterion of disability—inability to engage in substantial gainful activity—has remained the same, today SSA uses a five-step process for deciding whether an applicant meets the criterion, with two steps that explicitly use a functional approach to disability. The agency (1) determines whether the applicant is working at a level that amounts to engaging in "substantial gainful activity." If so, the applicant is ineligible. If not, the agency decides (2) if the applicant has a severe impairment, or (3) an impairment that meets or equals in severity one of the impairments from a long list that SSA maintains. If the applicant's impairment does not qualify under number 2 or 3 above, the agency (4) assesses the applicant's "residual functional capacity" and decides if the applicant can do the work she or he has done in the past. If the agency decides that applicant no longer has this capacity, the agency (5) takes into account the applicant's residual functional capacity, age, education, and experience to assess whether the individual could find some other work in the economy.[52] If the applicant is rejected, in most states he or she may ask for a reconsideration by the agency. Overall, in 2010 an average of 35% of applicants were accepted at the initial stage, and 8% of the rejected applicants were accepted at reconsideration.[53]

Denied claimants may bring an appeal to an administrative law judge, who decides the appeal "de novo," that is as if the claim was a new one, through an in-person hearing. The biggest changes in the SSDI application process have been at this appeal stage. First, the proportion and number of appeals has grown tremendously. In the initial years of the program only about 2% of denied claims were appealed; today about one in three are, about 800,000 per year. Second, today most of those appealing, nearly 80%, have representatives who help them argue their case at the appeals stage, and most of those representatives are lawyers; an entire industry of Social Security claims advocates has been created (Krent and Morris 2013: 6–7). Successful advocates can collect 25% percent of a back pay award, up to $6,000; the total payout in representative fees was $1.4 billion in 2010, a bounty that critics say has led some representatives to push the boundaries of honest advocacy (Paletta and Searcey 2011).[54]

But even with the increasing involvement of lawyer representatives, the appeals process retains many of the hierarchical elements of bureaucratic legalism. The hearing is conducted by the administrative law judge who calls on experts and questions the applicant. The SSA is not represented; the case is treated as an application to an agency rather than a dispute between parties. The claimant cannot argue that the standards the ALJ are using are unjust, as those standards are promulgated by the SSA and control the case. Indeed, even the ALJ is limited to the rules—though the ALJs have the title of "judges" in most respects they are fundamentally bureaucrats, a condition that has caused great distress among the ALJs as well as conflict between them and the SSA (Wolfe 2013).

Even so, the appeals system is a potential source of inconsistency, and thus from the perspective of the bureaucratic ideal a potential problem. News accounts of some judges who deny nearly all appeals and others who seem to grant nearly all prompted an investigation (Paletta 2011).[55] Overall, in recent years the ALJs have awarded benefits in roughly 60% of cases, but in one study a particularly stingy ALJ had a 4% rate while another on the generous end was at 98% (Krent and Morris 2013: 15). The SSA has used the final step in its process, the Appeals Council, to try to reduce inconsistencies. Applicants who are denied by the ALJ can appeal to the Council, but it is not required to review their claims. The Appeals Council can also review claims that were not appealed, which it does by randomly sampling. It has created a quality control program to try to identify and reduce errors in ALJ decisions (Krent and Morris 2013: 50–55).

The final step of the SSDI claims process, taken in less than .5% of claims, is an appeal of the SSA decision in a federal district court. But even that tiny percentage, 5 in a thousand, represents more than 10,000 cases in federal district court per year (Swank 2012: 4). These court appeals are surprisingly successful: district courts in recent years have remanded to SSA for reconsideration in about half of the appeals brought and in most of those case the appellant eventually receives benefits (Krent and Morris 2013: 9). A much smaller number of cases, about 500 per year, are appealed from a district court to a court of appeals.[56]

Even a small number of court rulings can powerfully affect a governmental institution, as for example the school board of Little Rock Arkansas could attest. Have federal courts, through their handling of disability cases, partly displaced SSA as the chief rulemaker for the handling of SSDI claims, and so moved the program from bureaucratic legalism to adversarial legalism? Litigation certainly has had a powerful influence in some cases, for example the *Zebley* decision, but the SSA has ways to resist the encroachments of the judiciary that most bureaucratic agencies lack. For years the SSA had a policy of nonacquiescence, meaning that when a federal court overturned the denial of an individual disability claim, the agency treated the ruling as good for that case only. In this way SSA limited the power of courts by ensuring that they affected only individual cases and did not set policy for the agency. The blanket policy of nonacquiescence was controversial. Under considerable pressure, the SSA in 1985 announced that it would drop its policy and acquiesce to federal court rulings (Derthick 1990: 138–152). In practice, however, this policy is much more hierarchical and bureaucratic than one might imagine: It is SSA that decides when a court ruling has made policy rather than merely decided an individual case, and it is the SSA that dictates to its ALJs, and to the state agencies what that new policy will be. It does this through "acquiescence rulings" that it issues. In 2012, SSA had 43 such acquiescence rulings actively in force (Swank 2012: 4). Even where SSA has acquiesced, it does so only for the district in which the ruling is made, not the whole country.[57] The SSA has no choice but to acquiesce to a Supreme Court decision, but of course the SSA can stop a case from going to the Supreme Court by giving in and providing a benefit. Thus even when cases end up in the federal courts, the SSA is able to shape the impact on its rules and procedures.

The greater propensity of applicants today to hire representatives to help them argue their cases, and to appeal, both to the ALJs and the federal courts, has transformed the application process, bringing elements of adversarial legalism to SSDI. In all fundamental respects, however, SSDI remains a bureaucratic program. A person who seeks SSDI benefits is an applicant, not a party to a dispute. The applicant faces a series of bureaucrats who apply the SSA's standards to determine whether he or she is eligible for the program. There is no neutral referee in this system who is empowered to decide whether those standards, or the process used to apply them, are fair. The government, on the other side, does not have attorneys to argue against the applicant's claims, as it would in an adversarial system. Even more fundamentally, the compensation provided is set by a bureaucratic formula, and comes from a social insurance fund rather than an individual defendant. SSDI is clearly a more adversarial program than it was at its origins, but the greater involvement of lawyers, lawsuits, and courts in the SSDI process has not reshaped its core—a social insurance program for those who, by reason of inability to work, deserve governmental support. More specifically, additional legal contestation has not changed the key mechanisms that we argue link policy design to its political trajectory. The program remains funded by a payroll tax and the core issues are framed in terms of need and eligibility, not blame and fault.

Discussion

Our case study allows us to build on the cross-sectional comparisons in the congressional hearings data and explore the politics of SSDI both across policymaking forums and over time. The hearings data suggested a quiet, fairly technocratic politics in which claimant groups and federal officials predominate. When we look in more depth at the politics of SSDI, however, we find a much more complex pattern. First, we find instances of furious political struggle, first at enactment and then during the fiasco that was the Reagan Administration's continuing disability review. Second, at the "microlevel" we find quieter, ongoing struggles in multiple forums, including courts, agencies, and Congress, during periods of expansion. Yet we are also struck by the way in which SSDI politics is contained, first at the level of interest groups, and then at the level of ideas. For all the money spent on SSDI, it remains an obscure program, certainly nowhere as politically prominent as Medicare, or Food Stamps, or AFDC, and a relatively small number of groups participate in its politics. At the level of ideas, both the disability movement and conservative thinkers have offered radical critiques of the program, but these have not gotten much of a hearing. The program has evolved in important ways, but its fundamental premises remain largely as envisioned by the policymakers who created it in 1956.

It is striking to compare the intense struggle over enactment of the SSDI with the relatively quiet politics of expansion from 1956 to 1980. The story begins as a classic illustration of redistributive politics, in which stakeholders square off against one another in a fight over who pays, how much, and to whom, as well as who should administer the program. During this period, labor, program officials, and their liberal allies in Congress took on businesses, insurance companies, and their conservative allies on the Hill along with the AMA (which feared that SSDI would be a step toward socialized medicine). As Martha Derthick argues, the politics were intensely contested but narrow. Unified, well-organized interests fought over the creation of the new program. Business groups in this initial period were both well-organized and passionate in their opposition to SSDI, so much so that advocates had to adopt a piecemeal approach and eventually settle for a program that was quite limited in its definition of disability and scope of coverage.

The politics of SSDI significantly shifted as the program entered a long period of growth. During this period of expansion, the politics were largely consistent with the general pattern of limited participation and relatively little conflict seen in the hearings data, as business groups largely deferred to a relatively small cadre of program administrators and congressional insiders. The quiet politics during this period was all the more striking given that program costs soared and many of the key concessions needed to pass the program were abandoned. Despite the fact that their worst suspicions about SSDI were confirmed and that they were already well organized, fluent with the issues, and ready for battle, businesses stayed mostly on the sidelines, deferring to a small circle of pro-program advocates and experts.

Beginning in the 1970s, unchecked expansion of the program inevitably resulted in problems, as the SSA struggled with its burgeoning workload and the increases in program costs threatened the program's solvency. A series of fiscal crises, as well as concerns that underserving claimants were defrauding the program, resulted in waves of retrenchment efforts. The politics of retrenchment were deeply contested, with program officials, liberal allies and interest groups representing the claimants on one side, conservatives and fiscal hawks on the other, and business interests largely sidelined. Moreover, unlike the asbestos case that will be discussed in the next chapter, claimants generally remained unified, fighting to preserve a broad functional definition of disability and resisting structural reforms that might cap benefits. There were admittedly some exceptions. The welfare reform law signed by Bill Clinton managed to isolate some of the most politically vulnerable recipients in the program, substance abusers and illegal immigrants, and sought to curb their benefits—mostly in SSI rather than SSDI because that is where these groups were concentrated. But disability groups objected to this singling out, and the cuts were soon blunted by congressional second thoughts about the immigration restrictions, as well as the ability of those suffering from substance abuse to requalify for benefits under the broad functional definition of disability. During an era in which American politics has turned sharply to the right, SSDI has survived largely unscathed; indeed it is rarely even attacked. The resulting picture then is one of a distinct pattern of political development, as the contentious politics of creation gives way to a quieter politics of expansion and a narrow politics of retrenchment among relatively united interest groups.

As noted at the beginning of the chapter, SSDI serves as our "control" case, a bureaucratic policy that provides the baseline for comparison with the adversarial injury compensation policies we analyze in the next two chapters. In this book we assess some standard claims about the politics of adversarial legalism: that adversarial legalism crowds out other forms of political participation, that it engenders a polarizing backlash, that it creates path dependent outcomes, and that it individualizes politics and so undermines social solidarity. Given our comparative framework, we can turn these criticisms around and measure the extent to which SSDI, a bureaucratic injury compensation policy, generates the political patterns that critics often associate with adversarial legalism. By doing so, we can get some insight on whether these patterns are generic across policy designs or specific to adversarial legalism.

One standard concern about adversarial legalism is that it acts, in Rosenberg's evocative metaphor, as "flypaper," trapping activists in a mode of political action, litigation, and the pursuit of legal rights that is often ineffective. We see no evidence of such a trap in the case of SSDI. Supporters of the program used an array of methods, including lobbying and litigating, to realize their objectives. When beneficiaries faced major retrenchment through the Reagan Administration's aggressive use of disability reviews, claimants contested these decisions through the administrative appeals process, congressional hearings, and the courts. Thus, claimant groups adroitly combined litigation, lobbying, and administrative strategies, especially in the critical fight over the meaning of disability, resulting in the significant expansion of the program, after some initial setbacks during the Carter and Reagan Administrations. In sum: no flypaper here.

Similarly, it is hard to find any evidence of a backlash in this case to the enactment and implementation of SSDI. The backlash hypothesis, remember, is that adversarial legalism, in cases like *Brown v. Board of Education* and *Roe v. Wade*, can stimulate counter-mobilization and polarize moderates, thus setting back the cause that the court decisions were supposed to move forward. The enactment of SSDI, however, seemed instead to demobilize opposition and moderate views about the program. In this case bureaucratic legalism clearly generated no backlash.

Indeed, there is much stronger evidence here of the opposite dynamic, path dependence. Remember that throughout this book we are assessing the claim that adversarial legalism engenders path dependence. We take this as a comparative claim, and so we use SSDI as a comparison point to assess the extent to which bureaucratic legalism induces path dependence, in part by identifying mechanisms of "increasing returns" that make it harder and harder for policymakers to move off the path. SSDI's basic structure has endured for more than a half-century, despite serious concerns about the program's financial viability and its administration, even among its proponents. The mechanisms of increasing returns are evident in the case study. SSDI, like other benefit programs, mobilized groups representing beneficiaries to defend the program from retrenchments, as they did first in the 1980s during the Reagan Administration's continuing disability review and then during the mid-90s when the rise of the House Republicans created another threat (Soss 2002). In both cases, defenders of the program took advantage of a basic fact about benefits, that it is extremely difficult politically to cut off recipients, especially given the likelihood that errors in administration will be made, so that "horror stories" will shape the politics of retrenchment.

If we look beneath SSDI's broad formal structure, then the story is more complicated, especially as it pertains to the definition of disability in SSDI. Although the social movement of people with disabilities was able, in coalition with the Bush and Reagan administrations, to create a new sweeping civil rights statute, the ADA, partly on the premise that people with disabilities are able to work, this movement thus far has had less of an impact on the eligibility criteria for SSDI. Disability groups successfully campaigned to move the SSDI standards award from a medically-based definition toward a more holistic, functional approach, but they have not been able to incorporate the more radical social model of disability into SSDI. As a result, the program still equates disability with inability to engage in "substantial gainful activity."

Is this fundamental stability in SSDI a result of path dependence? It is possible to imagine benefit programs for people with disabilities that do not have a work-based definition—the Veterans Administration in fact runs such a program for four million recipients—but it is hard to imagine SSDI

changing in this way, partly for reasons that relate to the dynamic of increasing returns. Opening up the program to people with impairments who work
could easily destroy the already precarious fiscal health of SSDI and could
raise concerns among all the current recipients of the program, who have
qualified under the demanding substantial gainful activity standard. Altering
SSDI in this way would literally mean throwing out the book on beneficiary
eligibility and rebuilding the entire review process, which currently considers
more than a million applications each year. Congress has never seriously considered any change to the "substantial gainful activity" standard, doubtless for
many reasons, but the mechanisms of path dependence are likely part of the
explanation.

We do not mean to suggest that all features of SSDI are "locked in" by
path dependence. Clearly the history of SSDI shows how programs can
change quite substantially, even in the absence of massive reform legislation. Most importantly, Congress has passed a series of piecemeal measures
that have over time vastly expanded the categories of recipients, and moved
the program from a medical standard to more functional standards of eligibility (recall Table 3.1). In addition to the formal revisions by Congress,
SSA and the courts have repeatedly altered the operations of SSDI through
administrative practices and reinterpretations of program requirements,
whether through the process of "bounce back," which directly contra-
dicted the law's limits on SSA's power of review, or the courts' attempts to
thwart the Reagan Administration's attempt to "purify" the rolls under the
disability review process. At this level, far from a story of path dependence,
the story of SSDI is one of constant institutional evolution, as stakeholders probed the limits of the program in multiple forums, moving from
Congress to SSA to the courts and back again. The result is a complex pattern of change and continuity. The formal structure of SSDI has remained
largely in place, but key aspects of the program have evolved over time
though its daily practice, much like a house that is remodeled but whose
foundations remain in place.

Our last question about adversarial legalism was its effect on stakeholder claims and patterns of mobilization. Adversarial legalism was said
to "individualize" social problems, creating a more fractious politics that
over time divides potential allies in society from one another. Did SSDI
have this effect? The case study seems to suggest the opposite, that SSDI
has engendered a relatively high degree of solidarity among stakeholders. To
help explain this, we need to reexamine the two main mechanisms that we
believe connect policy design to politics in the field of injury compensation,

the *distributional effects* that a particular design creates, and the *assignment of blame* that the policy engenders.

During the creation of SSDI, business groups acted as if the costs of SSDI were to be borne on their shoulders. They closed ranks with insurers to fight the expansion of the federal government into a policy realm traditionally dominated by means-tested state programs. After enactment, however, business groups were only sporadically involved in the politics of SSDI. On most of the occasions that there have been attempts to cut or even limit the growth of the program, business groups have not been part of the effort. How to explain this turnaround? The distributional effects created by a widely-shared social insurance tax appear to have an important influence. Because the SSDI tax is folded into the overall Social Security tax, and because that tax is paid by all who make income from work, it is a "smooth" cost that falls on all businesses in proportion to their number of employees, creating no competitive advantages for particular companies. It is hard in fact to see how the material interests of businesses are even affected, as the entire cost of the Social Security tax is likely passed on to workers in the form of reduced wages. (Business groups do have an interest in the ways in which SSDI interacts with workers' compensation and private disability insurance, and so could be expected to get involved when these issues are raised.) Thus business has not been a major factor in SSDI politics.

The distributional effects created by SSDI also influenced the other side, groups representing beneficiaries. At the outset, it was unions and liberal groups that joined forces with sympathetic SSA administrators to doggedly fight for the creation of SSDI, but as the program grew, groups representing disabled beneficiaries have taken the lead in defending the program. This is a familiar form of policy feedback, in which the creation of program benefits leads beneficiaries to coalesce and mobilize. In comparison with adversarial legalism, though, another aspect of the distributional effects created by SSDI is worthy of note: the relative evenness of compensation in SSDI may have a role in limiting conflict among beneficiaries, allowing them to unify to fight cuts in the program. In the struggle over asbestos injury compensation, the subject of the following chapter, some plaintiffs and their attorneys received massive awards, while others got nothing at all, and this created consequential political divisions among beneficiaries. In the case of SSDI, by contrast, the coalition of supporters have remained united, even when program opponents tried to drive a wedge between present and future beneficiaries, the old and the young, or between those with easier-to-prove illnesses and those with less "objective" ones. Of course, this solidarity has not been perfect. There were some divisions over tactics on Ticket to Work, and some groups were isolated during the Clinton era welfare reform, but these divisions were exceptional and short-lived.

Our finding of a well-organized coterie of beneficiary groups is consistent with another study that uses very different methods to explore the politics of SSDI. Joe Soss interviewed recipients of both SSDI and AFDC to understand the effects of these programs on their participation in politics (Soss 2002). Soss finds that while the AFDC beneficiaries felt stigmatized and vulnerable because of their participation in the program, SSDI recipients felt secure and confident in their interactions with government, and that this difference seemed to have political effects. AFDC beneficiaries had less confidence in their ability to be effective in politics and were less likely to vote than demographically similar individuals outside the program; SSDI recipients had the same levels of "political efficacy" and voting as non-disabled but otherwise demographically similar individuals. This finding is impressive because scholars have found that disability that results in withdrawal from employment depresses political participation (Schur 2000; Schur and Adya 2013). Disability is stigmatizing and dependency-inducing, particularly when it results in withdrawal from the labor force. In the absence of some policy response, people with disabilities who are unemployed may withdraw from political life. The SSDI program, by providing stable and predictable benefits, may be giving the resources and incentives for people with disabilities to participate more fully in public life.

But beyond the individual-level effects in the Soss study, the SSDI program undoubtedly has effects on the group mobilization of people with disabilities. Because the program puts recipients in a continuing relationship with a government agency that gives them benefits they feel they earned, and because it puts all recipients, whatever their disability, on roughly the same plane, it lowers the barriers to group mobilization. The unified mobilization of beneficiaries has been crucial to protecting SSDI benefits during periods of fiscal constraint, administrative failure, and conservative hostility, and in expanding the program during quieter periods. This unity, together with the general lack of interest from business groups, poses a steep political challenge for anyone who seeks a major retrenchment of SSDI. There simply is no strong constituency for such a retrenchment, and it would likely face united opposition from supporters of the program.

Here we see another mechanism that connects policy design to politics—blame assignment. Unlike in our adversarial legalism cases, in SSDI politics the issue of blame for injuries is made largely irrelevant, reflecting the eligibility standards built into the design of SSDI, in which questions of blame are superfluous. Indeed, after more than five decades in operation, the core idea behind SSDI, that society has a responsibility to compensate people for disabilities (an idea it shares with its younger, poorer sibling, SSI) is today almost unquestioned. There are cases in which blame for injury does seem to be an issue, for example in the case of the drug addicts who were stripped from the program. But even for "marginal" disabilities, the ones that arouse controversy, the dispute tends to be about whether the potential recipients are truly in need, truly unable to engage in substantial gainful activity. SSDI's policy design focuses politics on questions of need and away from questions of blame, in sharp contrast to the adversarial legal programs in our study.

The case of SSDI, then, suggests that bureaucratic legalism, rather than individualizing social problems, socializes them, with significant political effects. The people who collect SSDI benefits are diverse in class, race, and age, with a wide range of impairments, yet the differences among them seem to have played almost no part in the politics of SSDI. The "payees" for SSDI are such a broad group—all businesses that have wage workers, and all workers—that no group to represent their interests has arisen. Business in recently years has been almost uninvolved. All this has meant that for long periods, SSDI politics has been quiet, narrow, and technocratic, belying its extraordinarily contentious origins.

The Contrasting Case of the ADA

Before turning to the cases of asbestos and vaccine injury compensation, it is worth taking a brief detour to consider the politics of the ADA. The ADA is an anti-discrimination policy rather than an injury compensation policy, and so it is not strictly comparable to the other cases in this book. Nevertheless, the political history of the ADA offers a fascinating contrast to the story we have just told, of the enactment, attempted retrenchment, and growth of SSDI.

As we have suggested, the ADA and SSDI can be seen as rival approaches to the problem of disability. SSDI defines disability as inability to engage in "substantial gainful activity"; the ADA is premised on the principle that people with disabilities can work as long as physical, attitudinal, and institutional barriers to their participation in society are removed. Although the ADA has many bureaucratic provisions, empowering federal agencies to enforce regulations on the accessibility of facilities and programs, the law has an important adversarial component: it creates a private right of action that authorizes people who believe they have been discriminated against to bring a federal court case. Thus this component of the ADA can be analyzed as a federally created

adversarial legal disability policy and contrasted with SSDI, a federally created bureaucratic legal disability policy.

We can begin by analyzing congressional hearings data as we did in
chapter 2.[58] The patterns of participation and conflict in ADA hearings look
more like those we observed for hearings on adversarial policies than hearings on bureaucratic policies. As noted in Chapter 2, hearings on adversarial
policies featured an average of 13.96 witnesses representing 6.79 group types,
whereas hearings on bureaucratic policies averaged 7.86 witnesses representing 2.82 group types. The ADA hearings averaged 12.63 witnesses representing 4.57 group types. ADA hearings were also more similar to adversarial
hearings in the extent to which they featured witnesses who expressed conflicting views. Seventy percent of ADA hearings had conflicting witnesses,
closer to the 88% conflict rate we observed for adversarial hearings than the
42% rate in bureaucratic hearings.

Figure 3.5 takes a more granular look at the differences between the ADA
hearings and bureaucratic hearings. It is a radar graph just like the one in
chapter 2. (In this graph a score of 100% would mean that at least one representative of a group type participated in every hearing in the sample.) In

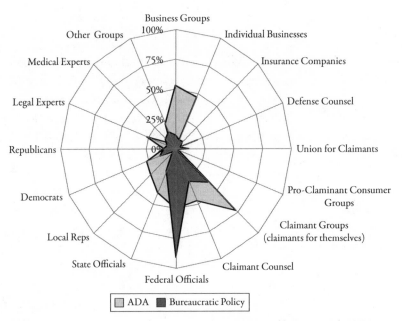

FIGURE 3.5 Participation rates of group types in congressional hearing on the ADA: 1988
to 2011 (compiled by authors)

chapter 2, we saw that the shape of the radar graph for adversarial legalism was relatively round when compared to that graph for bureaucratic legalism, reflecting the fact that a wide variety of groups appeared at the hearings. The graph for bureaucratic legalism, by contrast, was sharp and pointy, with federal officials appearing in 90% of hearings, beneficiaries in 40%, and other groups much less involved. As seen in Figure 3.5, the radar graph for the ADA hearings is also more rounded than its counterpart for bureaucratic policies (although not quite as round as the one for adversarial policies). Unlike the hearings on bureaucratic policies, a wide variety of groups, 10, appear in a significant percentage of the ADA hearings. Five group types participated in 50% or more of the hearings: business groups, individual businesses, claimant groups, claimant lawyers, and federal officials. Four groups participated in about 30 to 50% of the hearings: local representatives, state officials, Democrats, and legal experts. We see the same basic pattern when we compare ADA hearings to SSDI hearings. Hearings on the ADA featured a wider variety of participants, with 4.57 group types on average appearing compared to 3.92 groups for SSDI. Also like the adversarial hearings, business group participation in ADA hearings was relatively common, again in contrast to SSDI hearings. Business groups showed up at 53% of the ADA hearings but only 12% of SSDI hearings.

Of course, congressional hearings offer only a narrow window into politics of a policy area. As in our SSDI case study, it is important to consider the full political trajectory of the ADA, including events outside of Congress. When we widen our perspective, we see two major contrasts between the politics of the ADA and SSDI. First, the politics of creating the ADA was much less contentious than the politics of creating SSDI. Second, whereas the politics of SSDI cooled off after enactment, with business stepping aside, the politics of the ADA heated up, and business remained engaged.

SSDI and the ADA were both created by Congress, but the initial battle over the ADA was much less polarized than the epic struggle over the enactment of SSDI. This is in part because the process by which the ADA was created and enacted was, surprisingly from the perspective of the early twenty-first century, genuinely bipartisan. The law was nurtured in the Reagan and Bush administrations, and had high-profile support from congressional Republicans such as Senate Minority Leader Bob Dole. President George H.W. Bush enthusiastically endorsed it, and only 8 senators and 20 House members voted against it. Beneath the surface there was considerable conflict, but it was over the details of the legislation and not its overall approach. Business groups lobbied heavily over some of the language in the legislation they thought would affect future lawsuits. For example, a provision governing standards by which employers could refuse to hire a disabled person because of safety concerns attracted the interest of the restaurant lobby, which was worried about litigation by people with AIDS. Small business groups sought to expand an "undue hardship" defense and to limit many of the bill's provisions to employers with more than 15 employees (Burke 2002: 84). Most of all, there was a huge fight over the extent of monetary damages that plaintiffs could win in an employment lawsuit. That matter came down to a nearly party line vote in which the Democratic majority in the House prevailed (Burke 2002: 84–86).

Yet few in Congress criticized the goals of the legislation, or took issue with the main premises behind it, that the accessibility of programs and facilities should be regulated, and that people with disabilities should be given a right to sue individual wrongdoers for discrimination. The lack of any fundamental opposition can be attributed in part to the positive political valence of legislation aimed at improving the lives of people with disabilities, who, unlike other "minority" groups, are scattered among rich and poor, Democrats and Republicans. The prominent example of Bob Dole, a disabled WWII veteran, underlined this point. But the bipartisanship also reflected the vision behind the ADA, of individuals with disabilities leading more independent lives, a theme that appealed to both conservative and liberal sensibilities. For Republicans, the ADA could be sold as welfare reform, a way to reduce government expenditures on disability programs while giving individuals greater opportunity. Indeed, the Reagan-appointed commission that created the first draft of the ADA specifically cited a reduced SSDI and SSI caseload as one of the goals behind the law (Burke 2002: 77).

Also important, though, is that the ADA had the features that make adversarial legalism appealing to policymakers more generally. Because it relied in large part on private enforcement mechanisms, the ADA did not require the creation of a new agency, or for that matter any great investment of government dollars (see generally Farhang 2010; Burke 2002; Barnes 1997; Kagan 1994). The comparison with SSDI here is powerful, because SSDI's massive expansion of government and associated wage tax was precisely what made it initially so controversial. SSDI's socialization of the costs of disability sharply contrasts with the dominant feature of the ADA, which is to individualize costs by imposing them on organizations, particularly business, and further to individualize much of the cost of enforcement by empowering individuals to sue. This difference in policy design may be part of the reason the ADA's enactment was relatively consensual, whereas SSDI's passage precipitated a dramatic struggle.

A second contrast between the ADA and SSDI lies in their post-enactment politics. We noted that immediately after enactment, the politics of SSDI became less contentious, and the program began a long period of relatively quiet growth from 1956 to the Carter Administration. Conflict over the ADA, by contrast, only seemed to grow after enactment. If policymaking and implementation in the American system can be likened to a "dialogue" among the branches (Barnes and Miller 2004), the implementation of the adversarial component of the ADA was more like a shouting match. The drafters of the ADA attempted to smooth implementation of the law by using terms lifted from previous laws—"reasonable accommodation" and "undue hardship," and by retaining a definition of disability that had been litigated before. In the federal courts, however, a struggle developed over the meaning of all these key terms, though most of all over the statutory definition of disability, a "substantial limitation to a major life activity." Defense lawyers, realizing they could stop disability discrimination claims before trial if they could convince a judge that the individual was not eligible to bring a claim, litigated over what counted as a "substantial" limitation and what counted as a "major" life activity (Burke 2004). This litigation reached all the way to the Supreme Court in several cases during its 1999 term. The Court in those cases sided with the defendants, and considerably narrowed the definition of disability under the statute. For example, the Court ruled that in considering whether an individual was "substantially limited in a major life activity," judges should consider whether assistive devices—eyeglasses in one case before the Court— mitigated the limitation.[59] In this ruling, the Court turned aside the interpretation of the ADA by the Equal Employment Opportunity Commission, which had published guidelines ruling out consideration of assistive devices in determining whether the plaintiff was an individual with a disability.

Of course, litigation over who counts as disabled happens in SSDI as well; when applicants are rejected they can appeal all the way through the Social Security Administration to the federal courts. The ADA, though, is a more adversarial policy than SSDI because core issues such as the definition of disability are resolved through a "party-centered" rather than bureaucratically dominated process. Disability was defined in the ADA through the accretion of precedents in individual lawsuits by various plaintiffs and defendants; the EEOC, the relevant bureaucracy, was directly involved in only some of those lawsuits. The EEOC proffered its definitions through guidelines it issued, but those guidelines had no binding force in court, and in several cases the Supreme Court chose to ignore them.

The Supreme Court decisions angered disability interest groups who thought them outside the spirit of the ADA; they argued for deference to federal agency interpretations of the law, which were more in tune with their own. Steny Hoyer, a Democratic member of the House who had been deeply involved in congressional negotiations over the ADA, was so incensed by the Supreme Court opinions that he wrote an article addressed to Justice Sandra Day O'Connor, one of the authors of those opinions: "Not Exactly What We Intended, Justice O'Connor" (Hoyer 2002). But the disability groups, as upset as they might be, had no easy way to "overrule" the federal courts (Barnes 2004). Overruling a federal court in a statutory case requires amending the statute, which in turn requires Congress to act. By 1994, however, control of Congress had swung to the Republicans, and disability advocates were skeptical that opening up the ADA to amendment, particularly in the Republican-controlled House, would achieve their objectives.

Indeed, in the House the hearings that were held on ADA lawsuits from 1994 to 2006 usually featured the grievances of the *targets* of ADA litigation—business and professional groups, and local governments. Probably the most famous of the grievers was Clint Eastwood, movie star and mayor of Carmel, California, but also the owner of a resort that was sued for violations of ADA wheelchair accessibility requirements (Gaura and Gathright 2009). In 2000 Eastwood testified at a House hearing in favor of the "ADA Notification Act," which would have required prospective plaintiffs to notify organizations of ADA violations; the plaintiffs could only file an ADA lawsuit if the organization failed to correct the violations within 90 days of receiving the letter.[60] The ADA Notification Act, and other pro-defendant measures, went nowhere, but in the late 1990s and early 2000s the House was a place in which plaintiff complaints about the ADA literally could not get a hearing. So, while the politics of SSDI became quieter after creation, ADA's politics become more contentious.

With the return of Congress to Democratic control in 2006, plaintiff dissatisfaction with the implementation of the ADA resulted in the introduction of the ADA Restoration Act, a bill aimed at reversing some of the pro-defendant Supreme Court decisions. Business groups initially opposed the legislation, but perhaps realizing that pro-plaintiff groups now had the power on their side, representatives of the leading business groups joined with representatives of disability groups to forge compromise legislation. The result was the draft of what eventually became the ADA Amendments Act (ADAAA). It left the language of the disability definition intact, but made the "substantial limitation" and "major life activity" prongs more expansive, and gave the EEOC, seen to be sympathetic to disability groups, more power over defining them through regulation. Further, the Act specified that mitigating measures would not be considered, thus directly overruling the Supreme Court. The ADAAA sailed through Congress, approved by the Senate on a voice vote and in the House by a 402-17 margin. It was signed into law by George W. Bush on September 25, 2008.

The enactment of the ADAAA was a truce in the battle between business and plaintiffs over the ADA. Has the roughly two-decade period of highly contentious ADA implementation ended? It seems likely that divisions between stakeholders will re-assert themselves, as plaintiffs and defendants each seek to push their interpretations of the ADAAA in litigation, once again dividing groups from one another. The agreement of stakeholders embodied in the ADAAA runs against the generalization that adversarial legalism tends to divide interests from one another, but it seems a temporary agreement, driven more by the recognition that plaintiff interests had gained the power to legislatively reverse Court rulings against them rather than by any consensus on the law, or by the demobilization of business that occurred in SSDI (Hickox 2010).

The ADA/SSDI comparison developed here can be used to assess the claims we are evaluating in this book about the political effects of adversarial legalism. First, notice that there is no evidence here for the claim that adversarial legalism traps activists in the "flypaper" of litigation. Within the ADA case, disability advocates were active in all three branches, bringing lawsuits but also lobbying the EEOC and Congress. Indeed, some of the very same disability groups that were active on the ADA were also involved in lobbying on SSDI.

Second, we see the same complex pattern of stability and change under the ADA as we saw under SSDI. On one hand, many of the key terms under ADA—"individual with a disability" and "reasonable accommodation," as well as the basic adversarial structure of ADA's anti-discrimination policy—have remained undisturbed. On the other hand, the specific meanings of these terms have been the subject of great debate and change, even though they were written precisely so as to avoid surprises. The evolution of the ADA in the courts looks less like a case of generic program implementation and more like common law, with its flexibility, openness to new arguments and claims, and sensitivity to the context of particular cases and individuals. From this vantage, the ADA has been no more path-dependent than SSDI and maybe even less so, given that the meaning of key terms have been see-sawing ever since the passage of the ADA, with significant consequences for both plaintiffs and defendants.

Finally, there is the claim of backlash. At first glance, the ADA represents a great example of backlash—indeed a book written from the perspective of disability advocates on the tenth anniversary of the law was titled *Backlash* (Krieger 2003). ADA decisions against business regularly sparked backlashes; Clint Eastwood's high-profile campaign in support of the ADA Notification Act is just the most prominent example. It does not appear, however, that these backlashes had the effect that Klarman documents in the case of *Brown v. Board of Education*, of mobilizing countergroups, polarizing moderates, and hindering cross-stakeholder coalitions. No new anti-ADA groups appeared, there is little evidence of polarization around the ADA, and, most importantly, shifting, cross-stakeholder group coalitions have emerged after the policy's creation. The enactment of the ADA Amendments Act on an almost unanimous vote after a period of sharp conflict among stakeholders reflects this. ADA politics is far from peaceful, and the extent of controversy over it does not seem to be dying down, but neither is it an example of polarization.

The ADA/SSDI comparison, then, offers little support for several of the claims made about adversarial legalism that we are assessing. If the critics of adversarial legalism were right, we would find sharp differences between the politics of the ADA and SSDI. Yet in many respects the politics of these two cases were similar. Neither the adversarial design of the ADA nor the bureaucratic design of SSDI seemed to narrow the ways in which interest groups mobilized politically or generate a polarizing backlash, and the two designs seemed to produce similar levels of path dependence, with complicated mixtures of change and continuity.

In one respect, however, the cases clearly differ: the ADA case illustrates a distinct political trajectory, of expanding rather than diminishing conflict, that is quite different from the one we observed for SSDI. The battle to create the SSDI was an all-out legislative war between business and labor interests, but in the years since, business has largely demobilized and federal officials and beneficiary groups have dominated a politics that for many years has been relatively peaceful. The creation of the ADA was bipartisan, with business interests signing on, but since then there has been a ferocious struggle in the courts over fundamental aspects of the law, a struggle interrupted, though not likely halted, by the ADA Amendments Act. Of course, because the ADA is not an injury compensation policy like SSDI, we need to be careful in comparing them. As the next two chapters illustrate, however, the pattern of increasing conflict and factionalization seems even more prominent in injury compensation, where adversarial legalism's distributional and blame assignment effects are more pronounced.

4

Asbestos Injury Compensation: The Politics of Adversarial Legalism and Layered Policies

Introduction

The asbestos case offers an instructive contrast to the story of SSDI. Whereas SSDI is bureaucratic in design, asbestos injury compensation has been handled primarily through an adversarial structure. Asbestos policy, though, took shape through a complex process that left a layered mix of adversarial and bureaucratic elements. The layering of policy designs in asbestos compensation greatly complicates the story we tell in this chapter, but it also presents an opportunity to examine how different policy structures within the same issue area shape politics.

The evolution of asbestos injury compensation policy has not been neat or linear. It has been a process of fits and starts among the states, Congress, and the courts, as policies created in one institution generated problems that triggered responses in others, which in turn produced further reactions. We break this process into segments in order to streamline the narrative and facilitate within-case comparisons. We begin with some background on asbestos exposure as a public health problem. We then describe several stages of the development of asbestos injury compensation. The first step centers on state workers' compensation programs, their limitations in dealing with the problem of occupational diseases, and efforts to pass national workers' compensation reform from the late 1960s through the 1970s. The next (overlapping) step is the emergence of early litigation against asbestos mining and manufacturing companies, exemplified by the precedent-setting Clarence Borel litigation in the early 1970s, and efforts by some companies to lobby Congress for the creation of alternative compensation schemes. The third wave is the flood of asbestos litigation in the late 1970s and 1980s and the consequent battle over who should pay for its rising costs. This resulted in intense litigation between asbestos manufacturers and their insurance companies and a surge of judicial innovation, some of which was codified by Congress in the mid-1990s. The final wave emerges as asbestos litigation regains momentum in the late 1990s and serious efforts are made at passing comprehensive federal tort reform during the 2000s, including efforts to replace asbestos litigation with a no-fault compensation trust. As with the SSDI chapter, our account will by necessity be selective, focusing on key points and emblematic developments within a much larger and convoluted story. The goal is not to provide a comprehensive history, but instead to capture how the ebbs and flows of policy development have coincided with shifting patterns of interest group politics.

Asbestos as a Public Health Problem

Asbestos is a "magic mineral" (Tweedale 2000).[1] It is stronger than steel yet flexible enough to be woven into cloth. It is waterproof, corrosion proof, and fireproof as well as abundant and easy to mine. Given its remarkable properties, asbestos has been used in thousands of products, including battleships and hair dryers, roof shingles and children's modeling clay, gardening products and car parts, and much else (Virta 2003).

The problem is that exposure to asbestos can be fatal. It can cause asbestosis, a progressive scarring of the lungs; mesothelioma, a deadly cancer of the lining of the chest or abdomen; and lung and larynx cancer (IOM 2006; Roggli et al. 2004; NIOSH 2003, 2008). Dr. Alan Whitehouse, a physician in western Washington state, described asbestos-related diseases as "much worse than AIDS" (Bowker 2003: 109). Pat Cohen, clinic coordinator for the Center for Asbestos-Related Diseases in Libby, Montana—a once pristine town that had become a toxic waste site due to its asbestos mining operations—added that asbestosis causes "a slow, strangulating process, and there is nothing anybody can do about it" (Bowker 2003: 117). Asbestos exposure can also cause pleural plaques and thickening. These conditions can be asymptomatic and may not indicate the onset of serious diseases, but discovery subjects victims to years of stressful uncertainty because many of the worst asbestos-related diseases, including asbestosis and mesothelioma, can take 20 to 40 years to appear.

Although use of asbestos has dropped precipitously over the last 40 years (Virta 2003), its accumulated consumption in the United States remains high, and asbestos exposure continues to pose public health risks for a variety of reasons (see Figure 4.1). Part of the problem is that asbestos is still

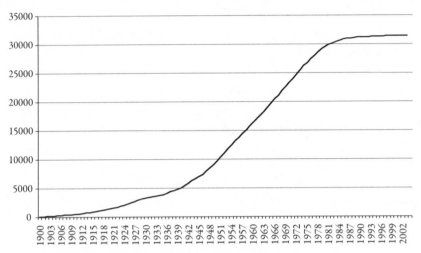

Note: Apparent consumption equals asbestos production plus imports minus exports.

FIGURE 4.1 Accumulated apparent asbestos consumption in the United States: 1900 to 2003 (in thousands of metric tons) (compiled by authors from Virta 2006)

legally used in the United States, and no one knows whether today's asbestos products—however safe at the moment—will become tomorrow's health problem. More importantly, asbestos does not evaporate, and its dangers do not diminish. If anything, some asbestos products, such as roof tiles and insulation, grow more dangerous as they age, becoming brittle—or "friable"—and hence more likely to release asbestos fibers into the environment. Asbestos also can be released when disturbed, as when older buildings are remodeled or destroyed, a fact tragically illustrated by the terrorist attacks on September 11, when the collapse of the World Trade Center released a toxic cloud of dust that included asbestos. Finally, asbestos occurs naturally, and epidemiologists have found higher rates of asbestos-related cancers in areas near asbestos-containing rock (Pan et al. 2005). As a result, even if U.S. followed other industrialized democracies and banned its use, asbestos would continue to present a public health hazard. Consistent with this assessment, the World Health Organization (2006) reported that asbestos is responsible for at least 90,000 deaths annually worldwide, and that the burden of asbestos-related diseases continues to rise, even in countries that prohibited its use in the early 1990s.

The exact scope of asbestos exposure and related health problems in the United States is hard to calculate: historical records are incomplete, some of the health risks remain contested, and long latency periods can complicate statistical projections. We do know that millions of workers in high-risk industries and occupations—asbestos manufacturing, shipbuilding, construction, insulation workers, automobile repair, and others—were exposed during the peak years of consumption from 1940 and 1979 (Nicholson et al. 1982). When these workers came home covered in toxic dust, they unwittingly endangered their families and greatly multiplied the number of people exposed. Meanwhile, in the mid-1980s, the Environmental Protection Agency (EPA) found asbestos in over 733,000 public and commercial buildings (EPA Report 1985), and Congress estimated that asbestos in schools affected 15 million children and 4.1 million school workers (House Report 1986; see also Ausness 1994; Lang 1985).

Whatever the final count, the list of victims is large and continues to grow. Widely cited reports estimate that asbestos-related cancers have caused about 55,000 to 77,000 deaths in the past 30 years (compare Walker et al. 1983 with Lilienfeld et al. 1988). The National Institute for Occupational Safety and Health (NIOSH) more recently reported that asbestosis deaths had increased nearly twenty-fold from the late 1960s to the early 2000s. Given this rise, asbestosis has surpassed black lung disease as the most frequent type of pneumoconiosis death in the United States (NIOSH 2003, xxiii, Tables 1-1, 2-1, 6-1). Data on mesothelioma are more limited but equally sobering. NIOSH has reported that mesothelioma deaths are rising and cost Americans aged 15 and above more than 32,000 years of potential life in 1999 alone, as mesothelioma may take years to manifest but kills quickly once it appears (2003, Table 7-3; 2008). No wonder asbestos has been called "the worst industrial accident in U.S. history" (Cauchon 1999: 4).

State Workers' Compensation Programs and Asbestos Injury Compensation

Asbestos injury compensation policy is often seen as a poster child for adversarial legalism (Kagan 2001). But the story does not begin in the courts or with a sudden surge of lawsuits. It begins in state workers' compensation programs in the early 1960s, when American asbestos workers and their families exposed during World War II began falling ill in increasing numbers. These programs were created during the Progressive Era, and were the forerunners of contemporary no-fault compensation programs. They were intended to replace negligence suits with employer-funded insurance programs. In many states they were supported by both labor and business groups who hoped that a social insurance approach to compensation would be more predictable and efficient than the tort system, the embodiment of American-style adversarial legalism.[2]

In design and practice, workers' compensation laws vary from state to state, but there are some general characteristics of these programs that represent a mix of adversarial and bureaucratic legalism. Among the adversarial aspects is that the programs rely on lawyers and dueling experts to argue claims (as opposed to SSDI, which primarily relies on officials to collect information and assess claims from the top down).[3] Although fault is not an issue, these programs afford ample grounds for contestation and, by the 1960s, they had become increasingly adversarial and legalistic in practice (Nonet 1969; Brodeur 1986; Schroeder 1986; Kagan 2001).

But in many other respects workers' compensation programs represent a significant step away from the tort system and toward bureaucratic legalism. Although claims are often contested, the process of resolving them is stream-lined relative to tort because the range of the dispute is narrowed; workers need not prove that their employer was negligent, only that the injury is work-related, and damages are typically fixed according to state-created for-mulas. Rather than the decentralized system of judges and juries that decide tort cases, workers' compensation claims are handled by centralized and spe-cialized administrative courts, a system much better structured to produce the bureaucratic ideal of uniform treatment of cases. The decisions of worker compensation courts can be appealed, but only under the "arbitrary and capri-cious" standard typically used for the decisions of regulatory agencies.[4] The funding mechanism for workers' compensation programs is somewhat more socialized than tort and so again more closely reflects the bureaucratic ideal. Workers' compensation claims are paid through a variety of mechanisms, but private and public insurance is predominant. While premiums are typically adjusted to reflect an individual business's previous payouts, insurance tends to spread the costs and risks of injuries across similarly situated businesses (Sengupta et al. 2011). Tort payouts can also come from insurance, but many businesses are uninsured or underinsured, and so the burden of successful claims often falls wholly on individual companies. In the case of asbestos, as discussed below, when defendants turned to their liability insurers for help, the scope of their coverage was unclear, which became another source of liti-gation as companies and their insurers fought over who should bear the bur-den of spiraling litigation costs.

A fundamental premise of workers' compensation is that it is the exclusive remedy for workers; they cannot normally bring a tort lawsuit against their employers. Thus it was understandable that asbestos workers would first turn to workers' compensation programs. But workers' compensation provided asbestos workers very limited relief. The problem was two-fold. First, workers' compensation programs were designed to address claims for traumatic injuries at the workplace, such as broken legs and arms, not slowly manifesting occupational diseases like asbestosis and mesothelioma. As a result, asbestos workers' claims did not neatly fit into the programs' preexisting categories of injury. Second, employers and insurance companies fought asbestos workers' claims at every turn during the 1960s, ensuring that these programs would be construed narrowly. They argued that smoking, not asbestos, caused workers' lung problems. They alleged workers suffering from asbestosis—a slowly debilitating disease—were not "totally disabled" as required under many state laws. And they insisted states' statutes of limitation barred many asbestos workers' claims because these provisions (at the time) required claims to be filed within one to three years of an injury; many of the worst asbestos-related diseases took decades to appear. The combination of new claims and institutional inflexibility resulted in what Jacob Hacker (2004) calls "drift," the creation of gaps in social welfare programs through shifts in the policy environment. In this case the emergence of new, unanticipated risks left asbestos workers and their families only partially protected.

The Contentious Politics of Attempted Congressional Workers' Compensation Reform

In response to the problem of occupational diseases such as asbestosis and mesothelioma, organized labor ramped up long-standing efforts to enact federal reform of state workers' compensation laws. The issue was squarely raised in Congress at the end of the 1960s during hearings on the passage of the Occupational Safety Hazard Act of 1970 (OSHA of 1970), as prominent advocates for asbestos workers and their families pushed Congress to act. Dr. Irving Selikoff, whose epidemiological studies of asbestos workers in the mid-1960s were critical in raising public awareness of the problem, testified that "[t]here are many parts of our country and many states in which the regulatory and legislative process have not caught up with the medical facts."[5] Albert Hutchinson, the president of the Asbestos Workers Union added, "I am afraid that unless something is done now, we are going to have a disaster in this country that will make black lung in coal miners look like a picnic."[6]

The early politics of federal workers' compensation reform were similar to efforts to expand the federal role in disability insurance. Reformers began by convincing Congress to create a national commission to study the problem. The blue ribbon commission, which was created by OSHA of 1970, did not mince words: "The inescapable conclusion is that the state workmen's compensation laws in general are inadequate and inequitable" (Gottron 1975, 1883; see also Gottron 1976). It went on to make 84 recommendations to improve state programs, 19 of which were deemed essential, including recommendations relating to compulsory coverage, the duration of benefits, the size of death benefits, the provision of death benefits to a workers' spouse, and the coverage of all medical costs. It further recommended that states be given a chance to adopt its recommendations and that Congress should revisit the issue on July 15, 1975. At that time, if necessary, Congress could take additional steps to encourage reform.

The states' responses to the Commission's recommendations were uneven. No state adopted all of the Commission's core recommendations; most adopted some, but a few adopted none (see Figure 4.2). In anticipation of the states' failure to meet the Commission's July 1975 deadline, Senators Williams (D-NJ) and Javitz (R-NY) introduced a bill (S. 2008) that was designed to take on the problem of occupational diseases, including asbestos-related diseases, such as asbestosis and mesothelioma, which were explicitly included in its definition of disease (see S. 2008 sections 2(a)(1), 3(8)). The bill would have required states to adopt all of the National Commission's 19 essential recommendations. It further empowered the Secretary of Labor to impose the federal Longshore and

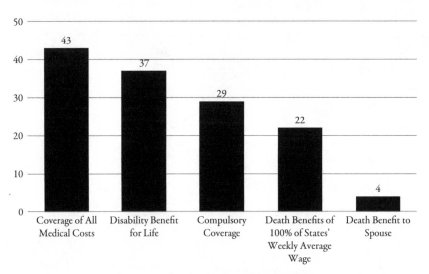

FIGURE 4.2 States and District of Columbia compliance with key national commission recommendations (compiled by authors from Gottron 1975)

Harbor Workers' Compensation Act on recalcitrant states, which would have effectively federalized their workers' compensation programs.

The Nixon Administration, which opposed the bill, sought to stall. The day before the Subcommittee on Labor of the Senate Labor and Public Welfare Committee was to begin hearings on the proposal, Nixon announced the creation of a new commission, the Interdepartmental Workers' Compensation Task Force. The Task Force was directed to report to Congress by the end of 1975, after the July deadline set by the original commission.

Javitz ignored the new Task Force and forged ahead with the hearings on his proposal. The hearings demonstrated that the affected interests were sharply divided. They featured 240 witnesses representing a wide array of interests, including business groups and individual companies, insurance companies, unions, claimant and defense counsel, individual workers, Republicans and Democrats, state and federal officials, and legal and medical experts. The hearings generated over 2,800 pages of testimony. In the next session, in the House, Dominick Daniels (D-NJ) proposed a bill (HR 9431) that would have forced the states to adopt the Commission's 19 essential provisions. Similar to the Senate hearings, the 1976 hearings before the Subcommittee on Manpower of the House Education and Labor Committee were contentious. They featured 78 witnesses representing the same array of interests and generated almost 1,500 pages of testimony.

Unions and their liberal allies in Congress supported federal action. Andrew J. Bienmiller, director of the AFL-CIO lobbying department argued that "As long as industrial injury and disease is such a common job risk, every worker in the nation must have the protection of an effective up-to-date workmen's compensation system based on uniform standards throughout the nation.... That is why the AFL-CIO gives whole-hearted support to the earliest possible enactment of S 2008" (*CQ Weekly* 1974a, 1441). Other unions joined the AFL-CIO, including the United Steelworkers, United Auto Workers, the Teamsters, United Mine Workers Association, the Air Line Pilots Association, Transportation Workers Union of America, the United Rubber, Cork, Linoleum and Plastics Workers of America, and the International Associations of Heat and Frost Insulators and Asbestos Workers (see generally *CQ Weekly* 1974b: 1696.)

Business, insurance groups, and their conservative allies, including members of the Nixon Administration, mostly opposed federalization and preferred the existing state programs. On the right, Lawrence Jones, president of the American Insurance Association, responded that, while federal minimum standards might be useful in the abstract, the application of the proposed standards would be "seriously detrimental" to the current system (*CQ Weekly* 1974a: 1441). Andre Maisonpierre, vice president of the American Mutual Insurance Alliance, added that the bill "would federalize all the important policy decisions and would create chaos in the state systems that ultimately a complete federal takeover would be necessary" (*CQ Weekly* 1974b: 1696). Douglas Stevenson of the Chamber of Commerce raised the specter of the federal reforms creating a class of malingerers, arguing that "as a matter of economic survival of our country in the long pull, we have to have more incentive for people to work rather than not work."[7] Michael Romig, who accompanied Stevenson, struck a more conciliatory tone. He conceded that many of the goals of the Commission were laudable in theory but that "we don't know enough about the problem to be able to fashion a solution to get from here to there."[8] Other business groups weighed in against the bill, including the National Association of Manufacturers, the American Retail Federation, Associated Builders and Contractors, Inc., the National Contractors Industry Council, and individual companies such as United Airlines and Arthur G. McKee Company.

It was a lineup that looked a lot like the 1950s hearings on Social Security Disability, a classic battle of business versus labor with an intriguing exception: a couple of business interests—tool manufacturers and professional groups representing architects—split off from their counterparts and publicly supported federal intervention. The defection appears to have been caused by the litigation risks that both groups faced. Frustrated by the limits of workers' compensation programs, claimants were beginning to bring product liability cases against businesses that supplied materials and expertise to the workplace, especially tool manufacturers and architects. Facing a surge of adversarial legalism, these business groups behaved very differently than those who were covered under the relatively more bureaucratic workers' compensation programs.

The two defendant groups argued that the federal government needed to step in not because the state programs were flawed, as unions insisted, but because the rising use of product liability suits against them undermined central policy goals of workers' compensation laws, including (a) the provision of a streamlined remedy in lieu of tort suits and (b) the spreading of costs and risks more evenly across industrial sectors. James Mack, National Tool Builders Association, explained as follows: "Today we are prepared to testify that, if H.R. 9431 is amended to include our proposal—and is revised in other ways which we shall indicate—we will actively support its passage. We say this recognizing that passage of H.R. 9431 will increase workers' compensation costs for some of our members.... This decision was not reached lightly.... It was reached, in the final analysis, after coming to the inescapable conclusion that the present system of workers' compensation simply doesn't work the way it is supposed to work."[9]

Carl Bradley, of the American Institute of Architects, agreed: "Increasingly, injured workers are suing architects since they are often the only available defendants. As workers' compensation systems have become less and less able to make the injured worker whole, the courts have increasingly used professional liability and the insurance system behind it to spread the uncompensated losses of the worker out to the entire society."[10] At the time, members of Congress responded that their focus was on workers' compensation reform, not tort reform, and that these groups should not muddy the legislative waters. The arguments of these groups, however, foreshadowed a recurring theme in the politics of asbestos injury compensation: businesses and professions facing high levels of litigation have tended to break away from other business interests and supported federal reform despite their stated inclination toward small government.

States also divided based on the degree to which the existing system imposed costs on them. Many states joined with business to oppose federal reforms of their programs. Michael J. Gillman, chair of the Michigan workmen's compensation appeals board, testified that the bill was "somewhat like recalling Secretary of State Kissinger from the Near East to negotiate a fence-line dispute between suburban neighbors" (*CQ Weekly* 1974b, 1696). Other states agreed, including Florida, New York, Texas, Arizona, Utah, and Wisconsin. Yet other states, especially those that had adopted a number of the National Commission's 19 essential recommendations, took a different view. Massachusetts, for example, had enacted 11 of the 19 recommendations, a relatively high number. Tip O'Neill, then Lieutenant Governor of the State, testified that his state generally supported the bill's creation of federal standards (while also recommending a study on the economic impact of the law and a phased-in approach to implementation). O'Neill further explained that Congress needed to act in order to push all states forward, so that some states would not be placed at an unfair disadvantage in attracting business. He stated, "It is unlikely that we will jeopardize our State's workers and the businesses that employ them by furthering our competitive disadvantage vis-à-vis other States. We must look to the Congress to require uniform benefit standards."[11]

Ultimately, Javitz's and Williams' efforts failed, although hearings on various versions of national workers' compensation reform continued at least until 1980, years after asbestos lawsuits had become common. Advocates could never overcome the coalition among business groups, the insurance industry, low compliance states and small government conservatives, despite some fissures among businesses that had faced a growing number of product liability suits.

Turning to the Courts: The Clarence Borel Era

During the struggle over federal reform of state workers' compensation, individual asbestos workers who had grown frustrated with workers' compensation programs increasingly turned to the courts. The story of Clarence Borel, whose lawsuit in the late 1960s culminated in the first major federal appellate court victory for asbestos plaintiffs against asbestos manufacturers, illustrates this process.[12]

Borel had spent decades insulating steam pipes, boilers, and other high-temperature equipment in shipyards and oil refineries using asbestos-laden products in the "Golden Triangle" region, a heavily industrialized area along the Sabine River that divides Texas and Louisiana. For most of his life, Borel had enjoyed steady work and reasonably good health. By the mid-1960s, however, constant exposure to asbestos began to take its toll. In 1964, his doctors warned him that his lungs were cloudy and that he should avoid further exposure as much as possible (Gifford 2010: 47). Borel, the father of six children, ignored this advice and continued to insulate pipes. His condition worsened. In January 1968, he developed pain in his chest and difficulty in breathing while working in a refinery for Fuller-Austin Insulation Company. Initially, he was diagnosed with pneumonia and sent to recuperate in a hospital in Port Arthur. During the next month, his condition deteriorated and doctors sent him to Houston for exploratory surgery. The surgery revealed that he was not only suffering from pneumonia but also had an advanced case of asbestosis. Later he would be diagnosed with mesothelioma. At the age of 57, Clarence Borel was dying.

Like many asbestos workers at the time, Borel did not initially file a lawsuit seeking compensation for his illnesses. Instead, in the spring of 1968, he filed a workers' compensation claim, which he eventually settled for $8,000 plus $5,081.10 in medical expenses—a total of $13,081.10 for injuries that amounted to a death sentence for a man in his fifties. Later that year, Borel decided to visit an attorney, Ward Stephenson, to see if he could claim further compensation in the courts to help cover his ongoing medical expenses and provide for his family.

When Borel arrived in Stephenson's office, he was visibly ill—pale, gaunt, and short of breath. He admitted that he knew asbestos dust was unhealthy and that he refused to wear a respirator at work because they were uncomfortable and easily clogged (Gifford 2010: 45). Nevertheless, Borel insisted that he never knew that asbestos dust could be fatal because he assumed that it would dissolve upon entering his lungs. He also maintained that he was never adequately warned of the dangers of asbestos. Instead, beginning in 1964, long after he began working, asbestos products provided generic warnings that "inhalation of asbestos in excessive quantities over longer periods of time may be harmful" (Gifford 2010: 47).

Two outside events in the 1960s strengthened Stephenson's hand. One was medical. During 1962 and 1963, three doctors began studying mortality rates among asbestos-insulation workers: Irving Selikoff of Mount Sinai School of Medicine; Jacob Churg, chief pathologist at Barnert Memorial Hospital; and E. Cuyler Hammond, vice president for epidemiology and statistics of the American Cancer Society. In October 1964, they presented their findings at an international conference on the biological effects of asbestos sponsored by the New York Academy of Sciences (Selikoff et al. 1965). These studies provided a scientific basis for Stephenson's claim that asbestos had caused Borel's illnesses.

The other was legal. In the spring of 1965, the American Law Institute (ALI) published the second edition of its *Restatement of the Law of Torts*. *Restatements* are commentaries by legal elites under the aegis of the ALI that both comment on developments in common law and attempt to influence judges to harmonize the law in certain directions. Section 402A of the *Restatement* set forth a new theory of products liability law, called "strict product liability." It stated: "One who sells any product in a defective condition unreasonably dangerous to the user or consumer or to his property is subject to liability for physical harm thereby caused to the ultimate user or consumer," even if the seller "has exercised all possible care in the preparation and sale of his product." The *Restatement* went on to explain, in "comment k," that unavoidably unsafe products would not be considered unreasonably dangerous as long as they were "properly prepared, and accompanied by proper directions and warning."[13] Before Borel's case, Texas had adopted Section 402A, which seemed a promising theory for suing asbestos manufacturers and mining companies on the grounds that they provided inadequate warnings in connection with their products containing asbestos.

Armed with Borel's detailed work records, Dr. Selikoff and his associates' medical findings, and Section 402A, Stephenson formally commenced Borel's lawsuit by filing a complaint in federal court for the Eastern District of Texas against 11 asbestos manufacturers from across the United States. The complaint sought $1 million in damages under Section 402A's theory of strict product liability for failing to warn.[14] Clarence Borel never saw his day in court. He died on June 3, 1970. However, under Texas law, his wife, Thelma, was able to take his place and the lawsuit proceeded. After a hotly contested trial, the Borels prevailed, winning damages of $79,436.24, more than six times the original workers' compensation award. It was the first time that a court held asbestos manufacturers strictly liable for failing to provide sufficient warnings about their products' health risks.

In the American legal system winning at trial is only the first step in the litigation process. The losers can appeal, and that is exactly what the defendants did in the Borel case. The manufacturers hired W. Page Keeton to argue their case before the Fifth Circuit of the U.S. Courts of Appeal. Keeton was the Dean of the University of Texas Law School, a leading expert on torts, and one of the architects of Section 402A. Keeton argued that the district court had erred as a matter of law, maintaining that strict liability should not be imposed simply because harm was reasonably foreseeable from a product's ordinary use. After all, harm is foreseeable from the use of almost any product, even seemingly innocuous items like cars, stoves, and antibiotics. Using Keeton's academic writings, Stephenson countered that it would be absurd to allow manufacturers to avoid liability by ignoring their products' dangers and concealing public health risks (Brodeur 1986: 66–68).

On September 10, 1973, in an opinion by Judge John Minor Wisdom, the Fifth Circuit rejected the manufacturers' appeal and affirmed the lower court.[15] In siding with Borel, Judge Wisdom leaned heavily on the manufacturers' failure to provide adequate warnings of the dangers of asbestos, stating as follows:

> In reaching our decision in the case at bar, we recognize that the question of the applicability of Section 402A of the Restatement to cases involving "occupational diseases" is one of first impression. But though the application is novel, the underlying principle is ancient. Under the law of torts, a person has long been liable for the foreseeable harm caused by his own negligence.... It implies a duty to warn of foreseeable dangers.... This duty to warn extends to all users and consumers,

including the common worker in the shop or in the field....Here, there was a duty to speak, but the defendants remained silent (*Borel v. Fibreboard Products Corporation,* at 1103).

Thus, with a stroke of the pen, the court created a new policy by adopting a broad interpretation of Section 402A, which significantly increased the potential liability of manufacturers of inherently dangerous products, even if the users of these products contributed to their injuries and knew they were harmful to some degree, on the theory that manufacturers are in a better position to detect risks, avoid future harms, and broadly distribute the costs of injuries (Gifford 2010: 52). Although the court stretched existing product liability law to recognize a new cause of action, the traditional issues of individual responsibility and fault were never far from its reasoning; *Borel* explicitly found that asbestos manufacturers had a duty to warn the public about the risks of their products and that they were liable for any damages stemming from their failure to discharge this duty. Indeed, Judge Wisdom's reasoning, quoted above, explicitly uses the language of negligence in interpreting the scope of Section 402A.

The defendants continued to fight. They asked for a rehearing but the Fifth Circuit refused (*Borel* at 1109). They then appealed to the U.S. Supreme Court, but the Court denied their petition (419 U.S. 869 (1974)). After these options were exhausted, the *Borel* litigation finally came to a close. Other federal appellate courts followed in Judge Wisdom's footsteps, holding that asbestos manufacturing and mining companies could be held strictly liable under Section 402A (see, e.g., *Karjala v. Johns-Manville Products Corporation; Moran v. Johns-Manville Sales Corporation*).

The Quiet Politics of Early Congressional Tort Reform Efforts: The "Johns-Manville Bailout Bills"

The defendants did not pin all their hopes on the judicial appeals process. They also lobbied Congress, seeking legislation that would provide an alternative to litigation and limit their liability. As early as April 1973, after some of the initial settlements but before the Fifth Circuit handed down the *Borel* decision and while Congress was considering broader state workers' compensation reform to deal with the problem of occupational disease, asbestos manufacturers pressed Congress for relief from asbestos litigation.

There was at least one asbestos compensation bill in every Congress from the early 1970s to the mid-1980s.

Some of these bills were referred to as the "Johns-Manville bailout bills" (Brodeur 1986) because they were introduced by members of Congress from districts with ties to the company, they were targeted to address asbestos-related injuries only, and they were generally seen as pro-industry. Some of the first bills were introduced by Representative Peter Frelinghysen, a Republican from New Jersey, and his successor, Millicent Fenwick, who represented the district that included the town of Manville, the location of Johns-Manville's large asbestos manufacturing plant. Senator Gary Hart, another early advocate of reform, served a state, Colorado, that was home to the headquarters to Johns-Manville starting in 1972.

The bills from Fenwick and Hart, both entitled the Asbestos Health Hazard Compensation Act, were supposedly written in consultation with Johns-Manville (Brodeur 1986: 194–195). Representative Fenwick's version of the bill (HR 8689), which was introduced in 1977, was a classic "replacement reform" (Burke 2002: 18). It sought to replace tort suits with a federal compensation fund financed by a combination of federal tax dollars and contributions from the asbestos and tobacco industries. In 1979, compensation for a totally disabled asbestos worker would have been $500 per month, while the maximum benefit for a worker with a dependent wife and two or more children would have been $1,000 monthly. Representative George Miller, a liberal Democrat from California, whose district included an asbestos plant and who chaired hearings on the cover-up of asbestos health risks by the industry, denounced the bill. Miller stressed the culpability of the asbestos industry, arguing that, under the bill, "the obligation of paying for decades of neglect, negligence, cover-up and lies would be foisted on the American taxpayer" (Brodeur 1986: 195).

Senator Hart's bill differed in its details but was attacked on similar political grounds. Instead of replacing litigation with a new federal program, Hart's bill banned asbestos-related tort suits and called for federal minimum standards for compensating asbestos workers through state workers' compensation programs. Under these new federal standards, compensation for total disability or death could not be less than two-thirds of a claimant's weekly wage during the highest three of five years preceding death or total disability. The federal standards, however, were voluntary, and workers who failed to receive adequate payments would have to apply for supplemental compensation to a federal benefits review board.

In contrast to measures aimed at reforming workers' compensation programs, which received considerable attention and generated extensive hearings, the early asbestos litigation reform bills were largely non-starters, dying in committee without hearings. As one interviewee explained, unlike workers' compensation reform that framed the issue of occupational disease as a societal problem, asbestos litigation organized claims into discrete lawsuits against a limited number of culpable businesses. Once this happened, asbestos-related injury compensation was seen as a "one-company problem," namely, Johns-Manville.

Given this understanding of the problem, there was little appetite in Congress to intervene and help companies that had intentionally concealed enormous public health risks. Reinforcing this view, the Federal Judicial Center, the federal research and education center for the U.S. federal courts, argued as late as 1985 that claims of an asbestos crisis were "greatly exaggerated" and that asbestos litigation was best understood as "relatively routine cases" (Willging 1985: 2, 5), suggesting that the issue was best left to the courts. Accordingly, while businesses and insurance companies with high exposure to asbestos litigation continued to work with sympathetic members to introduce various reform measures, some aimed at asbestos litigation specifically and others (in the mid-1980s) aimed more broadly at curtailing products liability law, such as the Uniform Products Liability Act, these efforts failed.

The Flood of Asbestos Litigation

Given the torrent of litigation that followed, it is tempting to assume that the *Borel* decision immediately opened the floodgates. It did not. *Borel* merely recognized a potential cause of action against companies that supplied asbestos-laden products to the workplace. This was crucial but only a first step. Having a right to sue and winning lawsuits are two very different things. Plaintiffs won only about half of the cases that went to trial immediately following *Borel* (Brodeur 1986). Defendants took advantage of the qualifications and defenses built into the decision. For example, under *Borel*, companies were liable only if they had failed to warn about "reasonably foreseeable" dangers (*Borel*, 493 F.2d at 1088) in connection with reasonably foreseeable applications (493 F.2d at 1090). The warnings needed only be "adequate" (1089) and "reasonably calculated to reach" the public (1091). Even if a seller acted unreasonably, the failure to warn must proximately cause the plaintiffs' injuries (1090). *Borel* also recognized the so-called "state-of-the-art" defense, which holds that sellers can only be liable for reasonably knowable risks, or the state of the art of existing medical and scientific knowledge (1089).[16]

Immediately following *Borel,* defendants typically asserted the state-of-the-art defense and claimed that they were unaware of the health risks associated with asbestos prior to the publication of studies by Dr. Selikoff and his colleagues in the mid-1960s. Early asbestos litigation, then, often hinged on what individual companies knew and when they knew it. It was a battle over facts and culpability, a sequel to the earlier battle over the law and potential liability. Together, these battles laid the foundation of modern asbestos litigation, and the subsequent surge in adversarial legalism.

A critical turning point in the battle over fault was the discovery of the "Sumner Simpson Papers." The papers were discovered in the course of a lawsuit against Raybestos-Manhattan, which was one of the largest asbestos manufacturers in the United States. The story is that Karl Asch, who represented asbestos workers at Raybestos-Manhattan's Passaic plant, obtained a routine subpoena in February, 1977, ordering William Simpson, president of Raybestos and son of its founder, Sumner Simpson, to testify at a deposition and to bring any documents pertaining to the plant's working conditions. During the deposition, Asch asked whether the company had hired any independent consultants to study the health effects of asbestos and, if so, whether there were any documents related to these studies. Defense attorneys directed him to a box of Sumner Simpson's personal papers that his son had dutifully saved. The box contained a treasure trove of correspondence between Sumner Simpson and his counterparts at other leading asbestos manufacturer companies, which showed these companies not only knew about the risks of asbestos for decades but also had commissioned studies on asbestos's dangers and concealed the results. Asch knew that he had "hit pay dirt" (Brodeur 1986: 111).

"Gold mine" might be a better description. The uncovering of the Sumner Simpson Papers and similar evidence exposed decades of willful corporate misconduct in concealing public health risks, destroyed the state-of-the-art defense, and unleashed a surge of successful (and highly lucrative) litigation. In the words of a leading 1985 study of asbestos litigation by RAND, "[b]y the late 1970s, the potential for plaintiff success had been widely recognized, and asbestos cases surged into the court system where worker exposure was common" (Hensler et al. 1985: vii). A new, adversarial injury compensation policy was established in which tort suits took precedence over workers' compensation claims without wholly replacing them (Hensler et al. 1985).

Asbestos litigation has grown exponentially since the late 1970s. In 2005, RAND published a comprehensive study of asbestos litigation that estimated 730,000 individual claims for asbestos-related injuries had been filed in the United States as of 2002, and projected that the number of new annual claims, while slowing down, would continue on an upward trend for the foreseeable future (Carroll et al. 2005: xxiv; Bhagavatula et al. 2001; see also Egelko 2013). Consistent with these estimates, NERA, an economic consulting firm that conducts annual reviews of corporate asbestos liability based on disclosures in SEC filings, recently found that new claims continue to be filed but at a slower pace, as the average number of asbestos filings has stabilized to about 20% of those filed in 2003 (Stern and Allen 2013: 7). Yet the *cost* of resolving claims has been increasing, probably reflecting the growing number of cancer-related claims being brought. According to a 2013 NERA report, the average amount spent to resolve claims since 2010 has been three times the average payments made in 2001 (Stern and Allen 2013: 2).

The story is not only the amount of litigation but also its scope. Asbestos suits have targeted over 8,400 firms, including companies in 75 of 83 categories of economic activity in the Standard Industrial Classification, which seeks to categorize all types of business activity within the economy (Carroll et al. 2005: xxv). In 2002, *Barron's* named 40 publicly traded companies with significant, and growing, asbestos-liability exposure (Abelson 2002). The list reads like a corporate *Who's Who*, including Dow Chemical, Daimler Chrysler, Ford, IBM, Kaiser Aluminum, Pfizer, Sears, Viacom, and even Disney.

Many of these companies had little or nothing to do with concealing the dangers of asbestos; they merely used asbestos-containing products in their businesses, or acquired firms that once produced asbestos products. Pacor, Incorporated offers a case in point. In the 1980s, Pacor was a medium-sized insulation company with annual sales of around $20 million. Pacor did not mine asbestos or manufacture asbestos products. It purchased insulation materials from the leading asbestos manufacturers and relied on them to supply high quality, safe products. James E. Sullivan, Pacor's chairman, explained the company's situation in testimony to Congress:

> We purchased insulation products from reputable manufacturers and used them in our business without any conception of their danger. We relied on manufacturers to test their products and make sure they were safe, as much as we rely on automobile manufacturers to test their vehicles and the ladder manufacturers to test their ladders. Purchasers

like insulation contractors simply do not have the money or expertise
to fully evaluate the composition and safety features of every product
they purchase.[17]

Nevertheless, under the rules of the tort system, which helps successful plaintiffs find solvent defendants, Pacor faced thousands of asbestos-related claims.
As a consequence of litigation, Pacor lost its insurance and credit rating. In
1983, Sullivan argued to Congress that "there has to be some sort of global
solution to the asbestos problem pretty soon, or most of us will not make it."[18]
Three years later, as Sullivan predicted, asbestos litigation overwhelmed Pacor
and it filed for bankruptcy. On top of the failure of his company, Sullivan was
diagnosed with mesothelioma and joined the ranks of thousands of asbestos
victims, like Clarence Borel, who unwittingly endangered their lives by using
asbestos products at work.

A cross-national comparison with The Netherlands helps place the
American policy in perspective. According to comparative legal scholars,
the incidence of asbestos-related diseases was five to ten times higher in
Dutch workers in the 1970s and 1980s, and, unlike American law which
channels most employee claims against their employers into workers'
compensation programs, Dutch law allows workers to bring tort suits
directly against their employers (Vinke and Wilthagen 1992). Yet only
10 tort suits had reportedly been filed in The Netherlands as of 1991. By
contrast, one of every three cases civil cases filed in the Eastern District of
Texas in 1990 was an asbestos case (Report of the Judicial Conference Ad
Hoc Committee on Asbestos 1991, 8 (hereinafter The Judicial Conference
Report)).

The Growing Critique of Asbestos Litigation
as a Means of Compensation

Asbestos litigation undoubtedly served important, even heroic policy functions at the outset (Brodeur 1986; Bowker 2003; Barnes 2009a; see generally
Mather 1998; Bogus 2001; Frymer 2003). For ordinary workers like Clarence
Borel, courts provided a forum to raise concerns when other branches and levels of government were not responsive. Asbestos litigation provided a means
to bypass the limited state workers' compensation programs, increase awareness of the dangers of asbestos, and uncover decades of corporate wrongdoing.

But as asbestos lawsuits proliferated, concerns about compensation and efficiency came to the fore, and many experts began to raise serious doubts about the costs and fairness of asbestos litigation. A 1983 RAND study showed that asbestos plaintiffs received only 37 cents of every dollar spent to resolve asbestos claims, significantly less than ordinary tort claims (Kakalik et al. 1983). Follow-up studies show that these patterns have persisted as administrative costs continue to consume over half of all compensation paid (Hensler et al. 2001; Carroll et al. 2005). By contrast, the administrative costs of the Black Lung Disability Trust Fund, which is often criticized as wasteful, accounted for only 4.5 to 5.8% of the Program's annual obligations from 1992 to 2006 (OWCP Annual Reports 2001, 2006, Table B-4).

These costs might be tolerable if asbestos litigation delivered consistent compensation, but it has been erratic. In Texas, five juries in a multi-plaintiff trial heard exactly the same evidence and ruled differently on specific liability and causation issues (Bell and O'Connell 1997: 22). Jury damage awards also have varied from case to case and jurisdiction to jurisdiction, providing similarly situated plaintiffs different compensation and providing those with harder-to-prove claims nothing at all (Sugarman 1989: 46). Meanwhile, some claimants herded into massive class action settlements were limited to lower recoveries than those who sued individually or happened to be swept into earlier class action settlements (Coffee 1995: 1384–1396), while payments to other claimants varied according to the solvency of defendants (Barnes 2007b; Austern 2001).

Asbestos litigation is also slow, as some, like Clarence Borel, died before their cases could be decided (Hensler et al. 1985: 84–85; see also Carroll et al. 2005). As early as the mid-1980s, experts began to document these delays, which varied across jurisdictions. After six or more years of asbestos litigation, the state court in San Francisco had completed only 11% of asbestos cases. In Massachusetts, the state court had resolved only 10 of 2,141 claims, or less than 1% (Hensler et al. 1985, 84–85). Even worse, asbestos litigation has reportedly become plagued by questionable and even fraudulent claiming practices that displace consideration of those suffering the most and unfairly burden business (see Schuck 1992; Koniak 1995, *Mealey's Litigation Report: Asbestos Bankruptcy* 2005; see also Coffee 1995). In short, asbestos litigation has come to embody many of the characteristic downsides of adversarial legalism as a means of compensation, including its costs, inconsistency, and delays as well as its potential for bogus and frivolous claims (Kagan 2001). These costs affect not only the targets of litigation but also some claimants, as some plaintiffs receive large settlements or verdicts while others with similar claims can receive little or nothing at all.

The Era of Judicial Policymaking

As the number of lawsuits escalated, conflict over asbestos policy grew both in the courts and Congress. In the absence of congressional action, courts made far-reaching policy decisions about the liability of insurers and how claims against bankrupt companies would be administered.

The insurance litigation

The question of who would pay for asbestos-related claims was complicated because asbestos manufacturing and mining companies had purchased millions of dollars of general-liability coverage insurance policies. These policies typically provided coverage of claims for "bodily injury," which included illnesses caused by an "occurrence," a term that included exposure to conditions that resulted in bodily injury during the insurance period. Unlike bureaucratic social insurance programs, which spread the costs of injury across economic sectors, private insurance for liability is arranged on a company-by-company basis. As a result, different businesses had different levels of insurance protection. Insurance companies also faced varying levels of exposure depending on the businesses they insured, whether they were primary or secondary insurers, or whether they had acquired re-insurance in order to share risks further. This complex web of private insurance coverage meant that the risk of litigation was not as evenly spread as in social insurance programs and that different individual companies had very different risk profiles.

During the early 1970s, before the stakes of asbestos litigation were clear, insurance companies and asbestos manufacturers generally worked together to defend product liability cases. But as costs and risks mounted in the late 1970s and early 1980s, insurance companies began to refuse to defend or indemnify asbestos companies under their general liability policies. This tension raised a fundamental policy question: what should be the scope of liability under these policies?

One of the leading cases involved the Insurance Company of North America (INA). In the late 1970s, INA informed Forty-Eight Insulations, a small asbestos manufacturing company owned by Forster-Wheeler Company, that it would no longer defend or indemnify suits in which asbestos-related diseases emerged after October 31, 1972, the expiration date of its comprehensive general-liability policies for the company. INA's argument was known as the "manifestation theory," which held that coverage was triggered only when asbestos-related diseases were diagnosed or when the victim should have known he or she was sick. Forty-Eight Insulations countered that INA's interpretation of its policies was too narrow, and that exposure to asbestos dust was the occurrence that triggered coverage. According to this theory, exposure to asbestos was a continuing tort, and all insurance companies that covered the company during the period of exposure were "on the risk."

INA sought a declaratory court judgment endorsing its narrow interpretation of the underlying insurance policies. It lost. The court adopted Forty-Eight Insulations' "exposure theory" and noted that INA had defended more than 150 cases on behalf of Forty-Eight Insulations and never raised the manifestation theory. INA appealed, but not all of the insurance companies involved in the case sided with INA. Travelers joined Forty-Eight Insulations in fighting the appeal, arguing for a pro-rated version of exposure theory that would apportion litigation costs among any company whose policy was triggered. Travelers' legal posture reflected its interests. Although it had issued primary insurance to many large asbestos manufacturers, including Johns-Manville, it had not issued a large amount of excess insurance, insurance that would kick in when the primary policy was exhausted, unlike INA, and insurers such as Lloyd's of London and the Commercial Union Insurance Company (Brodeur 1986). Under these conditions, Travelers had a short-term incentive in bringing as many deep pockets into the litigation as possible in order to share the costs. In the long term, if asbestos litigation continued unabated, and insurance coverage was construed broadly, Travelers' obligations would eventually be exhausted, but the cost of excess claims would fall on its competitors. Provided that asbestos litigation costs continued to spiral upward, the effect would be to shift asbestos litigation costs on its competitors long after Travelers had written off its initial losses.

In the end, the Sixth Circuit endorsed the exposure theory on the general policy grounds that insurance policies should be construed broadly in the case of ambiguity (*INA v. Forty-Eight Insulation, Inc.*; see generally Brodeur 1986). Other courts went further, adopting a "triple trigger" interpretation that held insurance coverage would be triggered by the initial exposure, continuing exposure *and* manifestation of a disease (e.g., *Keene Corp. v. INA*). Insurance companies sought Supreme Court review of these issues, but the Court declined to hear them. Like the early asbestos defendants, insurance companies with high levels of exposure called for congressional action, but gained little traction (Brodeur 1986: 190–192).

As the insurance litigation came to a close, it was clear that asbestos litigation would be funded by the deep pockets of the insurance industry in addition to asbestos manufacturers and, under the rules of joint and several liability, all other companies (and their insurers) in the supply chain. It was also clear that business groups and insurance companies would be deeply divided over the need for federal litigation reform depending on the degree to which they faced the risk of litigation costs.

Court-based tort reform

As litigation over insurance coverage percolated through the courts, another front opened in the battle of asbestos injury compensation policy, as defendants pursued a number of strategies to manage their liability through "court-based tort reform": the adaptation of existing legal rules and procedures to change who pays, how much, and to whom (Barnes 2007b). The most dramatic—and probably most influential—example was the Johns-Manville Corporation's filing for reorganization under Chapter 11 of the bankruptcy code.[19] Johns-Manville was the leading asbestos mining-and-manufacturing company in the United States and a primary target of asbestos litigation. In 1982, Johns-Manville filed for reorganization under Chapter 11 of the bankruptcy code, even though it was a Fortune 500 company and its day-to-day operations were profitable. Johns-Manville defended its unprecedented move on the grounds that mounting asbestos liability threatened the company's future solvency. Under these conditions, filing for bankruptcy promised several advantages commonly associated with any Chapter 11: it suspended pending litigation, it transferred all litigation to a single bankruptcy court where there is no right to jury trial and the debtor's attorneys' fees are reviewed by the court, and it offered the company a chance to reorganize its business, preserve assets for the benefit of all of its creditors, and prioritize payments.

Johns-Manville's Chapter 11, however, did more than rationalize the payment of claims and reorganize the company. It created a new administrative entity the "Manville Trust," with its own source of funding and rule-making authority, which was authorized not only to handle claims pending at the time of the company's bankruptcy but also to resolve future claims. The Trust itself has a complicated history, as the initial version dramatically underestimated the number of claims and became insolvent (Peterson 1990; Barnes 2011). The parties eventually restructured the Trust, creating a procedure for resolving claims with both bureaucratic and adversarial elements, the "Trust Distribution Process" (TDP). Like its predecessor, the TDP was intended as a move away from tort. It designated categories of asbestos-related diseases and set values for each. Once the Trust assigns a disease category, claimants are entitled to a percentage of its value set by the Trust. Disputed claims must go to arbitration, and lawyer fees are capped at 25% of the amounts actually paid to claimants. Moreover, while the TDP allows claimants to file tort claims, it discourages them. First, claimants can file a tort claim only if they select nonbinding arbitration and reject the results. Second, the TDP does not pay punitive damages, even if the claimant wins a tort suit. Third, if a tort claim exceeds the value of the amount determined through the TDP, that portion of the claim is not paid until all claimants receive 50% of the value of their claims, an unlikely prospect given that current payments are only 5%.

In crucial respects, however, the TDP is an adversarial policy. Unlike SSDI, or even a "mixed" policy such as a typical workers' compensation program, the TDP does not spread costs and risks across companies. It is primarily funded by a large equity stake in a single company, the Manville Corporation, and the channeling injunction still directs all claims to the Trust and away from the reorganized company. As a result, unlike workers' compensation programs that draw on broad pools of assets, the TDP relies on a limited pool of assets whose value is closely tied to the value of a single reorganized company. Distribution is made according to the Trust's ability to pay. The funding is private and individualized.

It can be argued, in fact, that the Trust (and counterparts created by other companies) actually augments adversarial legalism by providing proceeds to plaintiffs that are then used to fund additional litigation. Under the rules of joint and several liability, claimants can sue others in the chain of distribution for any remaining unpaid damages. Some argue that the TDP and others like it have become creatures of the trial lawyers, and thus are best understood as embedded in a set of inter-related complex litigation strategies. From this vantage, Chapter 11 trusts are an extension of adversarial legalism, not an alternative to it.

There can be no denying that the Manville Trust represents a significant source of asbestos-claim compensation. As of December 31, 2004—a month after the elections that preceded the last major effort to retrench asbestos litigation in 109th Congress—the Trust had settled almost 640,000 claims and distributed over $3.4 billion. In 2013, it had settled about 935,000 claims and paid almost $4.5 billion.[20] The Trust, of course, does not stand alone. By the time Congress considered replacing legislation following the 2004 elections, over 70 companies with asbestos exposure have filed for Chapter 11 reorganization, including such household names as Owens Corning Fiberglass and WR Grace Company. Like Manville, these companies have created trusts that have resolved hundreds of thousands of claims and distributed billions of dollars (White 2002).

The Chapter 11 trusts, according to one leading expert, provided neither "happy nor efficient" results.[21] On the one hand, Chapter 11 trusts have saved *individual* companies' transaction costs. Administrative costs of the Manville

Trust, the largest and longest running Chapter 11 trust, are about 5% of the total dollars spent on claims (Austern 2001). Assuming that attorneys limit themselves to 25% as required by the Trust, plaintiffs receive 70% of the total dollars spent as compared with only about 40% in ordinary litigation. In addition, once established, Chapter 11 trusts seem to reduce the time from filing a claim to payment when compared to tort suits (Peterson 1990). As of 2003, the average waiting time under the Manville Trust was about four months.

On the other hand, it is unclear whether these individual savings translate to overall savings or whether litigation costs are merely shifted as new defendants are dragged into court. The reason is that Chapter 11 trusts—unlike state workers' compensation programs—create limited funds that pay according to the trusts' liquidity, as opposed to the merits of the claims. Under these terms, payments have plummeted in some cases. In the Manville Trust, payments have dropped from 100% of liquidated value to 10% percent and currently 5%. Whether claimants will receive more hinges on their ability to find alternative "deep pockets" under the rules of joint and several liability (or other theories such as suing property owners and landlords whose buildings contained asbestos), which allow plaintiffs to sue any company in the chain of distribution for the full amount of damages, or some other theory. The net effect is that the cost of litigation and risk of insolvency falls on either (1) claimants who cannot find other solvent defendants in the supply chain or (2) non-bankrupt companies in the supply chain—many of which had nothing to do with the original concealment of asbestos-related risks. In addition, although Chapter 11 trusts may offer more consistent payments than individual tort suits, they do not ensure uniform payment, falling far short of the bureaucratic ideal. Trust terms and liquidity vary over time and across companies so that similar claims are not always treated the same over time or across trusts (Coffee 1995). Under these conditions, Chapter 11 trusts have not only failed to provide fair compensation and limit asbestos-related claims, they have also helped to spread asbestos litigation. As a result, the more individual defendants have used Chapter 11 to manage their liability, the more entrepreneurial trial lawyers have sought new targets for lawsuits, often using the money from the Chapter 11 trusts to fund litigation that has reached ever deeper into the chain of distribution, which stretches across thousands of businesses in the case of asbestos.

The Divided Politics of the Chapter 11 Trusts

The story of the Chapter 11 trusts, as with so many aspects of asbestos injury compensation, has both a judicial and legislative side, which adds a layer of complexity to the story but also provides a vantage point on the politics of these hybrid arrangements. When the first Manville Trust became insolvent and the parties renegotiated the new trust, there was doubt as to whether the bankruptcy court had authority to issue channeling injunctions that applied to future claims. These channeling injunctions were a lynchpin of the Chapter 11 trust strategy, because they directed all litigation to the trust, thereby shielding the newly reorganized company from future asbestos litigation.

Facing legal uncertainty, proponents of the Manville Trust appealed to Congress to codify the use of channeling injunctions by the bankruptcy courts and, in the process, formally recognize Chapter 11 as a tool for individual companies to manage their asbestos litigation liability. As with the insurance litigation, the issue of channeling injunctions internally divided business groups based on their exposure to litigation. The Chapter 11 trusts and companies that had filed for bankruptcy supported the codification of the channeling injunctions, while those who remained outside of Chapter 11 opposed them. Robert Falise, representing the Manville Trust, stressed the importance of legal certainty for maximizing the value of securities in the reorganized companies, which were a key source of funding. In his remarks to the Senate, he concluded, "potential buyers of the trust's securities or the underlying assets want to be assured that no asbestos liability would attach to them in the future, and that the underlying promise of Chapter 11, that the debtor emerges free and clear of all debts resolved in the reorganization proceedings, applies in this instance, as in any other successful reorganization. In our minds, and confirmed by the soundings of the financial community, the answer to our problem lies here with this Congress."[22]

John Camp, representing the Committee for Equitable Compensation, which spoke for businesses outside of Chapter 11, took a very different view of the issue. In his view, the Chapter 11 trusts unfairly shifted the burden of asbestos litigation to non-bankrupt companies, even though many of these companies were far less culpable than the original defendants, such as Johns-Manville, which had actively concealed the risks of asbestos. By allowing some businesses to escape future claims, Camp contended that Congress would force codefendants to "pay the bankrupts' share for claims arising in the future, [which] could decrease the resources otherwise available to those codefendants to pay claims and lead to additional bankruptcies."[23] At a minimum, Camp contended, Congress should give the courts a chance to decide the underlying legal issues.

The issue also divided claimant interests. David Mallino, a lawyer and lobbyists for the Laborers' International Union of North America, sided with the Committee for Equitable Compensation and testified against the bill, arguing that the trusts were underfunded, unfair to future claimants, and would encourage the filing of more bankruptcies. Robert Steinberg, from the California Trial Lawyers Association and American Trial Lawyers Association (ATLA) disagreed and favored the bill, even though trial lawyers had initially opposed the filing of these bankruptcies. Steinberg seemed almost apologetic for his support of the bill, claiming in his statement that he had "no love lost for Manville" and was "not an admirer of Manville's decision to seek Chapter 11 protection." However, once he overcame his initial "anger caused by Manville's abrupt removal from thousands of pending lawsuits," he realized that a viable reorganization was in his client's interests, and that the channeling injunction served to maximize the values of the trusts, which were funded by shares in the post-Chapter 11 operating company.[24] An interviewee offered an additional explanation: trial lawyers were instrumental in the creation of the trusts and often used the proceeds from Chapter 11 to fund litigation against business that had not filed for bankruptcy.[25] The splits between future and present claimants as well as reorganized companies versus non-bankrupt ones would persist through efforts to reform asbestos litigation, adding to the fragmentation of asbestos politics.

The Resurgence of Litigation and Attempted Legislative Retrenchment Efforts

Aside from the brief flurry of activity around the Chapter 11 trusts, the congressional politics of asbestos injury compensation quieted down after the mid-1980s. Members of Congress seemed disposed to wait and see if the asbestos crisis would pass. A prominent Washington lawyer and lobbyist explained, "You stop getting bills around 1986 … [because] everyone thought that this was really a solved problem. The [insurance] coverage issues were largely resolved; the people were getting into agreements that processed them more or less administratively."[26] Major reform proposals aimed specifically at replacing asbestos litigation with administrative alternatives dropped off during this period (see Figure 4.3).[27]

Yet some members of Congress were clearly watching and ready to intervene to correct deficiencies they observed in the tort process. In 1982, a leading proponent of asbestos reform in Congress, Representative George Miller (D-CA), maintained that a federal asbestos-injury compensation fund was

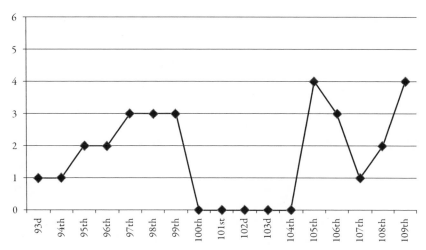

FIGURE 4.3. Number of replacement reforms in asbestos injury compensation: 93rd to 109th Congresses (compiled by author from Thomas bill summaries)

necessary because the existing system "failed to meet the needs of occupational disease victims."[28] The following year, Representative Miller convened a special hearing on the effect of bankruptcy cases and private settlements, arguing that the "testimony we will hear this morning will further establish the need to replace years of failure with a compensation system that can meet the needs of the disabled asbestos workers."[29] These arguments were echoed outside of Congress. The leading study of asbestos litigation in the mid-1980s argued that "[w]hether one believes that alternatives to the tort system, such as those proposed in recent legislation introduced by Congressmen George Miller and others, are necessary, should rest in part on an assessment of how well the tort system has processed asbestos claims" (Hensler et al. 1985: 4–5).

The case for congressional action seemed to grow stronger as the early efforts to provide alternatives to tort began to falter in the 1980s and 1990s. The continuing drumbeat of large verdicts in some jurisdictions, the rejection of mandatory class actions as a comprehensive settlement tool by the Supreme Court, the collapse of major private settlements, the growing costs associated with using bankruptcy as a means to manage asbestos litigation liability, and increasing tightening of credit for any business with any hint of asbestos liability risk all seemed to invite congressional reform. By the late 1990s, the Supreme Court was openly calling for legislation (e.g., *Amchem Products v. Windsor; Ortiz v. Fibreboard*: and *Norfolk & Western Railway Co. v. Ayers*). In *Oritz,* the Court declared "the elephantine mass of asbestos

cases...defies customary judicial administration and calls for national legislation" (*Ortiz*, 527 U.S. at 821).

In response to calls for legislative action, new reform measures targeting
asbestos litigation began to reappear on Congress' radar (see Figure 4.3). The
first serious effort was the Hyde-Ashcroft bill, which (among other things)
proposed to create an Asbestos Resolution Corporation (ARC) that would
review the medical eligibility of claimants and create an alternative dispute
resolution process. Under the bill, claimants could not proceed in court until
ARC issued a medical certificate and released them from mediation. If claimants received payment from ARC, the Corporation would seek to recover
costs from asbestos defendants. This bill failed in part because the publicity surrounding the devastating effects of asbestos on Libby, Montana—the
small rural town that was eventually designated a toxic waste site by the
EPA—made it difficult to limit access to the courts for asbestos victims, and
in part because Congress had little interest in creating an entity that would
make medical decisions.

The election of a unified Republican government in 2000 created a fresh
impetus for action. A coalition emerged between industry, insurers, and plaintiff lawyers like Steve Kezan, who specialized in bringing cancer cases. They
came together on what was called "medical criteria" legislation, whose core
idea was to give the most sick the highest priority for compensation. The initial momentum of this effort reflected a shift in perceptions about the asbestos problem. According to one interviewee, the perception that any attempt
to reform litigation would favor unscrupulous companies was changing. By
the late 1990s, litigation often targeted companies that had little to do with
concealing health risks, like Pacor, and the plaintiffs were often the "worried
well": claimants who had been exposed to asbestos but had not (yet) fallen ill.
Meanwhile, Nobel Laureate Joseph Stiglitz and his colleagues published an
assessment of the costs of bankruptcies that showed both management and
workers financially suffered (Stiglitz et al. 2002). In this environment, where
fault did not clearly reside in a handful of reckless companies, it was easier to
propose asbestos litigation reform without it being branded a "bailout."

The medical criteria approach, however, had significant policy limitations.
At its core, it sought to regulate claims by the worried well while allowing
other types of claims to proceed. Businesses facing large numbers of lawsuits
feared that controlling these cases would not provide them sufficient certainty over their liability. Others argued that the medical criteria approach
had to be joined with significant limitations of forum shopping that would
prevent trial lawyers from bringing cases in jurisdictions such as Madison

County in Mississippi that were seen by businesses as judicial "hell holes." For these reasons, trial lawyers adamantly opposed any effort to limit their ability to sue in these venues. Moreover, defendants were growing increasingly concerned about lung cancer suits, which the new bill would not limit and, indeed, might facilitate bringing to trial. Finally, lawyers who did not specialize in cancer cases opposed any regulation of their access to the courts, partly because these lawyers, unlike cancer specialists who tended to bring individual cases, tended to engage in group settlements, which benefited from combining a few cancer cases with claims of unimpaired claimants. If the worried well could not credibly sue for compensation, this strategy might lose its potency.

Thus the first plaintiff/defendant coalition effort disintegrated, and reform advocates advanced an alternative approach: instead of seeking to regulate the flow of litigation, they sought to replace litigation with a bureaucratic compensation program. The 2005 FAIR (Fairness in Asbestos Injury Compensation) Act proposed supplanting the court-based system of asbestos injury compensation with a $140 billion federal trust fund that would compensate claimants according to specific medical criteria and cap attorneys' fees at 5%.

At least from the perspective of the academic literature, the conditions seemed ripe for passing a replacement reform. The literature on legal reform identifies an array of factors that should set the stage for building winning coalitions that can overcome expected opposition to tort reform from trial lawyers, who predictably resist any attempt to lessen the flow of litigation that provides their meal ticket. These factors are (a) support from strategically placed policy entrepreneurs, (b) Republican majorities, (c) bi-partisan support, (d) judicial calls for legislation, (e) high legal costs and legal uncertainty, and (f) expert consensus on the lack of secondary policy benefits of litigation (see Burke 2002; Hausegger and Baum 1999; Ignagni and Meernik 1994; Campbell et al. 1995; Nolan and Ursin 1995; Elliot and Talarico 1991; Epstein 1988; O'Connell 1979; see also Esterling 2004; Patashnik 2000; Steinmo and Watts 1995). All were present during the 109th Congress (Barnes 2011).

Initially the prospects for reform seemed good. President George W. Bush convened a conference on improving the economy soon after his reelection and, in his opening remarks, the President insisted that a "cornerstone of any good program is legal reform."[30] He added, "I intend to take a legislative package to Congress which says that we expect the House and the Senate to pass meaningful liability reform on asbestos."[31] Several weeks later, Bush dedicated precious presidential time to visit Michigan and moderate a roundtable discussion specifically devoted to asbestos litigation reform, where he vowed to keep it on the "front burner" and expressed confidence that "we can get some-thing done."[32] Senator Arlan Specter (R-PA) echoed this sentiment, reporting that he was "very close" to reaching an agreement on a major reform proposal. Senator Patrick Leahy (D-VT) sounded even more optimistic: "I think we are very, very close to a bill" (Higgins 2005).

It might be tempting to dismiss these statements as cheap talk following an election, and it is probably true that President Bush's commitment to reform faded over time. Nevertheless, optimism about reform following the 2004 elections was not limited to politicians' sound bites in the media. Wall Street was also bullish. Stock values of companies with significant asbestos-litigation exposure, such as Armstrong Holdings and Owens Corning, jumped more than 80% at the outset of the 109th Congress (Higgins 2005). Other com-panies enjoyed a similar boost. From April 1, 2004, when the Senate filibus-tered a major asbestos reform effort in the 108th Congress, to mid-November 2004 following the 2004 elections when reform efforts regained momentum, stock prices of other major asbestos litigation defendants soared by double digits while the Dow Jones Industrial Average remained relatively flat, gain-ing about 1.7% (Barnes 2011).

Reform advocates capitalized on this momentum at the start, as Senator Specter managed a bi-partisan vote for the bill out of the Judiciary Committee, picking up support from all the GOP senators and three Democrats—Senators Leahy, Feinstein, and Kohl (Stern 2005). Almost immediately, however, oppo-sition emerged (Stern 2006a, 2006b). Conservative Republican Senators, including Senators Cornyn (R-TX), Coburn (R-OK) and Kyl (R-AZ), who voted the bill out of committee, began to question its substance, fearing that Congress would be forced to rescue the trust from insolvency at taxpayers' expense and create a permanent fixture in the federal bureaucracy. Their posi-tion was supported by the Congressional Budget Office's scoring of the FAIR Act, which stressed the difficulty of assessing its final price tag; a Government Accounting Office report on existing federal compensation trusts, such as the Black Lung Disability Trust Fund, which emphasized their long history of cost overruns; and a report by Bates White, a private consultancy recruited by businesses that opposed the FAIR Act, which predicted that the trust would dissolve within three years and accumulate a $45 billion debt (Hanlon 2006).

Meanwhile, liberals—including Senators Kennedy (D-MA), Feingold (D-WI), Biden (D-DE), Schumer (D-NY), and Durbin (D-IL) on the Judiciary Committee—feared that the FAIR Act was overly restrictive, underfunded, and tilted toward big business. Over time, opposition began to harden on both sides of the aisle (*Inside OSHA* 2005), leading Senate

Minority Leader Harry Reid (D-NV) to quip, "If anyone thinks they can bring up the asbestos bill and get it passed, I think we can get them a magic show in Las Vegas" (Knight 2005).

Reid proved prophetic. In the end, the FAIR Act failed when Senator John Ensign (R-NV), a conservative Republican, brought a budget point of order based on a prohibition against legislation authorizing more than $5 billion in spending during any 10-year period, starting in 2016. Under the rules, supporters of the FAIR Act needed 60 votes to waive the budget point of order. They fell just short. The final tally was 58-41, but the outcome was even closer (see Table 4.1 for a summary).[33] Senator Frist voted against the bill at the last minute, so that he could bring a motion to reconsider if proponents could find the missing vote. Senator Specter quickly insisted that he could deliver the 60th vote because Senator Daniel Inouye (D-HI), who was absent, had indicated that he would consider waiving the budget point of order if the Senate revisited the FAIR Act.

Inouye's vote never materialized, and opposition seemed to gain traction with each day. The problem was what one insider called "yes, but" support, in which actors expressed support for the idea of replacement reform but balked at the details of the FAIR Act.[34] On the left, Senator Kennedy had expressed sympathy for Senator Specter's efforts and seemed willing to work with him to create a new health program for asbestos workers and their families. In the end, however, Kennedy believed that bill was too narrow because, for example, it excluded a category of smokers from the trust fund provisions. Broadening the bill, though, would have alienated Specter's like-minded moderate Republican

Table 4.1 Roll Call Vote on Motion to Waive Senator Ensign's Budget Point of Order (Senate Vote 21, 2/14/2006)

Party	Yeas/Nays
Republicans[a]	44-11
Democrats[b]	13-30
Independent	1-0
TOTALS	58-41

[a]Senator Frist voted against the waiver (and thus against reform) to preserve the right to bring a motion to reconsider.

[b]Senator Inouye (D-HI) did not vote on the motion.

Note: A three-fifths majority vote (60) is required to waive the Budget Act and overcome a budget point of order. The FAIR Act was subsequently recommitted to the Judiciary Committee.

colleagues, like Senator Judd Gregg (R-NH), who were also open to passing asbestos litigation reform, but believed that the FAIR Act was already under-funded and that Congress would eventually be forced to cover its costs.

Meanwhile, conservatives, even those that seemed to initially support it, grew increasingly skeptical. Critically, Senators Coburn, Cornyn, and Kyl expressed growing hostility. Although they voted the FAIR Act out of committee and favored waiving Ensign's budget point of order, they made it abundantly clear that, if the FAIR Act proceeded to a vote, they would push a series of major amendments to the bill, including one that would substi-tute the House medical criteria bill for the FAIR Act. Others, like Senator Robert Bennett (R-UT), remained concerned about the bill's effect on small businesses, because the FAIR Act's formula for calculating contributions was based on historical rates of asbestos liability that tended to hit smaller firms harder than large, multinational corporations, such as General Electric and Honeywell. Perhaps even more importantly, by the time the FAIR Act had stumbled in the Senate, opposition to replacement reform had intensified in the GOP-controlled House, as conservative groups like FreedomWorks, led by former Representative Dick Armey (D-TX), publicly excoriated the idea of creating a new federal program, especially one that seemed to earmark $7 billion for trial lawyers (Stern 2006). In short, the FAIR Act was already in trouble when it fell on Ensign's budget point of order.

The complex and contentious party politics of the FAIR Act in the Senate mirrored its equally intricate interest group politics (see Table 4.2 for a sum-mary of interest group positions and Appendix III for an overview of our content analysis methods). On the plaintiff side, victims' groups split, mostly along the lines of their current health. The worried well favored a system that spread compensation among future and present claims, while those who were already ill and poised to bring lawsuits in search of huge jury verdicts generally opposed reform. Unions were also fractured. The United Auto Workers and Asbestos Workers Union supported the bill, but the AFL-CIO opposed it, in line with the union's growing alliance with trial lawyers under John Sweeney. Sweeney had become president of the union in part by opposing his predeces-sor's willingness to compromise on asbestos injury compensation issues.

Companies, meanwhile, divided mostly along the lines of their poten-tial liability. Companies with large and uncertain liabilities generally sup-ported the FAIR Act while others with more manageable liabilities favored a medical criteria bill. Some large and influential companies and their rep-resentatives, including General Electric, Viacom, the National Association of Manufacturers, and the Asbestos Alliance, strongly supported the FAIR

Table 4.2 Public Positions on the FAIR Act: January 2005 to January 2007 (compiled by author)

Group	For	Against
Business Groups	American Small Business Association Asbestos Alliance Asbestos Study Group National Association of Manufacturers National Association of Wholesalers and Distributers National Small Business Association Small Business and Entrepreneurship Council Women Impacting Public Policy	American Insurance Association Coalition for Asbestos Reform Common Interest Group National Association of Mutual Insurance Companies National Industrial Sand Association Property Casualty Insurance Association of America
Individual Businesses	Armstrong World Industries Dow Ford General Electric General Motors Georgia Pacific Honeywell McDermott Owens Corning Owens-Illinois Pfizer St. Gobain USG Corporation Viacom World Industries WR Grace	Borg Warner Exxon-Mobil Foster Wheeler NSI
Insurance Companies	ACE CNA Liberty Mutual	AIG Equitas Gen Re Hartford Liberty Mutual Travelers

(continued)

Table 4.2 (continued)

Group	For	Against
Plaintiffs' Groups	Asbestos Workers Union	AFL-CIO
	RetireSafe	Asbestos Disease Awareness
	The Seniors Council	Organization
	United Auto Workers	Committee to Protect
	Veterans of Foreign Wars	Mesothelioma Victims
		White Lung Association
Others	American Medical Association	FreedomWorks
	Council for Citizens Against Waste	Governor Rick Perry (Texas)
	in Government	National Taxpayer Union
	National Legal and Policy Center	Public Citizen

Act, arguing that the uncertainty resulting from asbestos litigation was unnecessarily hampering credit and creating a drag on economic activity (Investor's Business Daily 2005). Other businesses and their representatives vigorously opposed the bill, including Exxon-Mobil, Borg Warner, and the Coalition for Asbestos Reform. They argued that the Fair Act was underfunded and that its contribution formulas were unfair. Insurance companies divided along similar lines. Some companies with large liabilities supported the bill on the grounds that it replaced a hopelessly inefficient system, while others opposed it as too expensive and not robust enough to handle all future claims.

Companies that had filed for bankruptcy were particularly interesting on this front. In the early 1980s, when Congress held hearings on asbestos litigation reform, the companies with the highest exposure to asbestos liability, like Pacor, supported the creation of a "global solution" to the asbestos crisis.[35] By 2005, many of these companies had filed for bankruptcy and exited the tort system, creating a series of Chapter 11 trusts to deal with their remaining liability. The trusts took a very different stance toward asbestos litigation reform. They opposed the FAIR Act, arguing that its use of their assets to fund the new federal program was unconstitutional. The opposition of the Chapter 11 trusts was a double blow to the FAIR Act (Stern 2006a, 2006b; see also Nagareda 2007). First, the emergence of the trusts further fragmented an already divided group of business interests. Second, FAIR Act proponents were counting on Chapter 11 trust assets to partially fund the compensation system they proposed during its crucial start-up period, when experts expected a rush of claims. The threat of the trusts to hold up this funding by challenging the constitutionality of the FAIR Act in court only reinforced concerns about the fragility of the compensation system the Act promised.

It did not help that public interest groups were also at odds. Some, like the National Legal Policy Center, fully embraced the FAIR Act. The Policy Center argued that passing replacement reform would "end the circus of runaway asbestos litigation that has amply rewarded a handful of lawyers while leaving thousands of desperately sick people with a fraction of the compensation they deserve. This abuse of the legal system has already driven at least 70 corporations into bankruptcy and jeopardized thousands of America jobs" (PR Newswire 2005). Meanwhile, Ralph Nader's Public Citizen and Dick Armey's FreedomWorks attacked the bill from the left and the right, maintaining that the bill was a corporate bailout and a big government boondoggle.

The strange political lineups on the FAIR Act make perfect sense when one considers how the evolution of asbestos litigation has shaped the interests of various stakeholder groups (Barnes 2007b, 2011; see also Epstein 1988). Consider victims. As noted earlier, attorneys have developed different strategies for different types of claims over time. Under these circumstances, plaintiff groups came to very different stances on reform. Victims with cancers and other serious illnesses tended to do well in jury trials and typically opposed a national trust fund that would cut off access to the courts. The worried well, those who had been exposed to asbestos but had not fallen ill, were generally more receptive to the creation of a central program that would regulate payments to ensure that future claims would be paid.

A similar analysis applies to asbestos litigation defendants, whose material interests have been deeply shaped by judicial innovations (Barnes 2007b, 2011). The most straightforward illustration concerns judicial interpretations of legal liability rules. All things being equal, as liability rules are construed broadly, the targets of litigation should have a stake in seeking legislation that curbs or eliminates lawsuits. However, litigation risks do not always fall evenly on individual businesses and insurance companies. Some business sectors are exposed; others are not. Within business sectors that face a potential wave of litigation, some businesses are better positioned to absorb litigation costs because they are bigger, better insured, or have stronger legal defenses. Similarly, insurance companies' exposure to litigation risks varies depending on their underlying contractual obligations, portfolio of policyholders, and reinsurance policies. Why should defendants with lower exposure to litigation risks support legislation that benefits their high-risk competitors?

The factionalized politics that doomed the FAIR Act continues to evolve. Following the 2004 election, the number of Chapter 11 reorganizations began to increase again, as companies like Garlock Sealing Technologies, ASARCO LLC, Leslie Controls, Bondex International Hercules Chemical Company, and others took the plunge—and presumably joined the ranks of those who will now fight to preserve the status quo. The bottom line is that asbestos litigation, while tapering off, continues; the complex, layered asbestos compensation system remains in place; and adversarial legalism continues to generate a divisive and complex politics.

Discussion

The asbestos story gives us a chance to look back at the previous chapter on SSDI and compare the politics of adversarial and bureaucratic legalism side-by-side. The differences in the two cases should not be exaggerated. There is a lot of overlap, for example, in the cast of characters. In both stories, businesses, insurers, unions, claimant groups, and legal and medical experts each played some part. In addition, both the asbestos and SSDI cases featured periods of fierce interest group conflict that spilled across multiple policymaking forums. In an age of well-organized interest groups for claimants and payers left and right, injury politics has some generic features that stretch across programs, and in some respects those features trumped any effect of policy structure, our focus.

Nevertheless, the differences in the two cases are striking. There is a sharp contrast in their political trajectories: increasing conflict and factionalization in the case of asbestos, diminishing conflict over time in the case of SSDI. This divergence, we contend, corresponds to the differing patterns of blame assignment and distributional effects generated by bureaucratic and adversarial legalism. The fight over the enactment of SSDI was ferocious because it involved a fundamental shift in blame assignment, from individual to social responsibility for injury. The contending interests, business and labor, battled long and hard over the allocation of costs and benefits. Yet after creation, SSDI experienced an extended period of quiet expansion, as business groups ceded the field to a small coterie of experts and liberals in Congress. The fundamental issue of blame assignment—whether the government should be responsible for compensating injuries—appears to have been settled by the enactment of SSDI, and has not been refought since. The pattern of narrowed conflict over SSDI parallels the underlying distributional effects of a social insurance program that spreads costs and benefits relatively evenly and predictably. The smoothness of SSDI taxation allowed businesses to pass on much of the cost of SSDI to workers, and so diminished the incentive of business lobbies to mobilize against the policy. The relatively even and predictable benefits of SSDI, on the other side, had an effect on claimants, who organized into groups that usually stuck together to defend the program. When the growth of SSDI threatened its solvency and gave rise to retrenchment efforts, there was acrimonious conflict, but the claimant groups remained largely unified in their opposition, and business mostly stayed on the sidelines. This is not a political alignment conducive to major changes in public policy, and so the ambitions of SSDI reformers narrowed: drug addicts and noncitizens were (temporarily, in most cases) removed from the program, and relatively minor "welfare to work" policies have been enacted, but more fundamental reforms have not gotten a hearing. Bureaucratic legalism appears to have shaped a relatively narrow and quiet politics.

The contrasting effects of adversarial legalism, its particular distributional effects and blame assignment, can be seen in the asbestos case. When asbestos injuries first emerged as a health problem, these mechanisms worked together to dampen interest group conflict. Because asbestos litigation structured claims into discrete private lawsuits, asbestos litigation implicated only a small number of asbestos manufacturing and mining companies, most prominently Johns-Manville. At this stage it was easy for Congress to dismiss asbestos injury compensation as a "one-company problem" that did not merit a legislative response, even though asbestos was used widely and there was growing concern about the general problem of occupational diseases. Further, tort litigation unearthed the fact that companies like Johns-Manville had intentionally concealed the risks of asbestos from their workers and the public. These findings stigmatized the defendants, making it politically difficult for them to pursue legislative relief from the costs of litigation.

As asbestos litigation spread, however, it stopped looking like a problem caused by a few villainous companies and became a broad social and economic issue. At this point Congress grew more interested in intervening. Reformers, though, had to contend with the divisiveness of the distributional effects generated by adversarial legalism, which split both the defendant and plaintiff sides. The defendant divisions emerged relatively early in the case and persisted throughout, as businesses fought against their insurance companies over the scope of their coverage, insurance companies fought with each other over the interpretation of their liability, and Chapter 11 defendants squared off against those outside of bankruptcy over channeling injunctions and efforts at replacing litigation. The plaintiffs divided in part based on their degree of injury, with the worried well and their lawyers often opposed to cancer victims and their lawyers. In line with the quantitative data presented in chapter 2, adversarial legalism appears to have generated a fragmented, complex, and chaotic politics.

We have compared the politics of bureaucratic legalism and adversarial legalism across two policies, but we can also trace the effects of these two policy designs within the asbestos case. Recall that the creation of asbestos injury compensation policy unfolded on two tracks: before the tort suits ramped up, there was a congressional effort to broaden state workers' compensation programs, a relatively bureaucratic approach in contrast with the adversarial design of tort. This effort involved high-profile hearings in which business and labor groups squared off against one another to debate governmental responsibility for the cost of injuries. In other words, it looked a lot like the politics surrounding the enactment of SSDI, a bureaucratic policy, which featured a pitched battle between two polarized sides. The workers' compensation episode looks nothing like the rest of the asbestos case, in which the main constituencies—plaintiffs and defendants—became divided among themselves, and in which cross-constituency alliances, in which some businesses join with some victims, developed. The fight over asbestos injuries was unified and polarized when it was fought over a relatively bureaucratic policy, but fractionalized and divided when it was fought over adversarial policies. Even within the asbestos case, then, bureaucratic legalism and adversarial legalism seem to correspond to different brands of politics.

There were, you might remember, two exceptions to the unity of business groups in the fight over workers' compensation: groups representing tool manufacturers and architects broke ranks with other businesses and offered conditional support for reform. These are, however, exceptions that seem to underline the importance of policy design. The toolmakers and architects were, after all, not in love with the idea of a new federal workers' compensation program: they were simply terrified by the prospect of facing a cascade of product liability lawsuits. So even in this instance, the divisive effects of adversarial legalism—threatening two business groups while leaving others, for the moment, out of the fray—created a small fracture among interests that would usually stand together.

The case of asbestos injuries, then, reinforces the concerns of many theorists and political scientists that adversarial legalism individualizes politics and so reduces social solidarity. Adversarial legalism individualized first in the way it assigned blame. When, at the outset of the case, just a small number of companies like Johns Manville were being sued, this singling out of a few blameworthy defendants had important political effects on Congress's will-ingness to act. Asbestos exposure could have been framed as a public health crisis, one that the government had arguably fostered in part by requiring massive amounts of asbestos to be used during World War II in the building of ships and other armaments. Instead, when viewed through the prism of individual lawsuits, the problem was seen as the product of reckless conduct by a small group of companies. This framing isolated asbestos manufactur-ers politically, and made it difficult to build a coalition for a governmental response. Even dyed-in-the-wool liberals who would normally be receptive to the creation of new programs, like Representative George Miller, dismissed early efforts to create a governmental compensation fund as a "bailout."

Second, adversarial legalism individualized conflict in asbestos injury compensation through its distributional effects, which imposes costs and benefits unevenly. As the number of asbestos lawsuits soared, this lumpy dis-tribution of costs and benefits eroded solidarity among stakeholders, dividing them based on their expected losses and benefits. On the defendant side, this included the defection of the toolmakers and architects over the federaliza-tion of workers' compensation, the divisions between business and insurance companies over coverage, the divide between bankrupt and non-bankrupt companies, and the divide between low- and high-exposure businesses. Plaintiffs were also divided. Lawyers specializing in cancer cases divided with lawyers that brought large "inventories" of claims over some medical criteria bills that would have prioritized the claims of the currently ill over the wor-ried well. Meanwhile, the worried well tended to favor replacement reforms that would regulate payments over time, while those who were currently ill tended to oppose these reforms to preserve their access to the courts. The result was a fractious, chaotic, and individualized politics.

What about the other worrisome political effects that are often attached to adversarial legalism—that litigation crowds out other forms of political activity, or stimulates a backlash, or locks in through path dependence bad public policies? For the most part these claims are not supported by the case.

First, the argument that litigation crowds out lobbying, and thus "kills" interest group politics by diverting political struggle from ordinary chan-nels such as legislatures, proved largely unfounded. Asbestos stakeholders on all sides were willing to turn to both courts and Congress. Unions and their members, for example, simultaneously pursued broad federal workers' compensation reforms and products liability cases in response to the inad-equacy of state programs throughout the 1970s. Unions were still advo-cating for (and Congress was still holding hearings on) federal workers' compensation reform measures until the Spring of 1980, after the *Borel* decision established liability, the discovery of the Sumner Simpson papers demolished the state-of-the-art defense, and plaintiff counsel had gained valuable experience in bringing these suits—in short, after litigation had established a considerable foothold. There were, of course, some claimant groups who opposed congressional intervention because they wanted to preserve potentially lucrative lawsuits, but this was far from uniform. Some claimant groups, for example, joined efforts to pass replacement and medical criteria reform in the 2000s, seeking to regularize payments and the litigation process. On the other side, businesses also combined litigation with lobbying. Indeed, far from trapping business interests in the courts, adversarial legalism, with its characteristic costs and inefficiencies, drove them to Congress for relief. Business groups campaigned for various limits on liability, and some joined the coalition for a federal compensation fund, as in the FAIR Act. Thus, consistent with the hearings data, interest groups on all sides combined litigation with lobbying. In this respect, the politics of adversarial legalism seems consistent with the pluralist ideal (or hyperpluralist nightmare) of a multiplicity of interest groups pursuing competing agendas in a system of diversely representative, overlapping policymaking forums.

A second concern about adversarial legalism is unusually sticky, or path-dependent, so that a suboptimal outcome arrived at through litigation is resistant to change. The policy in asbestos compensation clearly became problematic over time, as the emphasis shifted from revealing corporate wrongdoing to providing compensation to victims. For decades, the inefficiencies and injustices created by asbestos litigation have been documented, and yet Congress, despite repeated efforts dating back to the 1970s, has failed to reform asbestos injury compensation. But as the previous chapter on SSDI suggested, bureaucratic policies can also be sticky, and it is not at all clear that adversarial legalism is any *more* subject to path dependence than bureaucratic legalism. Indeed, the pattern of development in which the formal structure of the policy remains stable but its practical implementation continues to shift through practice can be seen in both cases. So, in the asbestos case, while there was no fundamental legislative reform of the underlying adversarial legal policy, courts transformed the policy, first by reinterpreting product liability and insurance law and then adapting the Bankruptcy Code and procedural rules to fashion different modes of court-based tort reform (Barnes 2007b, 2011). The result was a reinterpretation of existing rules and the creation of entirely new entities like the Chapter 11 trusts.

Adversarial legalism, then, seemed to generate policy innovation in the case of asbestos, and so seems much *less* sticky than bureaucratic legalism, at least as it appears in the previous chapter on SSDI. The creation of SSDI mobilized a cohesive claimant lobby to keep the program in place, but no such cohesive lobby appeared in asbestos: there were plenty of splits among asbestos claimants, and this opened up the possibility of fundamental reform. Asbestos claimants with cancer have supported laws that would have limited the worried well's access to the courts. Some claimant groups have supported replacement reforms even as others have opposed them. Even lawyers specializing in cancer cases briefly broke ranks to join forces with some business interests to press for a medical criteria bill that would have regulated access to the courts. Asbestos politics has been highly fluid, certainly not sticky. Reform opponents have thus far used veto points in the process to prevent the passage of major reforms in the asbestos case, but their alliances have been more tenuous and temporary than the coalitions that have consistently supported SSDI.

We can also compare the path dependence of asbestos litigation to that of another policy touched on in this case, workers' compensation. In the 1970s, workers' compensation was more bureaucratic in design than tort because it partly socialized the costs of injuries, and because its processes were more hierarchical and somewhat less party-centered than court-based litigation. Workers' compensation seems to be "sticky" just like SSDI, certainly more sticky than asbestos litigation. Asbestos litigation got started, after all, in part because of the inflexibility of workers' compensation programs toward claims based on occupational diseases. Even though a congressional blue-ribbon commission recommended reform, political forces—business interests and states that benefited from the status quo—blocked significant change. Asbestos litigation, by contrast, has demonstrated a remarkable ability to reinvent itself from the initial recognition of new tort remedies in the early 1970s (over the objections of Dean Keeton, one of the architects of the strict product liability doctrine) to the multiple rounds of court-based tort reforms starting in the late 1970s and early 1980s. These judicial innovations included, among other things, the novel use of Chapter 11 to create ad hoc compensation trusts on a company-by-company basis, which fundamentally shifted who decides, who pays, how much and to whom. It also included the creation of massive settlements that helped transform the adjudication of individual common law lawsuits into the management of complex, multi-party litigation (Resnik 1982, 2000). Path dependence arguments are tricky—it is hard to measure the degree to which a program has changed over time, and harder yet to be confident about why programs resist reforms—but it seems to us very difficult to see in the SSDI and asbestos cases evidence that adversarial policies are particularly prone to path dependence. Indeed, the story of asbestos litigation reminds us instead of one of the proclaimed virtues of the common law, its ability to adapt to changed circumstances.

Another concern is that adversarial legalism produces a polarizing backlash that makes it harder to build coalitions across stakeholder lines. In their convincing analysis of the political construction of the tort reform debate, Haltom and McCann (2004) stress the ways in which business groups counter-mobilized against trial lawyers and the growth of tort liability. This is surely an important part of the asbestos story, and resonates with our findings about the campaign some business groups made against asbestos litigation, including their concerted efforts to change the narrative of fault from a story of reckless companies to rapacious lawyers representing the worried well. The backlash story, though, misses the divisions that adversarial legalism created among the targets of litigation. These splits among business groups were evident throughout the fight over the creation, expansion, and retrenchment of asbestos injury compensation policy. They help explain a number of key features in the politics of asbestos litigation, including the emergence of (short-lived) cross-stakeholder coalitions between some business and claimant interests. Business groups did not act in the simple way the backlash claim predicts. The backlash hypothesis, like the path dependence and crowding out claims, presume a kind of uniform behavior among interest groups that seems out of line with the chaotic, fractious politics that adversarial legalism appears to generate.

Conclusion

Consistent with the data on congressional hearings, the politics of asbestos injury compensation, a classic example of adversarial legalism, were often a free-for-all, featuring a wide number of interests with competing viewpoints. Moreover, the political trajectory of the asbestos case starkly differs from the one described in the last chapter. So, in SSDI, the creation of a bureaucratic compensation program featured high levels of interest group conflict in Congress, which seemed to dampen and narrow as business groups stepped aside during a long period of program expansion and several periods of attempted retrenchment. In asbestos, the political trajectory was reversed: the creation of an adversarial compensation policy seemed to dampen Congress's willingness to take on the issue, and the expansion of adversarial legalism seemed to increase conflict among interest groups. (This was the same pattern revealed in the previous chapter's brief examination of the development of the ADA, an adversarial disability policy.)

Two points bear emphasis. First, both case studies underscore the importance of temporal dynamics in understanding the politics of policy design. Whereas the congressional hearings data tell a simple story of cross-sectional differences in which adversarial legalism seems more contentious than bureaucratic legalism, the case studies make it clear that injury compensation policies always generate high levels of conflict; it is the *timing* of the conflict that varies. Second, both cases underscore the importance of two mechanisms that link policy design and political trajectory: the distributional effects and assignment of blame characteristic of the claiming process. Whether it is the story of SSDI, the ADA, attempted reform of state workers' compensation programs, the codification of asbestos trusts or congressional reform of asbestos compensation, distributional effects and blame assignment appear to shape the ways in which interest groups align. This suggests that what makes "law different" is not its reliance on precedent, not its particular tendency toward path dependency, not its propensity to divert interest groups away from the legislative process, and not its generation of polarizing backlashes. Instead, what makes law different in these cases seems to be its individualistic funding mechanism and assignment of blame, and the ways in which these features initially dampen and then amplify political conflict over time. The next chapter builds on these findings, taking a closer look at the politics of vaccine injury compensation, a case in which the policy abruptly shifts from an adversarial to a bureaucratic design.

5

Vaccine Injury Compensation: Shifting Policies, Shifting Politics

Introduction

Our last story spans more than a half-century of bitter political struggle, but it can be roughly summed up in the experiences of the families of three young girls: Anne Gottsdanker, Julie Schwartz, and Hannah Bruesewitz, each of whom developed a devastating illness after receiving a vaccination. In all three cases, a landmark legal/political battle for compensation ensued. From there the stories diverge. The Gottsdankers brought a lawsuit against a vaccine maker and won a historic jury verdict. The Schwartzes successfully campaigned for a new compensation program that provided payments to hundreds of families like their own. The Bruesewitzes, however, were denied compensation both in the program and in the legal system, where their dispute reached all the way to the Supreme Court. The stories of the three families mark three distinct periods in the politics of vaccine injury compensation, each of which featured a distinct policy design. They also illustrate the main theme in this book, the different ways in which adversarial legalism and bureaucratic legalism shape American politics.

The case of vaccine injuries and how American public policy has evolved in its approach to compensating them is obscure, but for our project extraordinarily useful. It is a rare instance in which an (admittedly rickety and partial) adversarial policy first developed in response to a problem and then, at a moment of crisis, was replaced by Congress with a more bureaucratic policy, the Vaccine Injury Compensation Program (VICP). That program was then retrenched in a way that, as explained below, moved the compensation process back toward adversarial legalism. Finally, there was an attempt to bypass the existing compensation policy altogether and revive the use of private tort suits as a means of resolving vaccine injury claims, an attempt almost entirely cut off in 2011 by the Supreme Court. Given that our goal is to trace the consequences of different public policy structures for politics, this shifting back and forth of dispute resolution and funding mechanisms is useful: it gives us a case in which the underlying issues remained largely the same, but the structure used to address them changed abruptly several times. This allows us to focus more carefully on the relationship between policy structures and political outcomes, offering multiple opportunities for within-case comparisons, which then can be compared to the patterns observed in earlier chapters. We begin with some background on the history of vaccination in the United States and then describe the evolution of vaccine injury compensation and its shifts over time.

Vaccination in the United States

American school children are required by state laws to be vaccinated against a wide range of diseases, including diphtheria, pertussis (or "whooping cough"), tetanus, polio, measles, mumps, and rubella. Every year, millions of children are safely vaccinated and, as a result, many of these diseases have been effectively contained, if not eradicated, in those nations where vaccination is common. Recent outbreaks of whooping cough in the United States, in which thousands are infected and a few die, may alarm Americans, but in the unvaccinated world pertussis takes an appalling toll. Whooping cough struck 16 million people in 2008 and killed 195,000 children. The World Health Organization estimates that in 2008 alone, vaccination against whooping cough saved 687,000 lives (World Health Organization 2010: 386). And whooping cough is just one of more than a dozen life-saving vaccines now routinely administered to children in the United States and other affluent nations.

Childhood vaccination has been a major public health triumph, but it comes at a price: a tiny percentage of those vaccinated suffer severe reactions. The size of this problem is a matter of great dispute, especially in the popular culture, where celebrities and talk shows readily proclaim the dangers of vaccines. Research suggests the scope of the problem is relatively narrow. In the 1980s, a government study estimated that vaccinations caused long-lasting or permanent disability in "probably no more than 100 or so" cases, and another 100–250 cases serious enough to require hospitalization (U.S. Office of Technology Assessment 1980: 8–9). In 1985, when the issue of vaccine injuries was first gaining prominence, an American Medical Association (AMA) study put the number at about 60 children per year (AMA Board of Trustees 1985: 1972). Numbers like this, however, seem overly precise given the extreme difficulties in studying vaccine injuries, particularly the rarer types. It is diffi- cult to conclusively establish causal relationships between vaccines and rare injuries, and even more difficult to definitively rule them out. A 2011 Institute of Medicine Report on eight vaccines considered 158 possible adverse reac- tions, finding that the evidence "conclusively supports" or "favors acceptance" of a causal relationship between the vaccine and the injury in 18 cases, "favors rejection" of the relationship in 5 cases, and that the evidence is "inadequate to accept or reject" a relationship in the remaining 135 cases (The Institute of Medicine 2011). But of course, critics of vaccines distrust the medical and scientific organizations that produce the research used to make these determi- nations, and so believe the injuries are not rare at all. The critics have alleged that vaccines are the cause of a range of devastating maladies that regularly strike children, including Sudden Infant Death Syndrome, profound devel- opmental disabilities, and, most famously, autism (Kirkland 2012a; Kirby 2005; Fisher & Coulter 1985).

Fears about the dangers of vaccines, and political struggles over purported vaccine injuries, are as old as vaccines themselves. In 1721, when Cotton Mather introduced variolation (a crude precursor to vaccination) to combat a smallpox epidemic in Boston, most of the town's elites rose up against him, and his house was firebombed. In a pattern that has been repeated many times since, the doctor who administered the variolation published a study show- ing that those variolated were much more likely to survive the epidemic, but opponents were unconvinced, one of them predicting that "Two or three years hence you'll see the dreadful effects of this wicked practice" (Allen 2005: 153). Vaccination, wherever it has been practiced, seems always to evoke concern and, often, fierce opposition. Much of the fear of vaccination historically has been based on superstition and bad science, but then again history is littered with horrific injuries caused by errors in the production process. In 1901, 13 children inoculated with the diphtheria vaccine died of tetanus because the horse used to produce the vaccine was infected; nine more children died from tetanus-contaminated smallpox vaccine. The ensuing furor led to the creation of the 1902 Biologics Control Act, the first direct federal regulation of medicine (Offit 2005: 5; Carpenter 2010: 75–76). Yellow fever vaccines contaminated with hepatitis B sickened 300,000 troops during World War II and killed 100 (Allen 2005: 153). During the initial round of polio vaccina- tion in 1955, vaccines made at Cutter Laboratories included a live, active virus that infected an estimated 220,000 people and resulted in 164 cases of severe paralysis and 10 deaths (Offit 2005: 89).[1] These historical episodes of production disasters reinforce the fear that often underlies public discourse about vaccination.

Vaccine injury politics are contentious because the stakes are so high. Vaccines are commonly given to healthy young children with many years of life ahead of them. While the number of children who develop a majority disability or illness after vaccination is small, the pain—and the costs—borne by families can be overwhelming.

The story of Julie Schwartz helps to put a human face on this suffering. In 1981, Julie, a four-month-old, received an injection of the diphtheria, pertussis, and tetanus (DPT) vaccine. A few hours later she was rushed to the emergency room with a massive seizure, the first of many that she would have for the rest of her life. The seizure scarred her brain, causing her to lose all function on the right side of her body, and giving her severe learning disabilities. Jeffrey Schwartz, Julie's father, summarized his family's experience in testimony before the Maryland Legislature:

> I can't find any way to express adequately the emotional cost Donna and I have had to endure without respite over the past 2 years—the fear, the pain, the sorrow, the confusion, the anxiety, the helplessness, the rage, the hopelessness, the stress, the unrelieved exhaustion, and the depression.
>
> These are the right labels for the feelings, but they cannot convey what the experience has been like. It has felt like a nightmare—with no waking, no escape. This is not to mention the direct financial costs and other indirect costs we have had to pay.
>
> Nor does this tally up what is perhaps the most important—the pain and loss that Julie has suffered, continues to suffer, and may well suffer for the rest of her life. Other families have suffered far worse than we.[2]

A year after this testimony, Julie suffered a final seizure that killed her.

As we have seen in earlier chapters, injuries give rise to demands for compensation. Because governments mandate that children receive vaccines, and because children like Julie suffer such severe disabilities, the claim of a right to some kind of compensation seems particularly powerful. But even granting such a right, hard political questions remain: Who decides whether a particular injury is compensable? By what standards? Who pays? How much? The difficulty of such questions is compounded in the case of vaccines, because the science on questions like whether DPT vaccine causes brain injuries is itself sharply contested. In the absence of a clear consensus on such questions, the politics of vaccination is often a struggle over how to balance uncertainty—were the injuries Julie suffered really caused by the vaccine?—with a host of other considerations involving public health. The fight over these questions mobilized a bunch of powerful constituencies, doctors, public health officials, pharmaceutical companies, and parents of injured children and their lawyers, each with a different perspective on the trade-offs involved.

The Rise of Adversarial Legalism: The Gottsdanker Era

Before 1988, parents who thought their child had been injured by a vaccine had only one route to obtaining compensation, a personal injury lawsuit. The first prominent instances of court-based vaccine injury compensation came in the wake of the infamous 1955 Cutter disaster, in which vaccines with live polio virus were distributed to children who then became infected and infected others. Lawsuits were filed against all the vaccine makers, but Cutter was the biggest target, sued 60 times. Most of these claims were settled, and Cutter ended up paying $3 million in damages (Offit 2005: 89).

The most prominent of the cases brought to trial was *Gottsdanker v. Cutter*. Anne Gottsdanker was a five-year-old child who had developed polio after being injected with Cutter's vaccine; her infection left her with severe paralysis in her legs. Her lawyer, Marvin Belli, the most prominent plaintiff counsel of the era, argued that Cutter had been negligent in producing the vaccine, but the jury disagreed. On another claim, that in making an unsafe vaccine Cutter had breached an implied warranty of safety, the jury agreed, and the Gottsdanker family received an award of $147,300.[3]

The Cutter incident was litigated during a period when product liability law was being transformed—and long before cases like *Borel*, the asbestos case described in the previous chapter, established the legal foundations for contemporary "mass tort" litigation. *Gottsdanker* was a viable lawsuit only because of the erosion of doctrines that had once made it difficult to recover for injuries caused by products. "Privity of contract," for example, was a long-standing doctrine under which warranties of safety existed only between the buyer and seller of a good. Vaccines, however, are typically distributed by doctors and clinics, so that the patient has no direct relationship to the vaccine manufacturer. Under the privity doctrine, the Gottsdanker family's breach of warranty jury verdict should have been thrown out. But when Cutter appealed the verdict on these grounds, a California appeals court, noting that "privity" had been abolished in sales of food, extended the abolition to vaccines.[4]

"Breach of warranty," interpreted as a guarantee of product safety, was a much more plaintiff-friendly cause of action than "negligence," the dominant concept in tort law (White 1985: 56–62). To win a lawsuit for negligence, a plaintiff has to show that a defendant had been at fault in some way, falling below some standard of conduct. The mere fact that a product has a defect—that for example, some live virus was distributed by Cutter—did not demonstrate that the company was negligent. Until the post–World War II era, tort law was primarily seen as a system for punishing misconduct through civil law, so anchoring tort law on questions of fault seemed appropriate. But in products liability, winning a negligence lawsuit by establishing fault could be difficult, as the *Gottsdanker* verdict suggested: even with a highly sympathetic plaintiff, the leading plaintiff tort lawyer of his generation (perhaps of the twentieth century) and a horrifying product defect, the jury did not determine that the live virus produced by Cutter was caused by its negligence.

This litigation, like the early asbestos litigation, occurred during a time when products liability law was haltingly and unevenly moving beyond negligence as the standard of judgment to "strict liability." The move to strict liability played out quite differently in the case of vaccines as compared to asbestos, the subject of the previous chapter. In asbestos, the chief effect of strict liability was to deemphasize the conduct of the plaintiffs, many of whom ignored generic warnings and failed to use protective masks. In vaccine litigation strict liability loosened the negligence standard, allowing plaintiffs in a few cases to recover even where the manufacturer's fault would have been hard to establish under older tort doctrines. One major factor in the move to strict liability was a shift in emphasis in product tort law to compensation, the plaintiff's side of tort, rather than punishment, the defendants' side. Edward White (1985: 146–153), in his intellectual history of tort law, links this shift to the rise of liability insurance, which gave manufacturers a way to smooth the costs of tort claims and price them into their products. Liability insurance may not have created the new focus on compensation, but it did facilitate new, more plaintiff-friendly doctrines, as did the realization that mass production put manufacturers in a powerful position both to surveil for possible dangers of their products and spread the costs of any dangers inherent in them.

In 1941 the great theorist of torts, William Prosser, in his influential textbook on tort law, argued for strict liability in product cases, arguing that it would allocate "a more or less inevitable loss to be charged against a complex and dangerous civilization, and [place] liability upon the party best able to shoulder it" (quoted in White 1985: 109). In 1944, in a widely cited concurring opinion, California Associate Supreme Court Justice Robert Traynor argued that the modern consumer economy made the negligence standard outdated:

> Those who suffer injury from defective products are unprepared to meet its consequences. The cost of an injury and the loss of time or health may be an overwhelming misfortune to the person injured, and a needless one, for the risk of injury can be insured by the manufacturer and distributed among the public as a cost of doing business.... However intermittently such injuries may occur and however haphazardly they may strike, the risk of their occurrence is a constant risk and a general one. Against such a risk there should be general and constant protection and the manufacturer is best situated to afford such protection....
>
> As handicrafts have been replaced by mass production with its great markets and transportation facilities, the close relationship between the producer and consumer of a product has been altered. Manufacturing processes, frequently valuable secrets, are ordinarily either inaccessible to or beyond the ken of the general public. The consumer no longer has means or skill enough to investigate for himself the soundness of a product, even when it is not contained in a sealed package, and his erstwhile vigilance has been lulled by the steady efforts of manufacturers to build up confidence by advertising and marketing devices such as trade-marks.[5]

Gottsdanker, decided 11 years after Traynor's concurrence, was not, technically speaking, a strict liability case; the jury's verdict was on breach of warranty. But as the judges in the case interpreted it, breach of warranty was a doctrine that seemed to make vaccine makers liable for anything caused by defects in their vaccines. A *Yale Law Journal* note celebrated the result, but urged a more forthright move to a strict liability standard, reasoning that it would "best assure compensation for the injured and best distribute the costs of compensation among those who benefit from the vaccine" (1955: 273).

In the years following *Gottsdanker*, courts found several creative ways in polio cases to find for the plaintiffs on a variety of grounds, including express warranties, negligence, and most of all, "failure to warn."[6] In *Reyes v. Wyeth*, a 1974 case, a federal appeals court upheld a verdict that Wyeth had failed to warn the Reyes family of the dangers of the Sabin oral polio vaccine, even though the company had included a warning in a package insert sent to the Texas clinic that had administered the vaccine. (The opinion was written by Judge Minor Wisdom, the same judge who authored the *Borel* decision that held manufacturers strictly liable for failing to warn workers adequately about the dangers of asbestos.) The court did not explain how, without depending on the clinics and doctors that administered vaccines, a vaccine maker was supposed to warn patients. Perhaps the most telling segment of the Court's decision was its statement that "Until Americans have a comprehensive scheme of social insurance, courts must resolve by a balancing process the head-on collision between the need for adequate recovery and viable enterprises...."[7]

Cases such as *Reyes* scared the vaccine industry and their insurers (Neustadt and Fineberg 1978: 49). When the federal government asked the pharmaceutical industry to produce the Swine Flu vaccine in 1976, insurers refused to cover liability, and manufacturers balked. This created panic that the vaccination campaign would be derailed. Acting with amazing speed, legislators drafted legislation making the U.S. government responsible for all liability claims arising out of swine flu vaccination, and passed the legislation within two weeks (ibid. at 60–61). The government then found itself in court defending against hundreds of lawsuits, and paying millions in claims, mostly in cases of Guillain-Barre syndrome.[8]

While it is clear that plaintiffs in vaccine injury cases made inroads from the 1950s to the 1980s, it is hard to know how many families made a claim, or how those that did fared during this time. We do not, unfortunately, have data on settlements or aggregate payouts. It seems likely, though, that the reported appellate cases were the exceptions, not the rule.[9] Vaccine plaintiffs faced formidable practical and doctrinal barriers in the adversarial system. Winning compensation involved an emotionally painful and uncertain legal struggle with a well-financed adversary. Just figuring out which manufacturer created the vaccine in their case was a potential barrier. For parents dealing with severely disabled children or the death of a child, the difficulties inherent in tort litigation loomed large.[10]

Judges may have been sympathetic to the plight of families with the injuries, and with Traynor and Prosser's call to create a kind of insurance system through product liability law, but they had to balance that with concerns about the impact of their decisions on the production of vaccines. This concern was embodied by "comment k" of the 1965 Second Restatement of Torts, which was briefly discussed in the previous chapter. While the Second Restatement strongly endorsed strict liability in product tort, comment k made an exception for "unavoidably dangerous products"—and specifically named vaccines as an example.[11] If "properly prepared, and accompanied by proper direction and warning," comment k says, unavoidably dangerous products like vaccines are not defective, and thus not liable even under strict liability. As with all of the recommendations in the restatements, courts across the country were free to interpret comment k as they wished, or to ignore it entirely. Judges' reactions to comment k varied, with some citing it as holding manufacturers to a much lower standard than strict liability.[12] Prospective vaccine injury plaintiffs had no way to know how much weight courts would put on the Prosser/Traynor arguments for strict liability versus comment k's suggestion that it was wrong to hold the makers of potentially life-saving products to this standard.

The leading cases after the Cutter incident mostly involved children who got polio from the Sabin oral polio vaccines, where issues of causation and design were relatively simple—no one denied that the Sabin vaccine was likely to cause a small number of cases of polio. For those who wished to sue for bad reactions to other vaccines, as in the case of Julie Schwartz that began this chapter, there were much more difficult questions. Causation is much more difficult to establish if, for example, the claim is that a child has an allergy or some other preexisting vulnerability to a vaccine. A symptom suffered after vaccination might be related to the vaccine, but as the saying goes, "correlation is not causation," and the symptom might have been caused by another malady that happened to surface in the same period. Even if the symptom can be linked to the vaccination, is difficult to label an allergic reaction a "defect" in the product, as strict liability calls for.

All these barriers were broken in another influential vaccine injury tort case, *Toner v. Lederle*.[13] In 1979, three-month-old Kevin Toner was vaccinated with a DPT vaccine manufactured by Lederle. Soon after, he developed transverse myelitis, a rare spinal condition that paralyzed him from the waist down. An Idaho jury found that Kevin's condition had been caused by the vaccine. Further, the jurors concluded that Lederle had been negligent because it had continued to manufacture the "whole cell" version of the pertussis vaccine when a safer "fractionated" design was available. The jury awarded $1.13 million in damages, and after some wrangling over comment k and Idaho state tort law, was upheld by the 9th Circuit Court of Appeals. Both on the causal issue and the design issue, *Toner* was an ominous case for manufacturers, not least because it came amidst a surge in DPT vaccine lawsuits. It was unclear how these lawsuits would be resolved, and whether *Toner* was destined to be a harbinger or an outlier. However, in the same year that *Toner* was decided, a jury handed down a $10 million verdict—$2 million for compensatory damages and $8 million in punitive damages—on another vaccine case involving the failure to warn parents that the Salk polio vaccine was safer than the Sabin vaccine that was administered. Although the verdict was eventually overturned,[14] the threat of so much liability rocked the vaccine industry.

As in the story of asbestos, the rise of adversarial legalism in vaccine injury compensation in the mid-1950s to the mid-80s was a double-edged sword. On the plus side, it provided some parents a means to seek compensation for losses that fell outside existing private and public social benefits systems, and served as a forum to raise concerns that some vaccines were poorly made and that the medical establishment had failed to provide adequate warnings of the risks. But adversarial rights tend to be slow, costly, and unpredictable, and this was certainly true of vaccine tort litigation. The Gottsdanker family, for example, had to win a tough jury trial and then an appeal; they received their payment five years after their daughter was paralyzed. The Toner family's claim took eight years.

The theory behind strict liability for products generally, and vaccines particularly, was that tort litigation could function as a kind of vast insurance system, financed by consumers through slightly higher prices on goods. What proponents of the theory might have overlooked was the diversity, complexity, and unpredictability of the American legal system. Plaintiffs and defendants faced not one unified system but 50 state systems. While the recommendations of leading elites like Prosser, Traynor, and the American Law Institute likely both reflected and reinforced a movement toward strict liability, when it came to vaccines that movement was hardly simple or uniform. The complexities of legal concepts such as "strict liability," "failure to warn," "implied warranty," and "unavoidably dangerous" played out differently across each case and each court, and there was no way to predict how judges and juries would calculate damages. The theorists of strict liability had imagined that manufacturers would manage the costs of litigation by increasing the costs of their goods and buying insurance. The problem was that as the risk of liability grew, it became increasingly uncertain and so difficult to manage.

As vaccine lawsuits began to percolate through state and federal court systems, there was little organized interest group mobilization on the issue of compensation. In the 1950s and 1960s, Congress held nearly dozens of hearings on vaccines, but none of them touched on liability issues. In the 1970s, Merck, a manufacturer of the MMR (Measles, Mumps and Rubella) vaccine took the lead in trying to organize manufacturers and the public health community to create compensation reforms, but found it impossible to find any consensus.[15] The 1976 Swine Flu fiasco was, in the terminology of John Kingdon (2011) a "focusing event" for the problems of vaccine liability and compensation. It generated congressional hearings that spilled beyond the immediate public health concerns to consider ongoing issues with influenza vaccine liability. But as often happens with focusing events, in the absence of any further crisis, and any easy consensus among the constituencies on what reform should look like, the energy behind the issue soon died out. The Centers for Disease Control, forced into narrowly targeting flu vaccination to high-risk individuals in part because of liability concerns, studied the issue in the late 1970s,[16] and the Office of Technology Assessment (1980) compiled a report on what an alternative compensation system might look like, but no further action was taken.

In the congressional hearings that did touch on liability in the 1970s, the focus was on the cost to manufacturers, and the possible effects of lawsuits on the supply of vaccines. Manufacturers and public health officials testified at these hearings, but there were no parents of vaccine-injured children, or plaintiff lawyers representing the interests of potential plaintiffs, and consumer groups raised concerns about injury compensation only sporadically.[17] In the adversarial compensation system created in the wake of *Gattsdanker* there were high levels of conflict among individual litigants—lawsuits could be hard-fought by plaintiffs and defendants—but until the early 1980s, this did not bring organized interests to mobilize in Congress for reform. To the extent there was a politics of vaccine injury in Congress, it was focused on the flu vaccine, and it was conducted almost entirely from the perspective of the effects on manufacturers. Problems of insufficient or unequal compensation for parents were largely ignored.

The Fractious Politics of Replacing Adversarial Legalism

Vaccine litigation demonstrated the characteristic costs and uncertainty of adversarial legalism. For parents raising severely injured children, the absence of a reliable and efficient compensation system caused hardship. Yet by the 1980s the legal environment was becoming a major concern for manufacturers. It hindered them in obtaining insurance against liability risks and eventually in maintaining the supply of childhood vaccines. As tort suits piled up, liability insurers pulled away from manufacturers, manufacturers dropped out of the business, and prices skyrocketed. The price of the DPT vaccine increased from 12 cents per dose in 1982 to $11.40 in 1986. In 1985, the Center for Disease Control advised delaying the vaccination of children to avoid a shortage of DPT vaccine (Hinman 1986: 529), and public health officials warned of a vaccine supply crisis.[18]

This created discontent on all sides, mobilizing manufacturers, doctors, public health officials and, eventually, parents. In 1982, Dissatisfied Parents Together (or DPT, the same as acronym given to the most controversial of the vaccines) was founded by four parents, including Jeffrey Schwartz, the father of Julie, who believed that vaccines had sickened their children. DPT came together when a television station in Washington, DC, aired a news report on the dangers of the DPT vaccine; the four parents were connected when they called the television station (Burke 2002: 146). DPT's main focus was on increasing awareness and research on the risks of the DPT vaccine, but the group also addressed compensation issues. As part of these efforts, the group reached out to the American Academy of Pediatrics (AAP), which had concluded that parents should be able to obtain compensation without bringing a lawsuit and proving that vaccine makers were at fault.

From the start, however, there were divisions among even these ostensible allies. Claimants under the "no fault" system would not have to prove a vaccine maker's negligence, but they would have to show their injuries were caused by the vaccine, and DPT and AAP sharply disagreed over who should make this determination. The pediatrician group believed that decision-making should be lodged with medical experts within the Department of Health and Human Services (HHS), but the parents' group, DPT, distrusted the medical establishment as over-zealous in its promotion of vaccination; it wanted a decision-maker independent of any group or agency with a tie to vaccines. The two sides also disagreed over the continuing role of adversarial legalism. DPT believed that tort played an important role in holding manufacturers and doctors accountable and thus wanted to preserve the right to sue. The AAP, by contrast, preferred that the no-fault program replace litigation entirely.

Realizing that any reform needed the support of DPT, AAP temporarily softened its position, and together the two groups released a draft bill. The compromise plan proposed a no-fault Compensation Program funded by a surtax on vaccines. Claimants would apply to the U.S. District Court in Washington, DC, which would appoint a special master to decide whether the injury was compensable based on a table of vaccine reactions. To win, parents only had to show that their child had developed a reaction listed on an official table of injuries after vaccination. If dissatisfied, parents could appeal the special master's decision the D.C. Circuit Court. Critically, parents retained the right to avoid the program entirely and, as before, sue in federal court.

Bills based on the AAP-DPT compromise were introduced into the Senate by Paula Hawkins (R-FL) and in the House by Henry Waxman (D-CA). After an initial round of hearings on her bill, Senator Hawkins introduced revised legislation aimed at gaining support from manufacturers. The revised bill restricted recovery to cases of injuries lasting at least a year or resulting in death, and narrowed the number of "on table" injuries deemed compensable. It locked claimants into the administrative remedy or a lawsuit, whereas the original bill allowed claimants to reject the special master's award and file a tort suit. The revised bill also made it more difficult for a plaintiff to prevail in tort by foreclosing the "duty to directly warn" theory of liability.

Some of the major vaccine manufacturers still balked. From their perspective, failure to replace litigation with an exclusive administrative remedy was the worst of all worlds—they would be forced to pay a surtax to support a program *and* they would still face the unpredictable threat of large jury verdicts. The Pharmaceutical Manufacturers Association (PHARMA) endorsed an alternative reform developed by a commission of medical experts and pharmaceutical groups in which health officials from HHS would administer a no-fault plan. Claimants could appeal the administrative decisions on only limited ground, and the parents' right to sue in court would be eliminated. The AMA endorsed this legislation, breaking ranks with the pediatrician group to oppose the new Hawkins-Waxman bill (Burke 2002: 152).

Manufacturers did not entirely unify behind the AMA/PHARMA Plan. Some coalesced around a new hybrid plan written by Lederle and supported by Wyeth. The plan, advanced by Representative Edward Madigan (R-IL), the ranking GOP member of Waxman's Committee, created 11 regional panels of medical experts that would arbitrate claims, with awards capped at $1 million. Eventually the pediatricians' group, AAP, abandoned its coalition with the parents' group and worked with pharmaceutical companies to float further alternatives. None of these coalitions made much progress, however (ibid.). The stakeholders remained divided over all the core issues in injury compensation politics—who decides, who pays, how much, and to whom.

In Congress this resulted in what political scientists call "fire alarm" oversight (McCubbins and Schwartz 1984; Lupia and McCubbins 1994). All the main stakeholders rang the alarm about the problems of the existing adversarial legal regime: its costs, delays, uncertainty, and potential threat to the supply of vaccines. Instead of negotiating with one another over a common plan, competing interests brought a welter of alternative solutions to Congress. In this environment, every issue seemed subject to question, as members of Congress and interest groups fought over the scope and nature of the underlying problem, the need for reform, and of course the many details of the competing plans. It was a fractious, chaotic politics quite similar to that observed in the previous chapter on asbestos.

The next step, however, makes the vaccine case distinctive. Henry Waxman, an unusually talented legislator, became determined to resolve the vaccine compensation problem. Waxman believed that legislative success hinged on building a broad coalition among parents, manufacturers, and doctors. Waxman reached out to these interests by pursuing a strategy of seeking "everyone's second choice" (ibid.). This attempt to build a cross-stakeholder alliance between plaintiffs and defendants is common in the politics of adversarial legalism; in the asbestos chapter there were several such attempts. As the asbestos chapter illustrates, however, bringing together such unlikely allies is challenging.

In the case of vaccines, one problem was that the manufacturers themselves were divided on the design of a no-fault program. Merck, the producer of the MMR vaccine, which faced relatively few liability claims, was supportive of a no-fault reform that preserved the tort option, though it also wanted reforms in tort law.[19] Lederle, the main (and at one point the only) producer of the DPT vaccine, was much more critical of the Hawkins-Waxman legislation, insisting that a no-fault plan that retained the tort option would be disastrous for the manufacturers.[20] Connaught, another producer of the DPT vaccine, was also critical of the non-exclusive remedy, and further challenged the socialization of risk built into the no-fault compensation scheme, favoring a system in which payments "would be made directly by the manufacturer of the vaccine alleged to have caused the injury."[21]

Waxman decided to exploit these divisions and seek out the most flexible of the manufacturers, Merck, to find a plan that would satisfy it and the parents' group. His staff conducted shuttle diplomacy, moving back and forth among the constituencies to come up with a plan that they could sign off on. The main issue was over the extent of tort restrictions in the legislation. Waxman found language that strengthened manufacturers' just enough to keep Merck on board but not so much that the parents' group, DPT, jumped ship. In the end, Waxman's diplomatic efforts produced a delicate coalition of DPT, Merck and some doctors' groups. With this coalition, Waxman managed to shepherd his bill, the National Childhood Vaccine Injury Act, through the House Energy and Commerce Committee, and eventually through the House.

In the Senate, vaccine legislation was also aided by strong legislative leadership by Senators Orrin Hatch (R-UT) and Edward Kennedy (D-MA). They worked with Waxman and Madigan to combine the Vaccine Injury Act with a bunch of other initiatives in a "Christmas Tree" bill—legislation that included enticements for every important constituency involving such unrelated matters as research on Alzheimer's disease.[22] The Christmas Tree strategy eventually worked, as the sponsors were able to get the Reagan Administration to convince a series of conservative Senators to release holds on the legislation, ensuring its passage.

Yet the possibility of a veto by President Reagan still loomed. The Reagan Administration was internally split, in a way that reflected the divisive politics of vaccine injuries at the time. Assistant Attorney General John Bolton set forth the case against the vaccine program in a memorandum to the Office of Management and Budget (OMB), arguing that the bill violated the Administration's core small government principles and inappropriately diminished the powers of the president by placing program administration in the hands of judges outside the executive branch. He also worried that the vaccine program undermined the Administration's tort reform agenda, which stressed the passage of "discouragement reforms"—measures aimed at discouraging litigation by making cases harder to bring or less remunerative—as opposed to "replacement reforms" that supplanted (or supplemented) private litigation with new government programs.[23]

White House Counsel Peter Wallison defended the bill. He argued that no-fault schemes were generally a bad idea, but vaccinations were a special case because the state required them and the number of claimants was inherently limited. Contrary to Bolton, he maintained that the no-fault program was consistent with the Administration's general tort reform agenda, as it took cases out of the courts and provided businesses with greater certainty.[24] In the end, President Reagan reluctantly signed, perhaps in part because he knew the program was passed without financing and that his Administration would have another chance to shape it during the funding process.

In fact, funding the program proved to be every bit as contentious as creating it. When Waxman took up a funding bill the following year, he struggled with budgeting for the thousands of claims dating from decades before, a particularly unpredictable aspect of vaccine injury compensation. He decided to restructure the program, splitting into pre- and post-program claims. Pre-program claims would be paid out of general revenues; post-program claims would be paid from a surtax on vaccines. Pre-program claims were capped at 3,500 in number, and awards were capped at $30,000 for attorney fees, lost earnings, and pain-and-suffering combined. (This left open the possibility of large claims for medical expenses.) Pre-program claimants retained the ability to sue in the tort system without applying to the Compensation Program. Post-program claimants had to go to the administrative program first, and could sue in tort only after rejecting the final judgment, but they were given more generous funding. Besides medical expenses, claims could include up to $250,000 for pain and suffering and $250,000 for the death of a child. Reasonable attorney fees were paid by the program even if the claim was rejected. All claims would be handled in the U.S. Claims Court, and the HHS could if it chose act as a kind of defendant and contest claims it considered ill-founded. If claimants lost in the administrative system, or received a payment lower than they felt was warranted, they could reject the decision and file a lawsuit, but as a result of the legislation, tort plaintiffs faced significantly greater hurdles than before. At the behest of the vaccine makers, Waxman had added significant defenses for them, making it particularly difficult for post-program claimants to prevail in tort.

If the final version of the vaccine program had been presented to President Reagan as a stand-alone measure, it most likely would have been vetoed. But proponents rolled the funding for the vaccine program into the massive 1988 Reconciliation Act, which President Reagan signed. Congress had succeeded in largely replacing an adversarial compensation system with a new, more bureaucratic policy.

The Structure and Operations of the VICP: The Schwartz Era

The VICP went into operation in October 1988. As of May 2014, VICP had paid out nearly $2.7 billion dollars to more than 3,500 claimants.[25] To initiate a claim, claimants file a petition along with the relevant medical records to the U.S. Claims Court. The Claims Court forwards the claim to the Division of Vaccine Injury Compensation within the Department of Health and Human Services, where medical experts recommend whether to compensate. A group of lawyers within the Justice Department who specialize in vaccine cases read the report and decide whether to contest the claim.

The program, then, retains a central element of an adversarial legalism: it can result in disputes between two parties, the claimant and the government, presided over by a neutral decision-maker, a special master within the Claims

168   HOW POLICY SHAPES POLITICS

Court. Further, in this dispute both parties are represented by lawyers who present testimony and expert witnesses. But in most other respects, the program represents a significant shift toward bureaucratic legalism. First, the process of resolving claims is streamlined because the range of disputing is narrowed; the claimant need not prove negligence, or failure to warn, or any of the other theories tort plaintiffs advanced, only that the vaccine caused the injury. Moreover, the legislation created a "Table of Injuries" that are presumed to be caused by vaccines. If the claimant can show that a symptom or set of symptoms on the Table happened within a defined period after receiving the vaccine listed in the Table, then there is a presumption in favor of the claim. Injuries that are not on the Table, "off-Table" claims in the parlance of the program, can also receive compensation, but in those cases the claimant has to demonstrate causation by a preponderance of evidence. The government also created a streamlined set of procedures. Cases can be disposed of without a hearing and, when hearings are held, they last one or two days, speedy by the standards of tort litigation. The program thus reduced one hallmark of adversarial legalism, dispute over the rules, both substantive and procedural. Similarly, disputing over the size of awards is reduced by strict monetary limits on pain and suffering damages and compensation for death.

Besides narrowing disputing, the program is bureaucratic in that it largely, though not completely, centralizes decision-making over vaccine injuries in a highly specialized court. Tort litigation is handled by thousands of courts in both the state and federal systems, and each state has its own set of precedents and legislation governing how the litigation is resolved. Moreover, jurors, who have no allegiance to any central authority, are key decision-makers. By contrast, the special masters in the vaccine program work only on vaccine cases and thus are in a position to develop not only expertise but also uniform approaches to cases. The structure is far from the bureaucratic ideal, however. The eight special masters are not bound by each other's precedents, leaving open the possibility of variance across the masters. Moreover, their decisions can be appealed to one of several judges on the U.S. Court of Federal Claims, potentially creating more variance. These judges handle a range of other matters besides vaccine injuries, and so are much less specialized. Further appeal is to the U.S. Court of Appeals for the Federal Circuit, an even less specialized court. The periodic intervention of Federal Claims Court judges and the Circuit Court has from time to time shaken up the rules under which the special masters operate, and it is not at all clear that the appellate courts have created clear guidance to the special masters in one of the biggest issues before them, determining causation in off-Table cases (Grey 2011: 343).

The funding mechanism for the compensation system marks the biggest shift to bureaucratic legalism from the tort system that preceded it. For pre-program injuries, funding (somewhat sporadically) came from general revenues; for post-program injuries, payments are made from a government trust fund supported by a surtax on vaccines. The program thus socializes the costs of vaccine injuries. In tort litigation, by contrast, the burden of successful claims falls on defendants and their insurers. This shift in funding is a crucial aspect of our story, for it greatly reduces concerns about injury compensation among manufacturers. In the tort system, decision-making was unpredictable, a typical effect of adversarial legalism. This made life difficult for manufacturers, because unpredictable and unevenly distributed costs are hard to insure against or pass on to customers. The surtax, by contrast, is extremely predictable and evenly distributed, and so manufacturers, whatever their concerns about the program, have not pressed for reforms.

We can call the initial years of the Compensation Program the "Schwartz era" for the family who fought for it as an alternative to the tort system. During this period the alternative was embraced by claimants. The number of DPT vaccine lawsuit filings dropped from a high of 255 in 1986, in the middle of the debate over the Compensation Act, to 19 in 1990, the second year of the program's operation, and continued to drop thereafter. The Compensation Program was clearly effective in displacing adversarial legalism, as the fear of the manufacturers—that they would end up financing both the Compensation Program and defending lawsuits—was soon proven groundless. In its early years the VICP was buried in a mound of old claims stretching back to the 1910s (Evans et al. 2008: Table 75-3, 1660). Between 1989 and 1995, the program's first six years in operation, 3,451 claims were resolved, resulting in payments of nearly $600 million to 827 successful claimants.[26] This was a period of relatively quiet politics, as stakeholders worked together to improve the program's administrative efficiency and funding structure, with Congress from time to time passing non-controversial legislation that fixed problems in the program's administration.

The Administrative Retrenchment of the VICP

The era of relative peace in vaccine injury politics ended in 1995 with a significant change in the program, an amendment to the Table of Injuries. The Table lists for each vaccine a set of injuries and a time period. If a petitioner can show that the injured party received a vaccine and suffered the injuries listed in the Table within the requisite period of time, there is a strong presumption in favor of the claim. If an injury is off-Table, the petitioner must show by a preponderance of evidence that the vaccine caused the child's injuries, a much more difficult enterprise. When DPT, the physicians, and the manufacturers negotiated over the shape of the Compensation Program in the mid-1980s, they focused much of their attention on the shape of the Table of Injuries, because it was thought that nearly all cases would be resolved through the Table. The sides negotiated the details of the Table so as to settle all the major existing disputes about vaccine injuries, principally the injury that Julie Schwartz had suffered, residual seizure disorder. The provision for off-Table injuries was added as a backup and a source of flexibility in case new issues arose, but not much thought was given to the standards by which off-Table claims were to be handled, particularly the type and quality of scientific data necessary to establish causation (Grey 2011).

The legislation creating the VICP also gave the Health and Human Services Department the right to use the rulemaking process to amend the Table of Injuries, a power that may have been more important than some of the groups negotiating the law realized. Because the Table of Injuries specifically recognized residual seizure disorder injuries and "hypotonic-hyporesponsive episodes," the most common bases for DPT vaccine claims, the compensation rate in DPT vaccine cases was relatively high. But officials in the Division of Vaccine Injury Compensation, the section of the Department of Health and Human Services that reads and evaluates all claims, thought that the scientific underpinnings of the link between the DPT vaccine and these injuries was questionable at best, and had been undermined by studies conducted after the enactment of the Compensation Program. Congress had mandated the Institute of Medicine to study several of the injuries on the Table, and those reports validated the suspicions of HHS officials. Through a rulemaking process in 1995, residual seizure disorder and hypotonic-hyporesponsive episode were struck from the Table, and encephalopathy was more precisely defined. This was a significant change in policy. If it had happened a few years earlier, the case of Julie Schwartz, which had helped to inspire the formation of DPT, would have been moved off-Table. The revisions on residual seizure disorder and hypotonic-hyporesponsive episode were the first and most controversial of many rulemaking processes, some of which removed other conditions from the table, others in which conditions were added. HHS was also granted the power to add any vaccine routinely given to children for coverage under the program, and so has added nine more, but has added few injuries associated with those vaccines to the Table (Evans et al. 2008: Table 75–76, 1664–1665).

The net effect of HHS's actions, starting in 1995, was to vastly reduce claims that could be made under the Table's streamlined administrative procedure, and to increase the number of off-Table claims. A 1999 GAO report noted that at that point about 45% of the claims awarded compensation, and about half the nearly $1 billion awarded had been for injuries subsequently removed from the Table (United States Government Accounting Office 1999: 14). Also, 72% of the claims the Compensation Program had considered up to that point were for on-Table injuries, and claims for on-Table injuries were three times more likely to be awarded than for off-Table claims (ibid. at 12). But after the amendments to the Table, off-Table cases predominated.

The institutional effect of the move toward off-Table cases has been to create a hybrid policy, one in which the bureaucratic funding mechanism remains, but the claiming process is increasingly adversarial. As compared to the Table process, the off-Table process is much less hierarchical and more party-influenced. The standard for demonstrating causation in off-Table injuries was left quite open in the legislation, providing lots of opportunity for the parties to argue its proper interpretation and application. The parties and their lawyers in off-Table cases frame the issues and gather the evidence, which is presented to the special master.[27] In these respects, the VICP today roughly parallels the tort law system it replaced, although the process is far more centralized than ordinary tort litigation. It is clear from reports that in the 1990s the amount of lawyering and adversarialism within the program grew after the initial years. Congress originally mandated that the program resolve claims within a year, but the 1999 GAO report found that it met this standard in just 14% of cases, with more than half the claims taking more than two years, and 18% taking more than five years (United States Government Accounting Office 1999: 8). Yet the program is still bureaucratic in its funding. The cost of successful claims, as well as the transactional costs of the claims process itself, including lawyers' fees, are socialized, paid from a trust fund rather than by individual plaintiffs and defendants.

The Politics of Bureaucratic Retrenchment

The amendments to the Table also changed the politics of the program. Not surprisingly, as in the case of SSDI, agency efforts to make claims harder to prove angered claimants. The parents' group, DPT, had by the late 1990s become the National Vaccine Information Center, and the leader of the Center, Barbara Loe Fisher, was outspoken in her criticism of the program (Fisher 2008). The biggest target of her criticisms were the changes made to the Table of Injuries.[28]

Fisher was not alone. Beginning in the 1990s, claimants' criticisms of the Compensation Program were aired in the media and in congressional hearings.[29]

From the perspective of parents and their lawyers, there were a bunch of problems that needed fixing. The greater delay and contentiousness in the program meant more work for claimant lawyers, and the law creating the VICP only authorized payments to them after claims were resolved, meaning that lawyers could wait for several years to be paid for their work. A provision authorizing the program to award interim attorneys' fees was sought. The original law had limited pain and suffering and death damages at $250,000, but had not included a provision for inflation, so the parents' groups wanted the amount to be raised. Probably the most important proposal, though, was to increase the three-year statute of limitations on claims made to the program. The parents and lawyers argued that because the VICP was so obscure, would-be claimants sometimes learned about the right to file for compensation after the time limit had expired. By the early 2000s, proposals to reform these and other aspects of the VICP had been made by an advisory committee within the program, by the Secretary of Health and Human Services, and by many members of Congress, including Waxman, who had helped create the program nearly two decades before.

Although discontent with the Compensation Program grew during this period, there was not a return to the fractious politics generated by adversarial legalism in the early 1980s, before the enactment of the VICP. Most strikingly, manufacturers, so active in the struggle over the creation of the VICP, were relatively silent on the bureaucratic retrenchment of the program. This is not surprising. The adjustments to the Table did not directly affect their interests; the surcharge on vaccines to fund the program would remain in place regardless of how specific claims were adjudicated. Besides, the program was solvent, and had resolved the problem that brought them to Congress earlier, tort liability. So, being relatively content with the program, they were disinclined to join the fray in battles over the details of the program's administration. Indeed, perhaps what is most notable is that manufacturers, far from fighting against the program, supported the inclusion of other vaccines in the program in order to take advantage of the predictability of its costs as compared to the tort system.

The Temporary Reemergence of Adversarial Legalism: The Thimerosal Litigation

It is tempting to try to imagine what might have happened to the politics of vaccine compensation if it had continued along the trajectory set in the late 1990s. Perhaps there would have been a further settling of the remaining issues, and some reduction in the dissatisfaction of parents' groups with the changes in the program. The resolution of old DPT vaccine claims, the move of manufacturers to a new, apparently safer "acellular" form of the pertussis component of the DPT vaccine and the replacement of the oral polio vaccine with the injected form all might have had the effect of reducing conflict. The stakeholder groups might have been able to reach some compromises on the procedural issues that had been raised.

We will never be able to observe this counterfactual, however, because by the early 2000s there was a new issue roiling vaccine injury politics, with a litigation threat of far greater scope than the old one over DPT. The issue was thimerosal, a mercury-containing preservative used in some vaccines since the 1930s. Concerns about thimerosal first gained prominence in the United States in the summer of 1999, when the Centers for Disease Control released a statement announcing that both the AAP and vaccine manufacturers had concluded that "thimerosal-containing vaccines should be removed as soon as possible." This conclusion had been reached even though the groups had not turned up any evidence that thimerosal was harmful; they wanted to further study the issue (Mnookin 2011: 126). The nuance of the statement was, of course, lost, and critics of vaccines seized on it as a concession about the dangers of mercury in vaccines. A kind of anti-vaccine social movement grew up, composed of parents of autistic children, sympathetic medical professionals, researchers, journalists and bloggers, and a few prominent celebrities (Kirkland 2012a). The parents, backed by this contingent of supporters, contended that vaccinations given to children had increased their exposure to mercury, and that this exposure played some role in the rise of autism among children in the United States. Parents of autistic children began filing claims with the Compensation Program, but autism claims were "off-Table," and claimants faced huge obstacles—the Justice Department was strongly committed to beating back the autism theory, and the science behind it was shaky at best. So some claimant lawyers attempted to bypass the program and file their claims against manufacturers directly in federal court. These lawyers argued that the Compensation Program did not cover claims arising from thimerosal because it was an "adulterant" or "contaminant" of vaccines, and thus fell outside the program's statutory scheme. More than 100 such claims were filed, but if certified as class actions they could have potentially represented millions of plaintiffs (Kirkland 2012b: 238).

The thimerosal suits represented a throwback to the days before the VICP, when court filings represented a major threat to manufacturers. Vaccine makers once again faced the fear that among the many state and federal courts handling vaccine lawsuits, some judges would accept the theory that thimerosal was not covered by the Compensation Program. This led the manufacturers to lobby Congress for a statutory change that would either immunize them from liability for thimerosal, or clarify that all thimerosal claims should be handled through the program.

The politics that resulted from the thimerosal issue seemed like a flashback to the 1980s, before the creation of the Compensation Program, with even greater intensity. Victims' groups charged that pharmaceutical companies were engaged in a mass poisoning of children. Dan Burton, an Indiana Representative who was convinced his own grandson had become autistic as a result of vaccines, each day read letters from parents of autistic children into the Congressional Record. On the other side, industry groups claimed that, just as in the 1980s, the proliferation of lawsuits threatened the supply of vaccines.

The vaccine makers had an ally in Senate Majority Leader Bill Frist, a cardiologist who was highly sympathetic to the pharmaceutical industry. To resolve the manufacturers' concerns, Frist realized that he would need to bring all the constituencies involved with the program together, just as Waxman had done years earlier. He began to work with the groups and their allies in Congress, including Senators Ted Kennedy, Christopher Dodd, and Judd Gregg, as well as Representatives John Dingell and Henry Waxman. To attract the support of parents and claimant lawyers, Frist included several of their favored provisions, most notably doubling the statute of limitations and giving those who had previously missed a deadline a one-year period in which to file a claim. The change in the statute of limitations issue was a major sticking point with manufacturers, however. They were not worried about potential for greater claims against the program—it was running a billion-dollar surplus—but they were concerned that the extending the statute of limitations would subject them to more litigation. Claimants who took advantage of the extension would be able to sue the manufacturers in court if they rejected the judgment of the program. Thus the effect of extending the program was to extend the statute of limitations in tort, and given the onslaught of thimerosal court filings the manufacturers were already facing, this was not a pleasant prospect.

As Frist continued to negotiate, someone in the House detonated the legislative equivalent of a bomb over the proceedings. In the lame duck session of 2002, a provision specifying that all claims involving thimerosal were to be resolved by the Compensation Program was quietly inserted into the bill that created the Department of Homeland Security. No one seemed to notice the add-on when the House voted to approve the Homeland Security bill; the provision was discovered when the bill reached the Senate. Democrats tried to scuttle it, but were unsuccessful, and after President Bush signed the legislation, the possibility of widespread thimerosal litigation seemed to have been averted. But when the insertion of the thimerosal provision became widely known, supporters of the victims' groups were outraged, and the whole episode was the subject of a media backlash. For a brief moment, vaccine injury compensation politics reached the front pages of newspapers and magazines. It is still not clear who added the thimerosal provision, though the House Majority Leader Dick Armey is the leading suspect; both Frist and Bush Administration officials denied any involvement (Stolberg 2002). Critics portrayed Congress's actions as a giveaway to the pharmaceutical industry; Eli Lilly, the target of much thimerosal litigation, had given $1.6 million in campaign contributions during the 2002 election cycle (ibid.). Moderate Senate Republicans aligned with Democrats in demanding the repeal of the provision. They succeeded in inserting a repeal into the 2003 omnibus appropriations bill.

After this fiasco, Frist continued to work on a compromise among the vaccine injury constituencies that would include the thimerosal provision. At several points it looked like a breakthrough was near, but Frist, unlike Waxman before him, failed to bring the warring interests together. Perhaps the blowback from the bungled Homeland Security bill episode clouded the effort. In any event, after Frist ended his efforts, Congress stayed away from the thimerosal issue and more generally seemed to give up on reforming the Compensation Program. While the VICP has had some outspoken critics in Congress, none have made any attempt to truncate or repeal the program. Even Dan Burton, the most vociferous and active critic of the vaccine industry and of the program, supported the program's continuing existence. Whatever his concerns about the thimerosal issue, he concluded that "it's not feasible for everyone to go to court" to resolve vaccine claims.[30]

The End of the Thimerosal Litigation: The Bruesewitz Era

The background to the dramatic conflict in Congress was a fundamental conflict among parents and program officials about the purposes of the Compensation Program. Parents and claimants' groups argue that the logic of the Vaccine Injury Act was political and legal, not scientific: the program was created as a kind of deal between the contending groups, and part of the deal was to base compensation decisions on standards for proof of causation that fell well below what might be required in a tort lawsuit. Program officials agree that the program was meant to "overcompensate," that is, pay claims for injuries that were not in fact caused by vaccines, and they believe it does this, but they balance the mandate for generosity with a concern about the effects of program rulings on public attitudes about vaccination.[31] A decision to compensate an injury that is not in fact caused by vaccines is problematic for them because it tells the public that the vaccine is potentially dangerous. The United States has among the highest vaccination rates in the world, but for public health authorities there are ongoing struggles with financing, production, and, most of all, public confidence in the safety of vaccines (Colegrove 2007: 54). Maintaining high vaccination rates amid public fear has always been a challenge, and what they see as overcompensation can complicate that challenge.[32]

Within the HHS, the perspective of public health officials is dominant; parents and claimant groups have little influence. Both parents and claimant lawyers serve on the Advisory Committee on Childhood Vaccines, which brings together all the constituencies in vaccine injury politics, but as the name suggests, the committee is purely advisory. The ACCV is consulted during rulemaking processes, but it has no formal power to block changes to the Table, or changes in procedures within the program. Parents who have served on the committee report that they have felt marginalized and disadvantaged relative to the public health officials and academics who dominate the proceedings. They are often dealing with severely injured children, and so struggle to find the energy to participate. One parent summarized her experiences:

> The doctors from Harvard and Hopkins are there with their computers. They are being paid to be there. Nobody wants us there. We're away from our children. We don't have many initials after our names. [33]

Parents and their attorneys, of course, participate more directly in the program through the claims process, which raises the same philosophical issues about the extent to which the program should be grounded in scientific standards. Here the main issue is the standards for causation in off-Table case, which has been the subject of rounds of litigation. The National Childhood Vaccine Injury Act, the law that created the program, is rather foggy on this, probably because the disposition of off-Table cases was not among the major concerns of legislators or interests involved (Grey 2011: 343). In a series of cases involving appeals to the Claims Court and Federal Circuit Court, the standards have been upgraded and downgraded, leaving confusing guidance for the special masters (ibid.). The issue of causation continues to be the subject of an ongoing struggle among parents, claimant attorneys, HHS, the Justice Department lawyers who fight the claims, the special masters, and the judges above them who hear appeals.

Faced with the increased disputing over vaccine injuries, including more than 5,000 autism-related claims, the special masters developed several innovations to tamp down adversarialism and speed up resolution of claims. The most important of these innovations are "omnibus proceedings," in which, as in the consolidated actions and class action suits in asbestos litigation, similar claims are brought together and decided in one fell swoop. To resolve the autism claims, the special masters created three "Omnibus Autism Proceedings" that judged three theories of the vaccine-autism link by examining six test cases in great detail. The outcome, a decisive rejection of all the cases and all claims of a vaccine-autism link, helped to further delegitimize the anti-vaccine movement, and embittered members of the movement against the Compensation Program. What under tort litigation would have been left to juries and judges in courts around the nation was instead put in the hands of three special masters. As one critic put it, in the Compensation Program "[g]overnment attorneys defend a government program, using government-funded science before government judges" (quoted in Kirkland 2012b: 254).

In the decentralized American judicial system, as opposed to the Compensation Program, there is always hope that a judge or jury will be more supportive of a claim about vaccine injuries. This is why the fight to keep thimerosal claims out of the adversarial legal system has been so intense. The punctuation to this fight is the story of the third of the three children we named at the outset of this chapter, Hannah Bruesewitz. In 1992, when Hannah was six months old, she was injected with a DPT vaccine that had been produced by Wyeth. Within hours of receiving the vaccine, Hannah had a seizure, and suffered 125 more over the next 16 days. At 20 months she was diagnosed as developmentally delayed, with no discernible speech, and with continuing, severe epilepsy. In 1995 her family applied to the Compensation Program, but with unfortunate timing: they applied just one month before residual seizure disorder had been removed from the Table of Injuries for DPT. After a long struggle a special master denied the claim in 2003, though the family was given $126,000 to pay attorney's fees and costs.[34]

The family then filed a tort lawsuit in Pennsylvania state court. Their argument was that Wyeth should be held liable for Hannah's injuries because it had stuck with a faulty design of the DPT vaccine. This was an echo of the claims made by Jeffrey Schwartz and Dissatisfied Parents Together in the 1980s. They had long argued that the "whole cell" version of the pertussis vaccine was dangerous, and that the United States should look to the example of Japan, which was administering a wholly different vaccine, the "acellular" version. Wyeth had continued to produce the whole cell version of the vaccine in an era in which other manufacturers were moving toward producing the acellural version. In 1991, the Food and Drug Administration licensed Lederle to produce acellular vaccines for children two years and above, and in 1996 it licensed an acellular vaccine for younger children.[35] The Bruesewitzes' principal claim, then, was for a "design defect"—Wyeth, they contended, should have known there was a safer design.[36] The case was moved to a U.S. district court in Pennsylvania, which concluded that the Vaccine Injury Act had preempted all vaccine tort claims based on a theory of design defect. The Bruesewitzes appealed to the 3rd Circuit Court of Appeals, which upheld the district court's decision, and finally to the U.S. Supreme Court.

Bruesewitz was a leftover from the Schwartz era, when the DPT vaccine was the dominant issue in vaccine injury compensation. By the time *Bruesewitz* came to court, there were few DPT vaccine claims still circulating either within the program or the judiciary. The real impact of *Bruesewitz* was on the thimerosal claims. The program had through its omnibus proceedings dismissed them, but if the Court ruled for the Bruesewitz family it would open state courts across the country to thousands of thimerosal claims, far outstripping in intensity the surge in DPT vaccine lawsuits that in the 1980s had stimulated Congress to act.

The core issue in *Bruesewitz* was the scope of the deal Waxman had made so many years ago in forging the Compensation Program. The parents' groups and their allies had bargained away some of their ability to sue in court in exchange for better compensation, but how much had they given? Unsurprisingly, the parties to the agreement differed on this key issue. The pediatricians and other public health groups argued in briefs for Wyeth that the National Childhood Vaccine Injury Act precluded any lawsuit based on a "design defect" claim like the one made by the Bruesewitz family. In this argument they were joined by the Obama Administration, and by the manufacturers, who argued that a ruling in favor of Bruesewitz would unravel the entire system of compensation, moving disputing back to state courts. On the other side, the successor to the parents' group DPT, the National Vaccine Information Center, filed a brief along with 24 other anti-vaccine groups in support of the Bruesewitz family. The brief was supported by all four of the parents who together had formed DPT, including Jeffrey Schwartz, the father of Julie Schwartz. It argued that the bargain made by DPT had not affected the right to sue for design defects.

The key phrase in the Vaccine Injury Act was this:

> No vaccine manufacturer shall be liable in a civil action for damages arising from a vaccine related injury or death associated with the administration of a vaccine after October 1, 1988, if the injury or death resulted from side effects that were unavoidable even though the vaccine was properly prepared and was accompanied by proper directions and warnings.

Was this a somewhat awkward attempt to codify comment k of the Second Restatement of Torts, which, according to one interpretation, merely invites jurors to decide for themselves whether the effects of a vaccine were "unavoidable"? Or was this, as the manufacturers urged, an implicit statement that of the three traditional grounds for product liability, manufacturing defects, failure to warn, and design defects, only the first two would be allowed in post-Vaccine Injury Act litigation?

By a 6-2 vote, the Justices sided with the manufacturers and their allies. Justice Scalia's majority opinion and the dissent by Justice Sotomayor both feature elaborate parsing of the paragraph above, replete with references to dictionaries about the meaning of words such as "unavoidable" and the phrase "even though." But also figuring prominently in the opinions are views about adversarial and bureaucratic legalism. In each of the opinions, the justices consider the question of whether decision-making about vaccine compensation should be placed in the hands of jurors across the nation in tort lawsuits, or whether is it better to leave these matters in the hands of a centralized bureaucracy, the Compensation Program. Scalia's majority opinion, for example, argues that the abolition of design defect litigation "reflects a sensible choice to leave complex epidemiological judgments about vaccine design to the FDA and the National Vaccine Program rather than juries."[37] Breyer's concurrence notes that to allow litigation in such cases would "substitute less expert for more expert judgment, thereby threatening manufacturers with liability (indeed, strict liability) in instances where any conflict between experts and nonexperts is likely to be particularly severe...."[38] Breyer, as is his wont, comes down on the side of the experts, and deference to an executive agency, HHS. Even Sotomayor, in her dissent, concedes that "reasonable minds can disagree about the wisdom of having juries weigh the relative costs and benefits of a

particular vaccine design," though she argues that neither the HHS nor the
FDA perform the same function that design defect lawsuits do, of encouraging manufacturers to adopt better designs for their drugs.[39] In any case, the
Court's decision is an endorsement of bureaucratic legalism that appears to
largely seal off a return to tort.

Discussion

We have framed the comparisons in this book in terms of ideal types, adversarial legalism and bureaucratic legalism, while acknowledging that in fact
there are few pure examples of either. Certainly this is case with the VICP.[40]
A purely bureaucratic compensation program would entrust decisions about
payments in the hands of unreviewable bureaucrats employing fixed standards; the VICP instead allows petitioners to bring disputed claims to a neutral referee, the special master, who, particularly in off-Table claims, has much
more discretion than the bureaucratic ideal would entail. Further, parents of
injured children dissatisfied with the VICP also had access to the courts to
challenge the program or do an end-run around it, though these judicial challenges have generally been unsuccessful.

As this case illustrates, policies in the American system are not always
static; they can shift between the poles of adversarial and bureaucratic legalism, sometimes creating novel hybrids. In vaccine injury compensation, the
problems created by the decentralization and consequent unpredictability of the adversarial system generated a political mobilization for a more
bureaucratic policy. That policy, once adopted, operated in relative calm for
a few years, but as often happens with bureaucratic systems in the United
States, over time it became more adversarial (Nonet 1969; Kagan 2001).
The most obvious cause of rising adversarial legalism was the amendment to
the Table of Injuries and the rising number of "off-Table" cases. This engendered considerable tumult both within the program and in federal courts
on the issue of causation. As a result, the amount of lawyering associated
with cases has increased; the system has become more "party-centered" and
less hierarchical, the outcome more dependent on the disputing process and
less based on fixed rules.

Nonetheless, as compared to the tort system that preceded it, the adoption
of the Compensation Program has had the net effect of centralizing power over
vaccine compensation, giving federal officials greater power to shape how compensation was awarded. The judiciary has reinforced this by generally fending

off attempts to bypass or end-run outcomes in the program. For anti-vaccine activists the centralization created by the program closed off some venues and so represented a loss, though for the parents who receive compensation it is hard to imagine they would have been better off in the tort system.

This complex pattern of institutional development corresponded with shifts in the politics of vaccine injury compensation. The shift in the mid-1980s from a tort system to the Compensation Program coincided with a change from a more fractious, internally divided politics to a quieter, more techno-cratic politics. This change seen in the case study is reflected in the change in the composition of congressional hearings on vaccine compensation before and after the adoption of VICP (see Table 5.1). The numbers are small, but the pattern is clear, and consistent with our large-n analyses presented in chapter 2.

Before the establishment of the Compensation Program, vaccine injury hearings featured witnesses from a greater variety of interests (5.5 on average) than after adoption (2.6). Business interests appeared in over 80% the hearings before adoption, whereas they appeared in 14% of hearings post-enactment.

Table 5.1 **Patterns of Congressional Testimony Before and After Enactment of VICP (compiled by the authors from CIS)**

Name	Pre-VICP	Post-VICP
Mean # of Group Types Participating	5.5	2.57
Conflict	1.00	.57
Business Participation Rates in Hearings[a]	.83	.14
Business Participation Rate Among All Groups[b]	.15	.06
Federal Official Participation Rates in Hearings[a]	.67	1.00
Federal Official Participation Rate Among All Groups[b]	.09	.39

Total Hearings: 6 adversarial legalism; 7 bureaucratic legalism.

Total Group Appearances: 33 adversarial legalism, 18 bureaucratic legalism.

[a] # of hearings group participated in/Total # of hearings.

[b] # of appearance in hearings by group/Total # of group appearances in hearings.

Federal government officials, meanwhile, became more prominent, appearing in 67% of the pre-adoption hearings but all of the post-adoption hearings (and accounting for nearly 40% of all group appearances). These hearings data suggest a politics that is much more centered on claimants and federal officials. The manufacturers do not show up—not because they have demobilized, but because they are satisfied with the program. Parents are unsatisfied, but they are represented.

The hearings, however, offer only a small window on the politics of vaccine compensation. We have shown that this politics takes place on many stages—on the floor of Congress, in state and federal courtrooms, and within the program itself. When we consider all these stages, the politics post-VICP looks much more polarized and pluralistic, including the battle in the popular culture and the debacle in Congress over the thimerosal amendment. Yet even so, the battle over vaccine injury compensation is in some respects contained. For all their differences—on the DPT vaccine, on the Table of Injuries, on thimerosal, on the science of vaccines, on the merits of the tort system—not even the most radical critical of the program in Congress, Dan Burton, has argued for abolishing it. That in itself represents a narrowing of differences. Anna Kirkland, one of the few social scientists who has studied vaccine injury politics, concludes that the program has served to defuse political tensions:

> While it often seems that no one is happy with the rulings of the vaccine court, it has functioned as a critical pressure release valve in vaccine law and politics. Its concessions that vaccines can have rare but terrible side effects have helped many families who would probably not have had strong cases in regular civil courts and prevented them from forming another arm of the anti-vaccine movement. Its extensive trial of autism claims provided a venue for airing a critical public debate and helped to bring it to a close (Kirkland 2014).

No public policy could possibly resolve the differences among parents, their lawyers, vaccine manufacturers, public health officials, and doctors over vaccines, but the Compensation Program has had the net effect of diminishing those differences rather than widening them.

Throughout our case studies we have treated the "political trajectory" of a policy field, the change in its politics over time, as a key variable. The political trajectory of adversarial legalism, at least as seen in the asbestos case, is toward increasing fragmentation of interests. The political trajectory of bureaucratic legalism, as documented in the SSDI case, is nearly the mirror opposite, with an intense and polarized conflict that diminishes over time. In the vaccine case one can observe both trajectories. As in the asbestos case, the vaccine case begins quietly with a series of lawsuits against particular manufacturers. The injuries are at first framed as the product of individual misdeeds—a company that fails to warn its workers about the dangers of asbestos, or produces an unsafe vaccine—and Congress does not become involved. But as the number of lawsuits increases, the social dimensions of the problem become apparent, and a debate ensues over who should be responsible for injuries and whether the government should be involved. In both the asbestos and the vaccine cases, efforts to replace tort with a bureaucratic alternative engendered intense and fractionalized interest group activity in Congress. Would-be asbestos reformers were unable to overcome this fractionalization, but in the vaccine case Henry Waxman took advantage of it to knit together a coalition of plaintiffs, defendants, and public health officials.

The result was the creation of a bureaucratic policy. Here begins the parallels to SSDI. In both cases, the creation of a bureaucratic program was hotly contested but, after creation, the politics became more subdued, with business interests largely withdrawing from the field. Further, in both cases there are attempts to retrench, and these attempts mobilize claimants to defend the program. The political outcomes of these fights differed, as SSDI beneficiaries have proven more effective than those seeking compensation for vaccine injuries, but the battle lines were similar. In the SSDI case claimants and administrators came to dominate a fairly quiet technocratic politics. The vaccine program has not settled down in this way, in part because of the rise of the thimerosal controversy, but also because claimants and administrators are at odds: the administrators are public health officials committed to vaccination who worry about negative publicity over purported vaccine injuries, but among the claimants and their representatives there is much more concern about the extent of injury and skepticism about the whole project of vaccination. The Compensation Program in many respects has quieted the politics of vaccine injuries, but it cannot resolve this fundamental divide.

What does the vaccine case say about standard accounts of the politics of adversarial legalism? In many ways, the story of vaccine injury politics suggests how normalized judicial politics is, the degree to which it is integrated with other modes of politics, and the extent to which actors can flip back and forth between judicial, legislative, and executive branch politics. From this perspective, the claim that courts and law can "crowd out" other forms of participation or act as "flypaper" for social movements and interest groups, pulling them away from more effective modes of political action, seems unfounded. Here the story is quite the reverse. First, litigation, far from a dead end, was an invaluable device for gaining the attention of legislators. It was only through an accumulation of lawsuits against the makers of DPT that pressure was applied to Congress to act. When the litigation became so intense that liability insurers dropped their coverage, the manufacturers threatened to get out of the business entirely, and the prospect of a public health crisis moved members of Congress to pay attention to an otherwise obscure problem. In the absence of the threat of litigation, it is hard to imagine that parents would have gotten Congress to take seriously their problem of paying for the services needed to raise sometimes severely disabled children. Nor did the parents' group, DPT, get trapped like flies in the flypaper of law. When the time came to make a pragmatic trade, in which parents would give up some of their ability to sue in Court, the main group that spoke for parents, DPT, was willing to forego some of their judicially created rights for the prospect of more certain compensation. True, the parents fought hard to retain the tort alternative, but in reading through testimony at hearings, statements made by the groups, and in interviewing one of the group leaders, Jeffrey Schwartz, we found that this was an entirely pragmatic strategy, grounded not in some metaphysics about rights, but about real distrust about the shape of the Compensation Program, and the need for an alternative mechanism as a failsafe.

The vaccine case, along with the earlier chapters, also casts doubt on the claim that law, courts, and rights are distinctively "path-dependent" so that, as in the flypaper metaphor, we may be stuck with adversarial policies that are suboptimal but cannot be escaped. Instead the case seems to illustrate the dynamism of common law, its ability to morph over time. The changes in product liability law that fostered the *Gottsdanker* case were path-breaking, as were the 1970s cases, *Reyes* and *Toner*. Even more striking, though, was the adoption of the Compensation Program, a transformation that is hard to square with claims of path dependency. The VICP broke with the tort system in many important respects, eliminating any kind of determination of fault, capping or eliminating damages, and socializing the cost of injuries through a surtax on vaccines. There are, of course, some continuities in vaccine injury compensation from *Gottsdanker* to *Bruesewitz*—vaccine claims are still handled through a type of disputing process, causation is still an issue in these proceedings, and claimants still retain a (greatly diminished) tort option—but we are struck much more by the discontinuities, the many ways in which policymakers broke new paths rather than following old ones.

Why was vaccine compensation not subject to increasing returns and path dependence? Partly perhaps because its path was never entirely clear. The doctrines governing vaccine litigation were ambiguous and varied from state to state and court to court. Nor was there, as in other areas of tort, a large body of lawyers making a living from vaccine litigation, and thus poised to oppose changes that might affect their livelihood. The VICP was created before the adversarial regime could get settled and institutionalized, so that the mechanisms of increasing returns never got established. Indeed if there is a case to be made for path dependence in this story, it is within the bureaucratic legalism of the Compensation Program, which has endured and resisted legislative change because the constituencies around it are stalemated, and cannot agree on even modest legislative reforms. In any event, the history of vaccine compensation certainly offers no reason to believe that adversarial legalism is any more path-dependent than bureaucratic legalism.

Finally, the argument that litigation produces a polarizing backlash that hinders coalition building found little support in this case. As with asbestos, business interests counter-mobilized against the surging costs of adversarial legalism, but they were far from unified in their resistance. Instead, adversarial legalism seemed to fragment interests, making the backlash productive: the fragmentation provided the raw material for Waxman's skillful political entrepreneurship, which culminated in a broad, albeit tenuous, coalition among plaintiff groups, a manufacturer and public health groups.

So does this case suggest that the politics associated with adversarial legalism is no different from that produced by other policy designs? Does it make no difference at all for politics whether vaccine compensation is administered through courts rather than executive agencies and legislatures? We do not think so. As with the cases of SSDI and asbestos, we are struck in this case by the ways in which adversarial legalism shapes both material interests and the interpretation of social life, and the effects this has on politics.

Here we return to the two primary mechanisms by which policy shapes politics in our cases, distributional effects and blame assignment. Consider first the distributional effects. Under adversarial legalism, plaintiffs and defendants were on their own, plaintiffs to try heroic tort lawsuits, defendants to guard against the tides of litigation, with uncertain and wildly varying outcomes for both sides. This seems to have had an effect on how the two sides mobilized politically. For the manufacturers, in the beginning the costs were low, and so there was little political mobilization in the 1960s and 70s.

As costs mounted in the 1980s and created uncertainty for manufacturers, they sought relief in Congress, but they were divided, in ways that tracked their differing material interests. In the 1980s Merck made the MMR vaccine, a relatively infrequent target of litigation, and was in the midst of developing a series of new vaccines for hepatitis B, chickenpox, and pneumonia. Lederle and Connaught, by contrast, came to the debate as makers of DPT vaccine, the subject of high and rising litigation. For Lederle and Connaught, stopping the flow of litigation was the primary objective, and any legislation that failed to guarantee this was defective. Merck might well have had a longer view, reasoning that if the Compensation Program proved successful, it would improve the liability climate for new vaccines, as it appears it has done.[41] Merck had less to lose if the program failed to eliminate litigation, and this appears to have shaped its political strategy.

Merck began a campaign for reform in 1975, well before the others, and it was always isolated in its approach. Even 12 years later, as Waxman was putting together financing for the Compensation Program, Merck could not get its fellow manufacturers to follow its position in support of a no-fault program that allowed parents to retain the option of filing in court. Lederle and Connaught, the two other main participants in the vaccine injury compensation debate, consistently and vociferously opposed the Compensation Program. There was no "industry position" on compensation issues; PHARMA, the industry association, did take a stand in favor of the Madigan reform bill, but that had no chance of being enacted in law, and outside of that position, PHARMA stayed away from congressional hearings on liability reform, leaving it mainly to Lederle, Connaught, and Merck.

Merck's endorsement was key to Waxman's coalition strategy, and the enactment of the Compensation Program. The adoption of the Compensation Program socialized the risks of liability for the manufacturers by creating a pooled compensation fund. This change in the distribution of costs seems associated with a change in the political behavior of the manufacturers. After the enactment of the Vaccine Injury Act they were both less active and less divided. This did not change even as the administration of the program grew more adversarial with the shift to more "off-Table" cases. As long as the costs of vaccine injury compensation were evenly distributed (and the program remained in surplus), manufacturers were content to let others fight over issues related to claim administration. Equally telling, when the thimerosal litigation raised the possibility of a return to tort, the highly pluralistic and contested politics of adversarial legalism returned, and manufacturers became more active. As with the earlier cases, the pattern of interest group politics seemed to mirror the distribution of costs.

The plaintiff side offers a somewhat more muddled story. From the 1960s through the early 1980s, we see no group mobilization of parents or others claiming to being affected by vaccine injuries. They either sued or "lumped it" and swallowed their grievances—and they did so apparently alone. On the rare occasions when Congress discussed vaccine liability issues, neither parents nor their lawyers were represented. That changed in 1982 with the organization of the parent group DPT, which was effective in its relations with Congress in part because (unlike the manufacturers) it presented a united front—there were no effective splinter groups. This seems surprising: the material interest of parents under adversarial legalism might be expected to vary, with those who had relatively strong legal cases, for example, having different interests from those who had no hope of getting anything out of tort litigation. In the asbestos case this difference among plaintiffs resulted in political splintering. The lack of (detectable) splintering in the vaccine case may be the result of the much greater uncertainty of winning a vaccine injury lawsuit. For even the best-situated plaintiffs, the prospect of compensation was dim at best. This uncertainty about litigation was probably helpful in organizing parents. In the adversarial legal regime no one counted on receiving anything, so all were united in looking for more from a compensation system. After the Compensation Program was enacted, parents and their lawyers remained highly mobilized, though often unhappy with the way the program has evolved. As in the SSDI case, claimant interests have stuck together to defend their interests.

Unlike the SSDI case, though, claimants are often in conflict with administrators. To a large extent this is because they disagree over the most fundamental issue, the extent of vaccine-caused injuries, which in turn affects differing views about blame assignment. Adversarial legalism is a system for assigning blame to individual actors, and as the asbestos case suggests, it can be difficult for reformers to reframe injuries as a social or governmental problem. For the administrators, and the larger public health community, vaccine injuries, to the extent they exist, are the unavoidable price paid for the social good of vaccination, so that it makes no sense to blame pharmaceutical companies for them. The groups that represented parents resisted reforms that eliminated the tort option in part because these changes took the vaccine manufacturers off the hook. The attempts by some parents to do an end-run around the Compensation Program were also at least partly motivated by the desire to hold manufacturers responsible for what the parents believed was their misdeeds. Yet at the crucial moment the parents' group, DPT, did sign on to a bureaucratic reform that partly socialized the injury compensation program ("partly" because it was funded by a tax on vaccines rather than general revenues). The adoption of bureaucratic legalism in this case tends to redefine vaccine injuries as arising from unavoidable social processes rather than corporate wrongdoing.

Conclusion

As with our previous cases, the story of vaccine compensation goes against many of the characterizations scholars make about adversarial legalism. Adversarial legalism did not kill vaccine injury politics; indeed it seemed to stimulate the organization and mobilization of interests. Vaccine litigation led to the organization of the parent group, DPT, and sent pharmaceutical companies to lobby Congress for intervention, setting the stage for legislation that transformed vaccine compensation. Adversarial legalism did not seem particularly prone to path dependence; the common law of vaccine injuries took all kinds of twists and turns. And while business certainly counter-mobilized against adversarial legalism in vaccine policy, the result was not polarization; it was more a case of factionalization, in which the various stakeholders for a time went in many different directions. In all these respects, adversarial legalism did not seem to generate a particularly unusual brand of politics.

But that does not mean that the politics of adversarial and bureaucratic legalism are the same, that policy design has no effect on politics. Adversarial legalism affects the distribution of costs and benefits, and the attribution of blame for injury, and this seems to have significant political effects. It tends to fragment interests, and makes it harder to reframe injuries as a social problem rather than the product of the sins of individuals. That offers many challenges to those who wish to reform adversarial policies, but as this chapter suggests, for skilled political entrepreneurs such as Henry Waxman there are opportunities as well.

The political trajectory of bureaucratic legalism, we have observed, is toward a calmer, more technocratic politics. That has not yet happened in vaccine compensation, in part because of some turns back to adversarial legalism. When the Table of Injuries was amended, and claims increasingly were handled "off-Table," creating a more adversarial disputing process, conflict between claimants and administrators intensified. Similarly, when claimants bypassed the program and brought thimerosal lawsuits, the threat of adversarial legalism remobilized manufacturers. These two shocks roiled all the arenas of vaccine injury politics in the "Bruesewitz era" from 1995 to 2011. Now they have been resolved, at least for the moment. Absent further shocks, the politics of vaccine injury, so ferocious in past years, may be headed for a quieter period centered on the expertise of health officials, with claimants and their representatives warily, often unhappily, looking on.

6

Conclusion

The Politics of the Litigation State

Judicialization, juridification, legalization, litigiousness: whatever term scholars and commentators use, they are intrigued by, as one book put it, "the global expansion of judicial power" (Tate and Vallinder 1995), and wish to understand its implications for politics and society. Our contention is that the best path to fuller understanding lies in comparison, both cross-sectional and longitudinal. We compared policies within the field of injury compensation that varied in their degree of adversarial legalism, first through a quantitative analysis, then through three case studies, focusing on patterns that emerged across cases, within cases, and over time.

Our quantitative analysis was, as is sometimes the case with such data, striking and deceptively simple. It suggested sharp and clear differences between the politics of adversarial legalism and the politics of bureaucratic legalism. The case studies, by contrast, reveal some of the conceptual and methodological difficulties involved in trying to sort out the consequences of employing litigation in public policy. They highlight the extraordinary, at times bewildering, complexity of the American litigation state, and the ubiquitous and protean role of litigation in American public policy. In our cases litigation took many different forms, from tort lawsuits against the makers of vaccines and asbestos-laced products, to administrative law challenges to the Social Security Administration and the Vaccine Injury Compensation Program (VICP), to claims in bankruptcy court. Indeed, litigation—for example, lawsuits challenging restrictive definitions of disability—was an important aspect even of our nominal control case, SSDI. The interweaving of litigation with legislation and executive rulemaking in each of our cases suggests the difficulties involved in separating out the consequences of litigation for politics, and so raises doubts about the enterprise of making grand claims about the politics of judicialization/juridification/legalization.

To address this problem, our approach moves away from considering the effects of particular lawsuits, legal doctrines, or lines of litigation on politics. Instead we take a more holistic approach, and consider how politics unfold in the shadow of two distinctive policy designs, adversarial legalism and bureaucratic legalism. A key advantage of this conceptual move, from our perspective, is its recognition that litigation can be important in both types of policies, but that its place in the policymaking process differs. In tort, our main example of adversarial legalism, litigation is the primary mechanism by which policy is created and implemented, whereas in social insurance, our example of bureaucratic legalism, legislatures and agencies generally take the leading role.[1] By comparing these different institutional arrangements—one is that relatively more court-centered and another that is more centered in agencies and legislatures—we can meaningfully engage the issues of whether and how "law" is different, while being careful to recognize that law and litigation serve important functions in many types of public policy.

Our approach stands in stark contrast to the dominant strands in the public law literature that have tended to separate out law and litigation from the rest of American politics. Much of this literature focuses on judicial voting behavior, especially at the Supreme Court level, and in the area of constitutional law. While this literature has yielded many insights into judicial decision-making, it has tended to divorce the study of law and courts from broader political processes and structures of authority (Shapiro 1994). The irony is that in an age in which courts reach into nearly every corner of our polity, the study of law, once at the heart of political science and American politics, has been marginalized. Our analysis seeks to push against this trend and to bring rights, courts, and litigation back into the mainstream of American political science.

This move builds on a long tradition of "political jurisprudence" scholarship, most importantly that of Martin Shapiro, and on themes in the law and society movement, exemplified by the early work of Stuart Scheingold; more recently we are influenced by the work of Robert Kagan, Martha Derthick, Shep Melnick, Michael McCann, Charles Epp, Malcolm Feeley, Edward Rubin and other authors who treat litigation as a form of policymaking that is distinct yet comparable to the activities of legislatures and executive agencies. If you are unfamiliar with this literature, you may, even having read our study, still find it strange that we treat tort law, which is not created by a legislature, implemented by agencies, or funded by taxes, as a public policy directly comparable to Social Security Disability Insurance. We remind you that all injury politics, indeed all redistributive politics, including the politics over tort law, is a struggle over the same core issues of who pays, how much, to whom, and who decides. Just as Congress holds hearings on the implementation of federal programs, it also holds hearings on the operation of the tort system. Moreover, as we have seen, a similar set of interest groups lobbies over the scope of tort law and other injury compensation programs, including claimant groups, businesses, and federal officials, though the patterns of their participation and engagement differ. So, even though tort law develops under a fog of legal jargon and specialized norms of professional reasoning, we believe that it is best understood as one of many distinct types of injury compensation policies in the United States.

Treating tort as a distinct type of injury compensation policy also aligns our work with recent scholarship on the American welfare state, which challenges an older account that characterized the American welfare state as limited or small (Hartz 1955; Lipsett 1996; Kingdon 1999).[2] Scholars now take a much broader view of what constitutes the welfare state and include mechanisms such as tax subsidies and regulated employer benefits. When we include this "welfare state nobody knows," as Christopher Howard (2008) puts it, we find that the aggregate size of the American welfare state is comparable to some of its European counterparts (Hacker 2002). What is different is the complex, layered structure of the American welfare state. In describing American disability policy, just one small corner of the American welfare system, historian Edward Berkowitz (1987: 1) notes a tangle of disjointed programs that are "born in many different eras [and] reflect many styles of policymaking." Our analysis builds on this literature, adding litigation to the grab bag of remedies underlying the American welfare state and to the possible sources of policy feedback in American politics.

Another parallel to the work of others, especially those working under the umbrella category of American Political Development, is our interest in tracing the historical path of policies and their politics as they move from periods of creation to expansion and attempted retrenchment (Orren and Skowronek 2004; see also Epp 2009). As noted in the opening chapter, this emphasis on the politics of developmental trajectories builds on Paul Pierson's argument (2004) that the politics of expanding welfare programs differs from the politics of retrenching them. We extend this idea by comparing the politics of creation, expansion, and retrenchment across different policy types. The result is a distinctive comparative developmental approach to understanding how policies shape politics, which we believe is particularly well suited for understanding the politics of increasingly layered and complex administrative states in economically advanced democracies.

Is the Politics of Adversarial Legalism Different?

We applied our comparative developmental approach to studying the politics of adversarial and bureaucratic policies in the field of injury compensation. We combined a quantitative analysis of 40 years of congressional hearings data with three process-tracing cases studies: (1) SSDI, a bureaucratic case, (2) asbestos injury compensation, an adversarial case, and (3) vaccine injury compensation, in which the policy wavered between adversarial legalism and bureaucratic legalism. Besides the comparisons we made between cases, we also made comparisons within cases. The SSDI case included a comparison to the Americans with Disabilities Act, an adversarial policy that, while not aimed at injury compensation, contrasted sharply with the bureaucratic approach to disability in SSDI. The asbestos case included an attempt to resolve chronic injury issues through federal workers' compensation reform, a policy that would have moved asbestos compensation in a bureaucratic direction. The vaccine case, finally, moves back and forth between adversarial and bureaucratic legalism. The combination of quantitative data, across-case comparisons, and within-case comparisons allows us to triangulate and so carefully probe claims about the political effects of using rights, courts, and litigation in public policy.

We find that the politics of adversarial legalism does differ from the politics of bureaucratic legalism, but not in some of the ways critics have suggested. In many respects the politics of adversarial and bureaucratic legalism were largely the same. In both there was conflict over the core issues in injury politics, including who decides, who pays, how much, and to whom, although the patterns of conflict differed over time. We were also struck in all of our cases by the degree to which stakeholders pressed their agendas in multiple forums, easily moving between different levels and branches of government and shifting gears from litigation to lobbying. On these dimensions, the imperatives of redistributive politics trumped any effect of policy design. Injury compensation politics involves transfers of money and how those transfers will be organized, and whatever the policy involved looks like, we should expect some commonalities across cases, especially given the high degree of mobilization among the contending stakeholders.

We observed, however, quite different political trajectories for adversarial injury compensation policies as compared to bureaucratic policies. In asbestos and vaccine litigation, the politics of adversarial legalism started in a decentralized way, in various courts whose decisions were not widely covered in the media and did not reach the congressional agenda. During this period, individual lawsuits were bitterly contested but there was little organized interest group conflict in Congress. If anything, the emergence of litigation encouraged Congress and interest groups to see the problems in terms of individual fault—the problem of a particular company—as opposed to a more systemic policy issue. This made the issue seem unworthy of a legislative solution, and made it easier for Congress to wait and see if the courts could resolve them. But when asbestos and vaccine litigation started to gain momentum, and the threat spread beyond a few individual defendants, alarm bells went off. A pluralistic and fractious interest group politics developed in Congress, reflecting the complex pattern of winners and losers in litigation.

SSDI had an inverse trajectory. Its creation was the most contentious stage, as well-organized interests on the left and right squared off against one another with bitter arguments about nearly every aspect of the policy. After the big bang of creation, though, a less-contested interest group politics developed around SSDI, with business interests receding; key members of Congress and experts adapted and expanded the program with encouragement from program beneficiaries. At politically opportune moments (particularly fiscal crises), there were attempts at retrenchment. Conflict over SSDI reemerged, but it tended to be narrower and less fragmented than at similar points in the trajectories of the asbestos and vaccine cases. In contrast to those cases, in which business interests were highly mobilized, in SSDI politics business participated sporadically. Another difference is that in the SSDI case claimants remained united against proposed cuts to the programs, whereas in our adversarial legalism cases we saw splintering among both plaintiffs and defendants.

These differences largely held up in our within-case comparisons. The politics around federal workers' compensation reform, which would have moved asbestos compensation in a more bureaucratic direction, looked nothing like the rest of the asbestos case. Federal workers' compensation politics was not fractious or chaotic; it was a clear-cut pitched battle between labor and business, very much like the struggle to enact SSDI. SSDI politics, in turn, was quite different from the politics around the ADA, an adversarial disability policy. The trajectory of ADA politics after enactment was toward increased rather than diminished conflict; the implementation of the law mobilized business groups for reform, but also disappointed disability organizations, and so the politics of the ADA never settled down as it did with SSDI.[3] In the vaccine case, increasing litigation created a fractious, chaotic politics, but the enactment of a bureaucratic compensation program began a period of narrowed conflict—at least until the thimerosal issue emerged, and litigation ramped up again. So even within each case, we see a correspondence between policy and politics.

Our findings raise questions about some of the standard arguments over the political costs of adversarial legalism. We found no evidence, for instance, that reliance on litigation crowded out other forms of advocacy or limited the types of demands made by claimant interests. In the asbestos case, claimant interests were able to pursue litigation and broad workers' compensation reforms simultaneously, while parents whose children fell ill after being vaccinated were able both to sue vaccine manufacturers and work with others to create a vaccine compensation program. Similarly, in the bureaucratic social insurance case, SSDI, beneficiaries skillfully combined lobbying and litigation to pursue changes to their program, while in the vaccine case parents and their lawyers were enormously creative in trying to find ways to revive adversarial legalism after it was ostensibly replaced by the VICP. In short, we find that, in a system where each branch of government can shape policy, and victory in any forum is uncertain, advocates fight in multiple forums using multiple forms of advocacy, whatever the structure of the underlying policy, bureaucratic or adversarial.

Nor did we find evidence that adversarial legalism was more path-dependent than bureaucratic legalism. On the "macrolevel" (Erkulwater 2006), the basic structures of both types of policies were institutionally sticky: asbestos litigation and SSDI persisted despite favorable circumstances for reform. On the more "microlevel," however, we were struck by the degree to which policies evolved, as asbestos litigation was constantly being remade by court-based tort reforms, the scope of SSDI's coverage was transformed by various reinterpretations of the core concept of "disability," and vaccine injury compensation switched from adversarial legalism to bureaucratic legalism to a hybrid. If anything, adversarial legalism seemed less path-dependent than bureaucratic legalism in our cases, reinforcing the idea that a strength of common law lies in its flexibility over time. These findings strongly resonate with the work of Shep Melnick (1986, 1994, 2004), who has persuasively shown the importance of litigation as a source of policy change in the absence of major reform legislation. They also add to the burgeoning literature on the evolution of modern welfare states in the absence of "big bang" formal legislative reform (e.g., Mahoney and Thelen 2010; Streeck and Thelen 2005; Hacker 2002, 2004; Thelen 2003; Schickler 2001; Clemens and Cook 1999).

Finally, we found little support in our cases for the idea that policy or legal change via adversarial legalism produces a polarizing backlash that hinders the creation of diverse coalitions. As one might expect, a proliferation of asbestos and vaccine lawsuits did generate strong counter-mobilization by business, and businesses remained far more mobilized in these cases than in our bureaucratic legalism case, SSDI. But the counter-mobilization to adversarial legalism was not a unified backlash; businesses divided depending on their exposure to litigation. These internal divisions enabled policy entrepreneurs like Henry Waxman and Arlen Specter to cobble together temporary reform coalitions between some plaintiff and defendant groups (see generally Melnick 1999). These coalitions did not guarantee the passage of reform, but they created a politics much more fluid than the backlash hypothesis suggests. Both the standard path dependence and backlash arguments miss the political contingency created by adversarial legalism: the fragmentation of stakeholder interests affords some opportunities to create reform coalitions among disgruntled plaintiff and defendant groups.

While most of the charges made against adversarial legalism find little support in our data, we did find evidence that by organizing social issues as discrete conflicts between individuals, adversarial legalism "individualizes" politics. Policy shapes politics in our cases through two mechanisms, *distributional effects* and the *blame assignment*. The distributional effect of adversarial legalism is to create unequal, unpredictable, and unstable costs and benefits. In our asbestos and vaccine case studies these costs and benefits divided defendant and sometimes plaintiff groups amongst themselves. Those who had lost out in court fought for reforms; those on the winning side sought to preserve the status quo. The effect was a chaotic, fractious politics in which social interests were divided from one another, though cross-stakeholder "strange bedfellows" alliances in favor of reform were also enabled.

The comparison to our bureaucratic case, SSDI, was striking. The creation of SSDI was deeply contested, as business groups and their conservative allies fought with unions and liberals over who should bear the costs of disability. But once in operation, SSDI had distributional effects that appeared to demobilize business interests. Because SSDI organized claims into a social insurance framework, it made costs relatively even and predictable. At a minimum this meant that the establishment of the program did not create competitive advantages and disadvantages among businesses, but it may have even allowed businesses to avoid the costs involved by passing them onto their employees. In any case, after SSDI was enacted, business groups took a less active role in the politics of the program, leaving beneficiaries and government officials to bargain over them. SSDI has had periods of sharp conflict over retrenchments, but business has not been an important player in those episodes, and for the most part SSDI politics has been technocratic and calm.

The vaccine case exemplifies the distributional effects of both adversarial and bureaucratic legalism. In the early period when vaccine injury lawsuits were gaining momentum, adversarial legalism threatened some vaccine makers but left others relatively free from worry. With their material interests so varied, the vaccine industry was divided on reforms. The enactment of the Vaccine Injury Act, with its surtax on all included vaccines, smoothed costs and so resolved the problems of all the vaccine makers; thereafter they did not participate in the hearings on congressional reforms of the Compensation Program. When, however, the threat of vaccine litigation emerged once again, the manufacturers that were most threatened lobbied Congress for relief. Each of the cases, then, is consistent with the general claim that policy creates politics in part through the ways in which it shapes material interests, as well as the more specific claim that adversarial legalism tends to divide interests from one another.

Injury compensation policy also affects blame assignment, and this in turn affects politics. In our cases, adversarial legalism's organizing of claims into private lawsuits focused blame on particular defendants—vaccine and asbestos makers—and this created a barrier to reform; opponents argued that socializing the cost of injury let the defendants off the hook. The bureaucratic policies, SSDI and the VICP, shifted politics away from questions of individual blameworthiness toward other concerns: need, deservingness, fiscal balance, and efficiency. The enactment of these policies seemed to settle the issue of social responsibility for injury—it was hard to find anyone who argued that either program should be dismantled—though there was continued conflict over the parameters of that responsibility.

In injury compensation the matter of blame assignment is perhaps particularly salient, but we think the contrast here between adversarial and bureaucratic policies likely reflects patterns that go well beyond our cases. Legal disputes typically involve a claim of the plaintiff that the defendant has done something improper, perhaps by not taking the proper care in manufacturing or labeling vaccines or fire-safe materials, or by discriminating against you because you are a person with a disability. There are examples of adversarial legal policies that do not involve blame (no-fault divorce, bankruptcy) but they seem marginal; for the most part the "adversarial" in adversarial legalism, its organization of social issues as dispute between parties, creates charges and countercharges about legal blameworthiness. Blameworthiness may be redefined, as we saw in the area of products liability law, which moved away from negligence, but there is almost always a focus on judging the conduct of individual actors.

Bureaucratic legalism, by contrast, often deemphasizes issues of blame. In our control case, SSDI, for example, there is no concern about why someone became disabled. If you shot yourself in the neck and paralyzed yourself, you would be just as eligible for SSDI as if you had acquired your injuries because your defective ladder broke and sent you tumbling to the ground. Similarly, if you apply to the VICP to pay for an injury, you need not make a claim that the vaccine manufacturer acted badly; the program's decision will not be based on culpability. This is not true for all kinds of bureaucratic legalism—a regulatory agency that enforces environmental laws, for example, certainly is assessing a kind of blameworthiness in its everyday operations. But note that the socialization of the problem of bureaucratic legalism still has an effect in this case: the company being penalized can claim that it is not guilty, but it cannot, as often happens in adversarial legalism, make countercharges about the other side or argue that the standards for blameworthiness should be reassessed. Moreover, for many types of bureaucratic policies involving taxes, subsidies, and grants, the issue of blame and fault never arises. The choice between an individual blame frame and the socialized frame that we saw in our cases is characteristic of many fields in which policymakers must choose between adversarial and bureaucratic designs. Our finding here is that this choice also has implications for politics, that the individualization of policy associated with adversarial legalism shapes subsequent political struggles.

Imagining policy alternatives in terms of individual fault versus societal problems brings us back to the criticisms of rights, courts, and litigation with which we began this book. The argument of critics of legal rights is that individualizing social problems is a terrible policy error based on a faulty understanding of society. It frames issues in terms of the fault of individual defendants and the particular situations of individual claimants rather than as social problems in which the whole society is implicated. From this perspective, the turn to adversarial legalism is a huge mistake, obscuring the broader social dimensions of a problem and potentially undermining solidarity among interests that should be working together. We can see this kind of claim in many other fields. In civil rights, it is the claim that trying to rectify inequalities through ferreting out individual acts of discrimination is a fool's errand, and that the life chances of oppressed groups (for example minorities, women, gays and lesbians, and people with disabilities) are much more likely to be improved through structural reforms (Freeman 1978; Tushnet 1984; Ford 2011; Roithmayr 2014). In environmental policy, it is the claim that punishing individual companies is much less effective and efficient in curbing pollution than systems of taxation and emissions trading. In poverty policy, it is the claim that policing the oppressors of the poor (landlords, payday loan lenders) is likely to be ineffective and that emphasis should be placed instead on direct support (Hazard 1971).

Of course, many might respond that it is the individualization of adversarial legalism that makes it so attractive. Locating social problems in the behavior of individuals or individual organizations gives us a tool of accountability and deterrence—we want to reduce the number of injuries by penalizing those who have caused them—and of upholding community morality, by demonstrating that those who violate social norms will be punished. The "fertile fear of liability," to use Charles Epp's evocative phrase (2009), can force stakeholders to rethink the status quo and push toward new policies. Our findings, if anything, add fire to this long-standing debate, by showing both sides that the policy choice between adversarial and bureaucratic designs can have fundamental political consequences. If you oppose the socialized approach of bureaucratic legalism, you might be particularly upset by the story of SSDI, which shows how the mechanisms of policy feedback protect such programs from attack. If you oppose the individualized approach, you might be particularly upset by the story of asbestos, which shows how reliance on litigation can undermine social solidarity and make it harder to build coalitions broad and stable enough to support comprehensive reform.

Implications

The academics who write about the effects of courts, rights, and litigation on politics are a diverse lot: law professors, political theorists, sociologists, Americanists, comparativists, and increasingly, scholars of international relations. In part because of that great diversity, the field abounds with interesting studies on widely varying substantive areas. At the same time, researchers often speak past each other rather than learning from one another's efforts. The proliferation of terms in this field is just one indication of the need for greater collaboration among scholars interested in studying the consequences of burgeoning judicial power. In the spirit of fostering such collaboration, it is worth thinking about how insights from our study, admittedly limited to the United States and to several cases within one policy field, might prove useful to researchers probing judicialization/ juridification/legalization in quite different contexts.

In our view, meaningful collaboration must begin with a frank acknowledgment that the study of judicialization's effects remains exploratory. This is understandable given the protean nature of judicialization, its growth in so many nooks and crannies of modern life, and the fact that we are just beginning to formulate concepts related to its apparent expansion in the United States and abroad. Given this state of knowledge, we decided to focus on cases that provide striking examples of our concepts and useful comparisons, recognizing that these cases are not generally representative. Tort law is in many ways the paradigmatic example of adversarial legalism, and the federal injury compensation programs, we believe, offer good illustrations of social insurance programs, classic examples of bureaucratic legalism. Moreover, asbestos litigation offers a particularly striking example of the policy trade-offs associated with using adversarial legalism as a mode of compensation; it has been enormously flexible and responsive to novel claims but also highly inefficient and unpredictable. The vaccine case, meanwhile, provides the rare instance of Congress replacing state tort law with a federal compensation program. By choosing these cases, we hoped to probe some of the underlying tilts and tendencies of different policy designs that might be hard to observe in cases with less striking features. So, we can think of our cases as a kind of engineer's stress test that seeks to reveal systemic tendencies that might be harder to observe in less extreme conditions.

The trade-off, of course, is that we worry about extrapolating from these findings. On the plus side, we are encouraged that some of our findings resonate with other studies that look at different policy areas using very different methods. For example, Michael McCann's in-depth research (1994) on activists within the pay equity movement also finds litigation did not crowd out other forms of advocacy or lock them into a legal mindset. Similarly, others have found that the political economy of adversarial legalism internally divides stakeholders, especially businesses (e.g., Melnick 1998; Epstein 1988; Leone 1986). Like us, Thomas M. Keck (2009) finds that the reaction to court decisions on gay marriage defies a simple backlash narrative, just as Alison Gash (2013) finds a complex set of reactions to the assertion of gay rights in the areas of marriage and adoption.

One important way in which our study is unusual is that it concerns common law rights and litigation. Much of the literature on judicialization/ juridification/legalization, both in the United States and around the globe, concerns constitutional law and the effects of judicial review on a policy field.

As we noted in chapter 1, claims about the path dependence of judicialized policies in such studies may be based more on the particular difficulties of amending constitutions, especially the U.S. Constitution, rather than any more general tendency of rights, courts, and litigation. But even in the special context of American federal judicial review, our study suggests several ways in which the path dependence claim might be more effectively analyzed. First, we would urge scholars to keep in mind the baseline of comparison. In our cases we certainly found instances of what looked like path dependence at work, in which the mechanisms of policy feedback prevailed over reform efforts: once asbestos litigation was established, Congress was unable to replace it despite strong policy reasons to do so and ostensibly favorable political circumstances. But the same was true of the bureaucratic programs we studied, SSDI and the VICP, whose basic structure endured despite powerful criticisms and occasional mobilization for reform. Indeed, overall there is a stronger case to be made for path dependency with the bureaucratic policies in our sample (SSDI, the VICP) than the adversarial policies (asbestos, vaccine product liability, and the ADA)—the adversarial policies took far more twists and turns and did not demonstrate the strong mechanisms of policy feedback, particularly unified interest group mobilization in defense of the status quo, characteristic of the bureaucratic policies.

Secondly, in assessing claims of path dependence, we would urge scholars to distinguish between macro-level and micro-level change as Erkulwater (2006) does in her study of the political resilience of SSDI. At the macro-level (or the basic structure of policies), change is unusual. The transformation in product liability law that helped to foster both vaccine and asbestos litigation, and the overhaul of vaccine compensation policy created by the Vaccine Injury Compensation Act, attract our attention precisely because they are atypical. The continuities in our bureaucratic cases, SSDI and VICP, whose basic structures have endured for more than 50 (SSDI) and 25 (VICP) years despite occasional political upheavals, seem to us just as significant. But all the policies in our sample, including SSDI and VICP, have changed in important ways since their first years, and so part of the methodological issue is to set a meaningful threshold for what counts as "off the path." We see the same issue in analyses of constitutional law, where precedents are rarely overruled, but often qualified, distinguished, or extended to new situations (Fisher 2004; Burke 2000–2001). The basic holding of *Roe v. Wade*, for example, remains in force, and this may be due to some of the mechanisms of policy feedback that produce path dependence. That said, *Roe's* doctrinal underpinnings have shifted, with great consequence—abortion regulations that were impossible before *Thornburgh v. Casey* are now taken for granted, a fundamental shift in abortion policy. So: Is the example of *Roe* evidence for the path dependence of constitutional law, or a case that goes against it? Researchers in the field have to be clear about the thresholds they use for making claims about path dependence.

Our study is unusual not only because it uses a common law field, tort, rather than constitutional law as the focus, but also because of certain properties of tort law and the social insurance alternatives to it. Because our cases concern injury compensation, they involve questions of material distribution, and this makes them different than many studies of judicialization/ juridification/legalization in significant respects. First, many analyses of judicialization do not focus on economics. The struggle over same-sex marriage, for example, certainly has material consequences; the right to marry includes rights to all kinds of governmental and non-governmental benefits. One could imagine a scenario in which business and other employer groups mobilize against same-sex marriage on these bases, but of course the focus instead has been on the cultural issues, and the opposition in the United States has come from conservative Christian groups. The distributional effects we have highlighted in our cases would not seem to have easy analogues for many of the issues—abortion and war powers (Silverstein 2009), school desegregation (Rosenberg 2008; Klarman 2004), school discipline (Arum 2005; Kirp and Jenson 1986), gender violence (Merry 2005)—on which scholars in this realm focus. We are tempted to turn this around and ask why so many studies of judicialization/juridification/legalization ignore economic issues, why do we not have more studies, for example, on the politics of property or contract or business or poverty law, to partly balance the focus in this field on human and civil rights. But another point here is that, even if there is no simple analogy to our finding about distributional effects, the primary mechanism—the relative unpredictability of adversarial legalism as compared to bureaucratic legalism—may shape politics in non-economic fields as well. The distributional effect, remember, is that adversarial legalism distributes costs and benefits in a relatively uneven and uncertain manner where bureaucratic legalism is relatively more even and predictable. The implementation of rights of other sorts through courts and litigation are also likely to be uneven and unpredictable, and this could have feedback effects on politics. When, for example, the Supreme Court strictly limits affirmative action in employment but gives more room for it in higher education, the politics of affirmative action is likely to be affected, as higher education interest groups are likely to take center stage while employers recede.

That said, it may be that the highly skewed and unpredictable distribution in our vaccine and asbestos cases brings to the fore some aspects of adversarial legalism that are less significant in other cases. In our one non-injury compensation case, the Americans with Disabilities Act, there was undoubtedly uneven consequences of implementation through litigation—plaintiffs with some forms of disability fared better than others (Swanson et al. 2011), and some industries were sued more widely than others—but it did not appear to fracture the alliances of disability or business groups who lobbied on ADA reform. In the asbestos case, before the scope of asbestos liability came into focus, business groups and their insurers maintained a unified front and cooperated in fighting the early suits. It was only when it became clear that asbestos liability could be devastating to companies that divisions within the business community emerged. Some issue areas where smaller stakes are involved, including injury compensation policies, may not generate the kind of highly fragmented politics we observed in our cases (see Barnes 1997). Further, even when adversarial legalism threatens to generate highly uneven results, there are mechanisms (such as insurance and mandatory arbitration of claims) that plaintiffs and especially defendants can use to insulate themselves from the uneven and uncertain distributional effects of adversarial legalism.[4]

The other mechanism we identified that shaped the politics in our cases, blame assignment, is more clearly applicable to a wide range of cases. Adversarial legalism, by organizing social issues as disputes between individual plaintiffs and defendants, frames them in ways that can shape politics. If asbestos or vaccine injuries result from the transgressions of individual companies, then there is no social responsibility for them, and no need to address them through a government program. Conversely, if disability or vaccine injuries are predictable social hazards, then government should address them in some way, and issues of fault are secondary. The "social construction of target populations" (Schneider and Ingram 1993), is particularly pronounced for adversarial legalism, tending to construct defendants as villains and plaintiffs as victims.

The extreme example is criminalization. Criminal law is adversarial, and criminalizing, say, the possession of marijuana, is an adversarial policy that is an alternative to other ways of combating the social and health effects of marijuana use. Less dramatically, lawsuits against polluters, or companies with a poor record of promoting women, or credit card companies that overcharge on fees, all construct the plaintiffs as victims and defendants as villains. These are, of course, just tendencies of adversarial legalism, not regularities. There are counterexamples; plaintiffs can be constructed as greedy whiners and defendants as victims of the legal system (Haltom and McCann 2004), or litigation may become so routinized that it no longer seems animated by issues of blame (Witt 2006). That said, we believe that the blame assignment effect is significant, and should be considered in any evaluation of the political effects of adversarial legalism. There is a model in this existing literature on how bureaucratic policies construct target populations. To take one example, Joe Soss (2002) finds that recipients of SSDI are constructed much more positively than those on AFDC, and this in turn has effects on the political behavior of recipients. There is a massive literature in sociology on the role that criminal law plays in the social construction of deviance (Gusfield 1967; Chambliss 1964). Aside from this, however, we have not seen a similar set of studies of adversarial policies in which the social construction effects of judicialization/juridification/legalization are evaluated. These are potentially important effects, and those seeking almost any policy aim, from racial or gender equality to consumer and worker safety to environmental health, the choice between adversarial and bureaucratic policies should include some thought as to the frames these policies generate.[5]

Teasing out the distributive and blame assignment mechanisms of adversarial legalism will require further cross-case comparison and longitudinal analysis. Our study focuses on cases in the United States, but there is no reason why a comparative developmental approach cannot be used to study judicialization/juridification/legalization in other countries. Indeed, Kagan's typology was originally designed to compare the American legal system with its counterparts abroad. Ran Hirschl's review of the comparative literature on judicialization distinguishes three spheres in which it operates: "the juridification of social relations," in which the language and routines of the law seep into social institutions; "the judicialization of public policy outcomes," which refers to the growing role of courts and litigation in public policy; and "the judicialization of mega-politics," which is the use of courts to resolve the grand conflicts that roil whole polities (Hirschl 2008). Our study seems most relevant to the second sphere, involving ordinary public policy, though it might have relevance to the other two as well. Particularly interesting is whether the tendency of adversarial legalism to individualize social issues has the same political effect in countries that have more communitarian political values, stronger political parties (and unions), and more corporatist structures. Stakeholder interests may be more cohesive and coordinated in other democracies and thus more likely to resist the politically fragmenting effects of adversarial legalism. In any event, we see no reason why the approach we have used here cannot be taken outside the borders of the United States.

We urge other scholars to take up the challenge of studying the political effects of judicialization/juridification/legalization both comparatively and developmentally, as we have done here. There is certainly no shortage of potential cases to study. Adversarial legalism is deeply engrained in contemporary American society (see Atiyah and Summers 1986; Melnick 1986, 1994; Barnes 1997; Kagan 2001; Burke 2002; Farhang 2010), and it appears to be growing around the world, if the use of labels such as "Eurolegalism" (Keleman 2011) the "legalization of world politics" (Goldstein et. al 2001) and "juristocracy" (Hirschl 2004) can be trusted. We have suggested that one consequence of this expansion is to individualize politics, that is, to divide social interests from one another, in a way that grows out of the individualization implicit in adversarial legalism, with its characteristic divisions between plaintiffs and defendants, winners and losers, victims and villains. The scale and complexity of the mechanisms by which rights, courts, and litigation operate in social life raises questions about the generalizability of these findings. Yet that scale and complexity is the reason the concerns probed in this book, which go back as far as critical commentaries on rights by Burke and Marx, are so important, and why the comparative developmental approach we have used here could be so useful in probing them.

Appendix I

Hearings Data

To identify our sample, we conducted general text searches of the CIS hearing summaries for the terms such as "tort or products liability," "black lung," and "SSDI or Social Security Disability," and culled through the results to identify hearings on compensation issues, generally meaning hearings that touched on questions involving who pays, how much, to whom, and who decides. The abstracts were coded along a variety of dimensions including: (a) total number of witnesses; (b) the diversity of stakeholder interests and group types that testified, meaning the range of constituencies that appeared at the hearings; and (c) the levels of conflict in the hearing testimony, meaning the extent to which the hearing reflected opposing viewpoints. In addition, we recorded a range of background variables such as the committee conducting the hearing, the date of the hearing and congressional session number, and whether the hearing involved a specific bill, budgetary matter, or information gathering. (Appendix II further describes the variables and their measures.)

To be useful, the coding of these data needs to be reliable, meaning it needs to reflect actual variation and not merely the idiosyncrasies of the coders. One of the authors and a research assistant did all of the coding. To test for reliability, the author independently coded a random sample of data coded by the research assistant, representing over 100 observations. An analysis of inter-coder agreement using Kappa suggests that had the cases been coded randomly (but with the probabilities equal to the overall proportion of cases), we would have expected agreement in about 52.91% percent of the cases. In fact, there was agreement in 95.31% of the cases, which is significantly above that which would be expected by chance (p > .00005). We also ran the Kappa test without weighting the results, so that *any* disagreement would be coded as total disagreement, even though some of the categories were non-dichotomous. Even using this very strict rule for coding agreement, our coding still proved reliable, as indicated by high levels of inter-coder consensus. After the Kappa tests were run, and we were confident that our measures were reliable, the author double-coded all the cases.

These data are, of course, far from perfect. For starters, they are observational, not experimental; the processes for selecting witnesses by committees are political, not random, and there is no public record of why or how witnesses are chosen. Moreover, groups that do participate are unlikely to represent all of their constituents perfectly and not all groups may participate through hearings (Strolovtich 2007). After all, there are back as well as front channels in Washington, and one could imagine groups that actively lobby members of Congress but do not testify publicly in hearings. Alternatively, groups might be active on a policy issue as a general matter, but believe their participation in a specific hearing would be fruitless, and hence voluntarily turned down an opportunity to testify. Conversely, groups may testify even though they are small, ephemeral, unrepresentative, and weak, reflecting superficial "Astroturf" political activity as opposed to meaningful action. Accordingly, participation in congressional hearings might provide a distorted picture of the politics of a given policy by either under- or over-counting the role of groups in the lawmaking process.

We believe these concerns are overstated. In theory, if we assume that members of Congress have limited time and resources for hearings, they would rationally engage in "fire alarm" oversight, and wait for interest groups to bring issues to their attention (Schwartz and McCubbins 1984). Once on the agenda, members of Congress would conduct hearings with an eye to learning more from the contending stakeholders. Moreover, as Jeffrey Berry argues (1999: 19), groups have strong incentives to testify, because testifying before Congress may legitimize participation in the policymaking process down the road; it may provide valuable public relations fodder for the group's newsletters and fund drives, and it may serve as a public platform for the group's leaders. In addition, as an empirical matter, groups indicate that they routinely testify before Congress. Kay Schlozman and John Tierney's survey of Washington lobbyists found that 99% of their respondents testified on Capitol Hill (1986: 150). From this vantage, although participation in hearings is probably not a reliable indicator of *influence* on Capitol Hill, it seems a reasonable lens for viewing interest group participation in federal lawmaking process (see Baumgartner and Jones 2002; Miller 2010).

Alternatively, if we assume that members of Congress use hearings cynically to create an illusion of broad participation in the legislative process, this bias should exist across policy areas, and all hearings should feature a range of interest groups, even if the final outcomes tend to favor particular interests. Under these assumptions, congressional testimony might provide a particularly difficult test for our underlying argument that the politics of adversarial legalism will significantly differ from those on bureaucratic legalism. In short, regardless of our assumptions about the nature of hearings, we believe that finding significantly different patterns of participation in congressional hearings on adversarial versus bureaucratic policies using the same data during the same time period is at least suggestive of variation in patterns of politics.

Model of Hearing Participation

There is no accepted theory of which groups are selected for hearing participation in Congress. However, a number of factors may plausibly affect interest group participation. Analytically, these variables can be divided into the following categories: (1) hearing type variables (2) committee-level variables, (3) Congress-level variables, and (4) congressional session/time. Each is discussed below.

Hearing type variables. Although there is little theory on why specific witnesses are called, it makes sense that different hearing attributes might affect the types of witnesses called. For example, not all hearings are substantively equivalent. As noted in chapter 2, we focused on three different types of hearings. We coded for hearings on specific reform proposals, which we expected to generate more participation, as one of the few regularities in politics is that people are more energetic about preserving benefits that they already have than seeking new ones. We also coded for hearings on yearly budgetary reviews and routine appropriation hearings, which we expected to generate less interest because the politics of policy change seem more likely to generate interest and conflict than the politics of policy maintenance (see generally Pierson 1994). Finally, we coded for oversight hearings in which Congress sought to gather information about problems related to court and agency practices. Common topics include the reasons for delays in processing lawsuits or claims, or the unintended policy consequences of the rising costs of claim adjudication. We controlled for these categories by coding each hearing as a dummy variable. (See Table AII.1) In the model, budgetary hearings were the omitted category.

Committee-level variables. It also makes sense that a variety of committee-level variables would potentially affect hearings, including (a) whether the committee is a House or Senate committee, as each chamber is organized differently and represents different types of constituencies; (b) the type and specific identity of the committee, on the theory that money committees that are responsible for balancing fiscal concerns might conduct different types of hearings than policy committees and that specific committees may have their own practices; (c) the party, seniority, and ideology of the

Table AII.1 Hearing Type Variables

Variable	Measure
Referral	0 if the hearing does not consider a specific bill or reform proposal concerning who pays, how much, to whom, or who decides; 1 if it does
Oversight	0 if the hearing considers a specific bill or is a routine budget hearing; 1 if the hearing focus on gathering information about court or agency practices related to injury compensation policy, such as issues related to the cost of resolving claims, delays in claim processing, problems in administration
Budgetary	0 if the hearing considers a specific bill or gathers information about agency or court practices; 1 if the hearing is on yearly appropriations

committee chair, on the theory that liberal and conservative chairs are likely to call different types of witnesses; (d) the party and ideology of the ranking member, on similar grounds; (e) the ideological distance of the chair from key players in the process, including the ranking member, the majority leader, the median voter in the chair's chamber, and the president, given that a chair who is ideologically alienated from the leadership and median voter of their chamber might conduct different types of hearings than those whose preferences align with those key players; and (f) the committee chair party's risk losing its majority (see generally Binder 1997; Farhang 2008), as we might expect that committee chairs whose majority is threatened might conduct hearings differently than those who anticipate retaining their positions. Table AII.2 summarizes these variables.

Congress-level Variables. Variables at the level of Congress might also potentially influence the conduct of hearings. Because this is not well theorized, we used a control for each session of Congress in our sample on the theory that this would represent the broadest possible control for variation in Congress. (It also doubled as a control for time.) In alternative models, we used more refined variables, including whether the Congress involved divided government, ideological distance between chambers, the distance between the chambers and the president, and the ratio of seats in Congress controlled by the party opposing the president. These variables are listed in Table AII.3.

Time Control Variables. A final issue concerns how to control for time, as the data span a period of 40 years. We used a variety of alternative measure to control for time: (a) congressional session; (b) year; (c) administration; (d) pre- and post-1994; and (e) the number of the session (1 through 40), this number squared, and then cubed Table AII.4.

Table AII.2 Committee-level Variables

Variable	Measure
House Committee	0 for Senate committees; 1 for House committees
Committee Type	0 for policy committees; 1 for money committees
Committee Name	Dummy variables for each committee in the sample
Chair Risk of Loss	Gains or losses as a proportion of total seats in the next election by the majority party in the relevant chamber
Chair Political Party	0 for GOP chair; 1 for Democratic chair
Chair Seniority	Cumulative number of years served as chair for a specific committee
Chair Ideology	Poole and Rosenthal's Common Space NOMINATE first dimension
Ranking Member Political Party	Common Space NOMINATE first dimension
Chair-Ranking Member Ideological Distance	Absolute value of the difference between Common Space NOMINATE first dimension scores of Chair and Ranking Member
Chair-Median Voter Distance	Absolute value of the difference between Common Space NOMINATE first dimension scores of Chair and Median Voter of relevant chamber
Chair-Chamber Leader Distance	Absolute value of the difference between Common Space NOMINATE first dimension scores of Chair and majority leader of relevant chamber
Chair-President Distance	Absolute value of the difference between Common Space NOMINATE first dimension scores of Chair and President

Note: All common space NOMINATE data were downloaded on July 25, 2011.

As noted in chapter 2, using these variables, we ran a number of alternative models using different combinations of controls. Our results with respect to the relationship between hearings of adversarial legalism and the number of group types were robust across the models and alternative specifications (see Table 2.5).

Table AII.3 Congress-level Variables

Variable	Measure
Congressional Session	Dummy variable for each congressional session in the sample
Divided Government	0 for undivided government; 1 for divided government
House-Senate Ideological Distance	Absolute value of the difference between CSN-1 scores of median voter of each chamber of Congress
Interbranch Conflict	Absolute value of the greatest difference between CSN-1 scores of median voter of each chamber of Congress and the President
Opposition Seat Ratio	Proportion of seats held by the party opposite the President averaged across chambers

Table AII.4 Time Control Variables

Variable	Measure
Congressional Session	Dummy variable for each congressional session in the sample
Year	Dummy variable for each year in the sample
Administration	Dummy variable for each presidential administration in the sample
Session Number, Session Number Squared and Cubed	Session number (1 through 40) and these numbers squared and cubed

Content Analysis of Interest Group Positions on the FAIR Act in the Media

To generate the content analysis of interest group positions taken in the media that was reported in chapter 4, we searched several publications including *CQ Weekly*, the *New York Times, Philadelphia Inquirer, Washington Post, Wall Street Journal*, and the *National Journal*, in addition to searching the LEXIS-NEXIS database for all major newspapers from January 2005 to January 2007. We searched using the terms "asbestos," "Congress," FAIR Act," "FAIR," and "Fairness in Asbestos Injury Resolution." In combing through these articles, we looked for reported support and opposition for the FAIR Act and cross-referenced these groups with their organizational websites. As a check on validity, we circulated the results to lobbyists who were familiar with the negotiations. Despite our best efforts, a few caveats are worth noting. First, the goal of the exercise was very modest. We were not trying to establish the universe of positions among all stakeholders or the intensity of their preferences, but only that there were conflicting views on the FAIR Act among various stakeholder groups. Thus, even though there was some disagreement about particular entries in Table 4.2 among the experts we consulted, there was little disagreement that the FAIR Act was divisive or that divisions existed within and across stakeholder groups. Second, some of the groups were described as fronts for individual interests and, as such, there may be some double counting in Table 4.2. The key point, however, remains: despite ostensible benefits to reform, interest groups remained remarkably divided on asbestos litigation reform.

Notes

CHAPTER 1

1. The quote comes from an interview with a man on public assistance, and was used by Sarat to summarize an aspect of the legal consciousness of poor people on welfare, but we think it equally appropriate as a summary of the role of law in American public policy.

2. Gerhard Teubner's analysis of the concept of "juridification" demonstrates the slew of ways in which the concept has been deployed in law and social science, most of which have little to do with comparing the work of courts and legislatures. Teubner, for example, approves Jurgen Habermas's use of the concept of juridification to mark the " 'constitutionalization' of the economic system," the growing use of purpose-oriented laws to regulate social life (Teubner 1987).

3. If you insist, for example, that a civil rights law like the Americans with Disabilities Act has been ineffective, is your comparison point some idealized agency-based policy that you imagine a legislature might have adopted instead, or just the conditions of people with disabilities before the ADA was adopted? On this point see Burke 1997.

4. Shapiro, for example, noted that judges are typically generalists, whereas agency officials tend to be specialists, and that courts often exercise negative power by striking down laws through judicial review as opposed to agencies, which shape policy through the promulgation of specific regulations (1968: 44).

5. We can think of our analysis as searching for patterns that are consistent across five types of comparisons: (1) cross-sectional comparisons of policies that feature different types of institutional structures (i.e., adversarial versus bureaucratic policies); (2) cross-sectional comparisons of policies that feature similar types of institutional structures but address different compensation areas (e.g., asbestos litigation, vaccine litigation, medical malpractice, product liability, and securities fraud litigation); (3) cross-sectional comparisons within policy areas where different policy types co-exist side-by-side (e.g., asbestos litigation and workers' compensation); (4) longitudinal comparisons across and within policies at different

stages of development (e.g., the politics of creating asbestos litigation versus the creation of SSDI or the politics of creating, expanding, and retrenching vaccine injury compensation); and (5) longitudinal comparisons within a policy where one type of regime replaced another (e.g., the vaccine compensation program and vaccine litigation).

6. U.S. v. Windsor, 570 U.S. _____ (2013) (Docket No. 12-307).

7. Ibid. (Scalia Dissent), pp. 25–26.

8. Commentators often decry judicial policymaking as inherently undemocratic and "counter-majoritarian," as Scalia did in *Windsor*. Our finding of intentionally shared policymaking powers adds to the long list of reasons for questioning simplistic arguments that judicial policymaking is necessarily less "democratic" than its legislative counterparts (see Barnes 2004; Friedman 2001, 1993; Whittington 2001; Peretti 1999; Feeley and Rubin 1998; Mishler and Sheenan 1993; Klarman 1994; Graber 1993; Rosenberg 1992). At its core, this argument—the so-called counter-majoritarian difficulty (Bickel 1962)—presupposes that the president and Congress are majoritarian and represent the "will of the People" simply by virtue of their elected status. Elections clearly matter in any democracy, but they do not guarantee majoritarian results, given low voter turnout, incumbency advantages, gerrymandering, unregulated campaign financing, and many other staple features of today's elections. Even if we accept that elections produce members of Congress that fairly represent the preferences of a majority of citizens in their districts or states (and effectively resist pressure from well-organized and wealthy groups)—a big "if"—no guarantee exists that a majority of lawmakers will be able to act given the large number of veto points in the American legislative process, including a host of supermajority requirements in the Senate. Conversely, majority rule legislative processes may not produce laws that reflect a clear majority preference of elected officials, much less concerns about public opinion; preferences cycle and votes can be manipulated (Arrow 1963; Shepsle 1992). Moreover, legislation can reflect a variety of motivations and purposes, some of which are plainly inconsistent with the majoritarian ideal, such as credit claiming, blaming shifting, and providing benefits to groups that can help officials get reelected (Mayhew 1974; Fiorina 1989; Arnold 1990). By the same token, federal judges are not heedless of public opinion simply because they are appointed for life (see, e.g., Mishler and Sheenan 1993; Marshall 1989; Feeley and Rubin 1998; Peretti 1999: 178–180 (collecting authority); Devins 2004). The question then is not whether judicial policymaking is *inherently* anti-democratic or counter-majoritarian; it is how reliance on litigation shapes the ongoing inter-branch colloquy on significant policy matters and whether it advances important democratic activities, such as broad political participation, coalition building among divergent interests, and deliberation within diversely representative branches and levels of government. That is why, in this book, we move beyond simplistic criticisms of judicial policymaking based on the counter-majoritarian difficulty and explore how adversarial legalism

shapes the underlying interest group politics that drive inter-branch relations over the making of policy.

9. See Powell (2006: 318), quoting Charles Evans Hughes, *Addresses of Charles Evans Hughes* 185 (1916). As Powell notes, Hughes did not literally believe that the Supreme Court controlled the meaning of the Constitution, and lived to regret the way the quotation was used.

10. We recognize that the term "mechanism" is deeply contested. In a thoughtful review, John Gerring (2010: 1500–1501) finds no less than ten definitions of mechanism in the relevant literature, some of which are contradictory. We have no desire to become bogged down in this debate, nor is it necessary to do so. In using the term "mechanism," we simply mean a pathway or link between an explanatory variable and an outcome, which is analogous to an intervening variable (see Weller and Barnes 2014; Gerring 2004, 2007).

CHAPTER 2

1. We are not alone in using congressional hearings data to probe patterns of political participation in public policy fields. Other scholars have used data drawn from CIS hearing abstracts in leading journal publications in both American politics and socio-legal studies (e.g., Sheingate 2006; Miller 2010).

2. One could argue that ATRA should be coded as a business group instead of falling under the "other" category. Because we believe that conservative public interest groups might have distinct perspectives on injury compensation programs, and, in fact, business groups were often split on issues related to tort reform, we coded it as a separate interest. Nevertheless, we coded it both ways in our sample and the results were nearly identical regardless of how we coded this particular group.

3. The coding of Judge Becker and Jeffrey Robinson's participation raised issues that illustrate some of the choices (and challenges) we confronted in coding these data. With respect to Judge Becker, the hearing abstract listed Becker as "Judge, U.S. Court of Appeals, Third Circuit," raising the question of whether he was testifying as a federal official representing the courts or as a legal expert explaining the bill. To decide this issue, we read his testimony, which focused on his explanation of many technical legal aspects of the bill that he helped craft. (Senator Cornyn called the legislative proposal under consideration the "Becker Bill" because of the Judge's role in writing it. Judiciary Committee, "Hearing on the Fairness in Asbestos Injury Resolution Act," 109th Cong., 1st Sess., January 11, 2005, 6.) Accordingly, we coded him as a legal expert. Similarly, the hearing abstract listed Robinson as "attorney, also Equitas Reinsurance Ltd., also Equitas, Ltd." Here, we had to decide whether to code him as counsel (and, if so, defense or claimant) or as another representative of insurance companies (whose testimony was redundant of other insurance representatives). Again, we turned to his testimony to make an assessment, which made it clear that he was a defense lawyer and a member

of a prominent law firm (and not general counsel of an insurance company). Moreover, unlike the other insurance representatives that testified to their general concerns about a federal asbestos injury compensation fund (such as that the bill's overall funding mechanisms be fair and that it provide certainty from future tort suits), Robinson focused on narrower issues about the representation on a commission that would determine contributions to the compensation fund from the perspective of his clients (foreign reinsurance companies). As such, his testimony added a distinct perspective to the hearings and we coded him as defense counsel. It should be added that close cases were coded both ways and that the alternative coding did not change our core findings. For more on our coding of these data, see Appendix I on the hearings data.

4. We expected our crude measure to be biased toward finding conflict, as the bar for finding conflict was set very low (a single set of reported opposing views on a key issue constituted conflict) and members of Congress may have incentives to create the appearance of vigorous debate in the process. Because this tends to diminish the range of the conflict variable, the bias toward conflict should tilt our conflict analysis *against* our finding of significant differences between the politics of adversarial and bureaucratic legalism.

5. The Nixon and Ford administrations were combined because there were no hearings on adversarial injury compensation programs during the Nixon Administration in our sample and hearings on bureaucratic policies featured similar levels of group type participation (2.30 under Nixon and 2.37 under Ford).

6. This is the political science corollary to Kahneman and Tversky's (1979) finding that people are risk-averse toward losses but risk-seeking toward gains.

7. We thank Sean Farhang, Keith Whittington, and Steve Wasby for pushing us to consider this issue in the hearings data. We take a much closer look at developmental dynamics in the case studies in Chapters 3–5.

8. In the model, budgetary hearings are the excluded category.

9. There are other types of committees, such as reelection committees, but our sample was divided among money committees and policy committees.

10. We thank Ann Crigler for suggesting this possibility.

11. As reported in Table 2.5 and discussed in Appendix II, we ran both Poisson, negative binomial and OLS regression analyses and a number of alternative specifications. Because the likelihood-ratio chi-square test for the dispersion parameter alpha was small and thus $p \geq .05$, we focus on the Poisson regression results. However, the results were nearly identical using both methods and alternative specifications.

12. Incidence rate ratios provide a change in rate of the dependent variable given a unit change in the key variable, holding others constant.

13. The concern is that just looking at participation rates at individual hearings could be misleading, because the number of hearings on bureaucratic legalism is more

than double that of adversarial legalism. For example, suppose that 100 different group types appear in 10 hearings on adversarial legalism and 20 hearings on
bureaucratic legalism collectively. At the level of all group types, the patterns of
participation would look the same: 100 different group types appeared in each
type of hearing. The patterns of their participation at the level of individual hearings, however, would look very different if 10 different witnesses testified in each
adversarial legalism hearing but only 5 appeared in each bureaucratic one: namely,
it would appear that the adversarial legalism hearings were twice as diverse. This is
why it was important to look at participation rates at the level of individual hearings *and* participation rates among all group appearances.

14. Recall that a group type appearance means that at least one representative of the
group appeared in the hearing. So, for example, if the Chamber of Commerce and
National Association of Manufacturers testified, this would count as one group
appearance for business groups. This coding helped correct for the situation in
which many witnesses would appear on behalf of a single group. For example, it
was not unusual for the hearings to feature a large panel of individual victims, not
all of whom would testify or who would testify as a group.

15. Specifically, we calculated a Herfindahl Index (also known as a
Herfindahl-Hirschmann Index or HHI) for our data, which economists and
anti-trust lawyers use to assess the amount of competition in markets. HHI is the
sum of the squares of the share of participation. Using this index of concentration,
the hearings on bureaucratic legalism scored 33%, while the hearings on adversarial
legal policies scored 25%. (We used decimals for the percentages instead of whole
numbers (i.e.,.0447 as opposed to 4.447), so that the scale would range from 0 to
100%.) Note that if participation was spread evenly among the five interests, so that
each accounted for 20% of the group appearances, the HHI would have been 20%
$[(.02)^2*5)]$. Conversely, if one group accounted for all of the appearances, the HHI
would have been 100% (1.00^2).

16. These numbers were calculated using the numbers in Figures 2.2 and 2.3. So, for
example, business stakeholder interests accounted for 35.88% of all group type
appearances. Business groups, such as the Chamber of Commerce, made up 11.29%
of all group type appearances and thus about 31% of all business stakeholder interest appearances (or 11.29%/35.88%).

17. The Nixon and Ford administrations were combined because there were no
hearings on adversarial legal injury compensation programs during the Nixon
Administration in our sample and hearings on bureaucratic legal policies featured
similar levels of conflict (.19 under Nixon and .26 under Ford).

18. More precisely, using odds ratios, moving from a hearing on bureaucratic policies
to adversarial policies more than doubles the likelihood of finding conflicting testimony in our sample.

19. The point is not that these interests perfectly represent their constituencies. As
the literature on intersectionality shows, members of multiple subgroups that

have been historically disadvantaged are less likely to be vigorously represented by broad public interest groups, even when the leaders of these groups are committed to doing so (e.g., Strolovich 2007). The point is that the well-organized interests and policy entrepreneurs in this area—ranging from Dick Armey's Tea Party-affiliated FreedomWorks to Ralph Nader—will reflect a diversity of viewpoints.

20. In addition to any substantive limitations of the hearings data, these data also face other, more generic limitations. One is that they are cross-sectional, offering lots of opportunities to compare patterns of participation across policy areas but relatively fewer opportunities to trace politics over time or make within-case comparisons (other than the vaccine and asbestos cases). This type of cross-sectional data is particularly vulnerable to arguments that other, unmeasured factors or processes are driving the results. Given all differences across the policy areas in our sample and the fact that cases of adversarial legalism center on state tort law while the cases of bureaucratic legalism center on federal programs, it is admittedly problematic to attribute all of the differences in participation to underlying institutional differences. This is precisely why we emphasize within-case comparisons in our case studies, which give us better leverage over this problem. Equally important, although we tried to control for some temporal and developmental aspects in our analysis of the hearings data, the case studies provide a much richer set of data to observe the politics of policies as they shift from creation to expansion and (attempted) retrenchment.

CHAPTER 3

1. Individuals who demonstrate they are disabled but don't have the work history receive Supplemental Security Income (SSI), a less generous benefit.

2. The tax is part of the Social Security tax, currently 12.4%. For wage workers, half the tax is paid by employers and half paid by employees.

3. SSDI is also the biggest of the U.S. disability compensation programs. SSI, a program for disabled and aged people without a qualifying work history, has about eight million recipients, and the veterans disability program has roughly four million recipients. *Social Security Administration, SSI Annual Statistical Report, 2012* (July 2013), Table 4, 21; *Department of Veterans Affairs, 2013 Performance and Accountability Report* (December 16, 2013), I-11.

4. Social Security Administration Office of Retirement and Disability Policy, *Annual Statistical Report on the Social Security Disability Insurance Program, 2012* (November 2013).

5. Social Security Administration, "Disability Insurance Trust Fund, 1957–2012," http://www.ssa.gov/oact/STATS/table4a2.html; Board of Trustees of the Federal Old-Age and Survivors Insurance and the Federal Disability Insurance Trust Funds, *2013 Annual Report*, 4. Congress can shore up the Disability

Insurance Trust Fund by reallocating a small portion of the 10.6% tax on wages currently financing the Old-Age Trust Fund. It has reallocated between the old age and disability programs on 11 occasions, the last in 1994 when the Disability Fund was close to depletion (Reno et al. 2013).

6. Senator Tom Coburn (R-OK) in 2012 expressed frustration with his colleagues' unwillingness to take an interest in SSDI. "Nobody wants to touch things where they can be criticized." Even Paul Ryan, the House Republican leader on budget issues, expressed little interest, noting that the program "is not a driver of our debt" (Faler 2012).

7. Advisory Council on Social Security, *Recommendations for Social Security Legislation: A Report to the Senate Committee on Finance from the Advisory Council on Social Security* (Washington: GPO, 1949): 71 (emphasis added).

8. U.S. House of Representatives, "Social Security Act Amendments of 1949, Part 2: Old-Age, Survivors and Disability Insurance," March 24–April 27, 1949, 1554.

9. Ibid. at 1555.

10. Ibid. at 1556.

11. Advisory Council on Social Security, 91.

12. Congressional Record, May 19, 1952, p. 5471–2.

13. U.S. Senate, Finance Committee, "Hearings on the Social Security Amendments of 1955," Part II: 649.

14. Ibid., 672.

15. Alvin David, remarks at "The Disability Program: Its Origins-Our Heritage, Its Future-Our Challenge," Social Security Administration Disability Symposium, Savannah, Georgia, January 21, 1993, accessed at: http://www.ssa.gov/history/dibforum93.html.

16. It should be added that Eisenhower was no stranger to vetoing legislation. During his administration, he vetoed 181 bills. This number was less than his immediate predecessors, President Franklin D. Roosevelt, who vetoed 635 bills, and Harry S. Truman, who vetoed 250 bills, but far more than any of his successors. Ronald Reagan vetoed the most bills in the post-Eisenhower era and he vetoed only 78 bills, less than half of Eisenhower's total. George W. Bush, by contrast, had a grand total of 12 vetoes (Peters 2013).

17. House Ways and Means Committee, Subcommittee on the Administration of Social Security Laws, "Hearings on the Social Security Amendments of 1960," March 11, 1960: 3.

18. House Subcommittee on the Administration of Social Security Laws, *Disability Insurance Fact Book* (Washington DC: Government Printing Office, 1959): 35–37, 58. The remaining 22,200 (1.5%) of the cases were pending, 11,400 at the reconsideration level and 10,800 at the ALJ hearing level.

19. "Hearings on Social Security Amendments of 1960": 11–12.

20. *20 CFR sec. 404.1501(d)* quoted in *Disability Insurance Fact Book*: 19.

21. "Disability and Social Security Booklet" quoted in *Disability Insurance Fact Book*: 34.

22. *Disability Insurance Fact Book*: 29.

23. "Hearings on Social Security Amendments of 1960": 21.

24. Ibid.

25. Ibid.

26. In 1960, the federal government contracted with 52 state jurisdictions; in four jurisdictions, there were separate agencies for providing benefits to blind people.

27. "Hearings on Social Security Amendments of 1960": 12.

28. *Annual Statistical Report on the Social Security Disability Insurance Program, 2010*, Table 3, page 20.

29. U.S. Senate, Committee on Finance, "Social Security Act Disability Program Amendments," October 9-10, 1979, 67.

30. Ibid. at 129.

31. Ibid., 135.

32. Ibid., 102–103.

33. Ibid., 149.

34. Ibid., 152.

35. A particularly prominent early example is Jacobus Ten Broek, a professor of law at UC-Berkeley who was blind. He wrote a widely cited 1966 essay on "The Disabled and the Law of Welfare" (ten Broek, 1966).

36. 42 USC 126.12021 (2)

37. 42 USC 126.12101.a.1.

38. 42 USC 126.12101.a.9.

39. *Board of Trustees, Federal Old Age and Survivors Insurance and Disability Trust Funds*, 1994 Annual Report, 15.

40. Perhaps for accounting reasons, Congress slightly shifted the reallocation over time. From 1994 to 1997 the DI portion of the tax was 1.88%, from 1997 to 2000 it was 1.7%, and from 2000 on it was 1.8%, the current rate. (PL 103–387 Sec 3a).

41. Testimony of Jane L. Ross, General Accounting Office, Senate Special Committee on Aging, "Problems in the Social Security Programs: The Disabling of America?" March 2, 1995, 40.

42. Ibid. A report by the National Academy of Social Insurance attributed the growth in SSDI primarily to the early 1990s recession and a reduction in people leaving the benefit rolls (Mashaw & Reno 1996: 34).

43. Testimony of Jane L. Ross, General Accounting Office, 40.

44. Ibid., 32.

45. Cohen held hearings, had his staff investigate the issue, and even produced a Washington Post op/ed on it, "Playing Social Security for a Sucker." *The Washington Post*, February 23, 1994, cited in Berkowitz and DeWitt (2013).

46. The law was signed by President Clinton, who emphasized another provision that made SSA an independent agency, a move prompted by concerns that the agency

had been too vulnerable to political influence in episodes like the disability review fiasco in the Reagan Administration.

47. U.S. House of Representatives, Subcommittee on Social Security, "Barriers Preventing Social Security Disability Recipients from Returning to Work," July 23 and 24, 1997: 47.

48. The pilot projects turned out to be a bust. In a 2004 report, the Governmental Accountability Office found that the pilot projects in the Ticket to Work law had been so poorly implemented by the SSA that they had little impact on efforts to improve the return to work rate of disability beneficiaries. See William R. Morton, "Ticket to Work and Self-Sufficiency Program: Overview and Current Issues," Congressional Research Service Report for Congress, September 13, 2013, available at https://www.fas.org/sgp/crs/misc/R41934.pdf.

49. For a particularly powerful argument on this point, see Paul Longmore's account of struggling to publish his dissertation because royalty payments might affect his disability benefits in an essay titled "Why I Burned My Book" (Longmore 2004).

50. See Stapleton et al. 2008, 213–214, who find an upper-bound estimate of impact of .1%, but say in their conclusion that the effect is "too small to detect with any degree of confidence" (237). Liu and Stapleton argue that the .5% figure is misleading, missing the large number of beneficiaries who work at some point after receiving an award, and severely underestimating the percentage who leave the program, which in their sample is closer to 4% (Liu and Stapleton 2010). Some of the limitations of Ticket to Work stem from problems with implementation, see General Accounting Office, *Ticket to Work Participation has Increased, but Additional Oversight Needed*, May 2011, available at http://www.gao.gov/assets/320/318098.pdf.

51. Social Security Administration, "Disabled Worker Beneficiary Statistics," *Selected Data From Social Security's Disability Program,* http://www.ssa.gov/oact/STATS/dibStat.html#fi.

52. Bernard Wixon and Alexander Strand, Social Security Administration Research and Statistics Note No. 2013-01 *Identifying SSA's Sequential Disability Determination Steps Using Administrative Data* (June 2013), available at http://www.ssa.gov/policy/docs/rsnotes/rsn2013-01.html.

53. Social Security Administration, *Outcomes of Applications for Disability Benefits,* Table 59 and 61, http://www.ssa.gov/policy/docs/statcomps/di_asr/2011/sect04.html. The acceptance rate has been dropping for several years; it was 56% in 2000.

54. The issue of waste in the program was also raised on the radio program "This American Life" in an episode entitled "Trends with Benefits, Act Two" *This American Life*, March 22, 2013, available at http://www.thisamericanlife.org/radio-archives/episode/490/trends-with-benefits?act=2.

55. For a summary of the results of the investigation, see Krent and Morris 2013.

56. U.S. Courts, *Federal Judicial Caseload Statistics*, Table B7, available at http://www.uscourts.gov/Statistics/FederalJudicialCaseloadStatistics/ FederalJudicialCaseloadStatistics2012.aspx.

57. Derthick (1990: 150) notes that through their handling of class action lawsuits judges have been able to get around some of SSA's control over acquiescence.

58. We used the same basic methodology for coding the ADA hearings as described in chapter 2. We performed a broad search for hearings that referred to the "Americans with Disabilities Act" and identified hearings related to its anti-discrimination provisions and/or litigation under the ADA (as opposed to, for instance, changes in communications technology that might improve access to the internet). We then coded participation by group types in the hearings using the categories described in chapter 2 and the related Appendices.

59. *Sutton v. United Air Lines*, 527 U.S. 471 (1999).

60. U.S. House of Representatives, Subcommittee on the Constitution, "ADA Notification Act," May 18, 2000.

CHAPTER 4

1. Much of the background for this chapter comes from Barnes (2011).

2. Employers and unions, in this view, both gave up some benefits in the tort system as a quid pro quo for the greater predictability promised by workers' compensation (Rodgers 1998: 245–250). The employers gave up the traditional tort defenses and agreed to pay for any accident arising out of employment, not simply those caused by the employers' negligence. The unions gave up the ability to collect larger damages, including pain and suffering payments, from the tort system. Fishback and Kantor (2000) capture the state-by-state jockeying by which the two big interests, employers and unions, designed a system geared to their respective interests, with insurance and trial lawyers also playing an important role. Some historians, by contrast, see the workers' compensation laws as an attempt by business interests to rein in juries, create a "captured" regulatory state, and forestall greater social regulation (Bellamy 1997; Weinstein 1981). Witt, in his wonderful account of the rise of workers' compensation, emphasizes the growing use of statistics and probabilistic thinking in its political appeal: if industrial accidentals were statistically predictable, then classical tort doctrines, which put the emphasis on fault, seemed beside the point. It became hard to justify denying benefits to workers, as the existing tort system often did (Witt 2004).

3. A 1988 study by the Workers Compensation Research Institute found that dueling attorneys were involved in all—100%—of permanent disability claims in New Jersey; 79% of these cases involved competing medical experts; and administrative fees gobbled up 46% of payments to claimants. (Not all states have the same track record. In Wisconsin, "functional impairment" claims generated 14%

administrative costs, dueling attorneys were involved in 32% of the cases, and competing doctors appeared in only 6% of cases (WCRI, 1988)).

4. For example, section 5952 of the California Labor Code, which governs the nation's largest workers' compensation programs provides as follows: "The review by the court shall not be extended further than to determine, based upon the entire record which shall be certified by the appeals board, whether: (a) The appeals board acted without or in excess of its powers, (b) The order, decision, or award was procured by fraud, (c) The order, decision, or award was unreasonable, (d) The order, decision, or award was not supported by substantial evidence, (e) If findings of fact are made, such findings of fact support the order, decision, or award under review. Nothing in this section shall permit the court to hold a trial de novo, to take evidence, or to exercise its independent judgment on the evidence."

5. Senate Subcommittee on Labor of the Committee on Labor and Public Welfare, "Hearings on Occupational Safety and Health Act, 1970, Part 2," 91st Cong., 2nd Sess., 1970, 1084.

6. Ibid. at 1083.

7. House Committee on Education and Labor, "Hearings on National Workers' Compensation Act of 1975," 94th Cong., 2nd Sess., 1976, 1389.

8. Ibid. at 1392.

9. Ibid. at 875.

10. Ibid. at 1399.

11. Ibid. at 668.

12. This condensed account of the Borel trial, the rise of asbestos litigation, and the costs of such litigation is drawn largely from Barnes (2011), *Borel v. Fibreboard Paper Products Corporation*, Paul Brodeur's *Outrageous Misconduct: The Asbestos Industry on Trial* (1986), and Donald Gifford's *Suing the Tobacco and Lead Pigment Industries* (2010).

13. *Restatement of the Law of Tort, Second Edition* (St. Paul, MN: American Law Institute Publishers, 1975), §402A.

14. Borel's case was filed in federal court under "diversity jurisdiction," which allows federal courts to hear cases under state law that involve parties from multiple states and involve a threshold amount of damages. This is how the federal courts came to interpret Texas's version of Section 402A.

15. Ward Stephenson himself died of cancer on September 7, 1973, three days before the Fifth Circuit officially handed down *Borel*. Fortunately, Stephenson reportedly learned of his victory before passing away (Brodeur 1986: 67).

16. In the mid-1980s, about decade after *Borel* and after plaintiff lawyers had uncovered evidence of deliberate concealment of the dangers of asbestos, several state court decisions abandoned the state of the art defense (*Beshada v. Johns-Manville Products Corp.*, 90 N.J. 191 (N.J. Sup. Ct. 1983); *Elmore v. Owens-Illinois, Inc.*, 673 S.W.2d 434 (Mo. Sup. Ct. 1984)).

17. House Committee on Education and Labor, "Hearings on Effect of Bankruptcy Cases of Several Companies on the Compensation of Asbestos Victims," 98th Cong., 1st Sess., 1983, 45 (hereinafter "1983 House Hearings").

18. Ibid. at 45.

19. It should be stressed that the treatment here is not exhaustive, as it could easily encompass other examples, including class-action lawsuits, group settlements, and the creation of defense consortiums, such as the Asbestos Claims Facility or the Center for Claims Resolution (see Hensler et al. 2000; Coffee 1995; Peterson 1990; Fitzpatrick 1990). It also could include efforts by judges, such as Judge Robert M. Parker, appointed in 1979 to the federal district court of the Eastern District of Texas, the home of the Golden Triangle, where Claude Tomplait and Clarence Borel worked as insulators, to streamline the process by the use of standing orders to regulate discovery, collateral estoppel, innovative trial practices, and multi-district litigation (Hensler et al. 1985; McGovern 1989; Schuck 1992; Hensler 2001; Behrens and Lopez 2005; Barnes 2007; see, e.g., *In re USG Corp.* 290 B.R. 223 (Bankr. D. Del. 2003); *Sophia v. Owens-Corning Fiberglass,* 601 N.W.2d 627 (Wis. 1999); *In re Report of the Advisory Group,* 1993 WL 30497 (D. Me. Feb 1, 1993); *Hardy v. Johns-Manville Sales Corporation,* 681 F.2d 334, 348–352 (5th Cir. 1982)).

20. See *Financial Statements and Report of the Manville Personal Injury Settlement Trust (Third Quarter 2013),* filed with the U.S. District Court, Eastern District of New York, October 30, 2013, page 2.

21. Interview with author on March 26, 2006. (Unless stated otherwise, all interviews for this study were conducted in confidentiality, and the names of interviewees have been withheld by mutual agreement.)

22. Senate Subcommittee on Courts and Administrative Practice of the Committee on the Judiciary, "Hearing on Need for Supplemental Permanent Injunctions in Bankruptcy," 103rd Cong., 1st Sess., 1993, 20).

23. Ibid. at 30.

24. Ibid. at 45.

25. Interview with author dated August 5, 2004.

26. Ibid.

27. Business groups did, however, continue to press (unsuccessfully) for more general federal reform of products liability law, such as the Uniform Products Liability Act.

28. House Committee on Education and Labor, "Hearings on Occupational Health Hazards Compensation Act of 1982," 97th Cong., 2nd Sess., 1982, 93.

29. 1983 House Hearings, 2.

30. White House Press Release, Transcript, December 15, 2004, 1.

31. Ibid.

32. White House Press Release, Transcript, January 7, 2005, 4.

33. It is notoriously difficult to interpret roll call votes. The final vote on the waiver may, in fact, not been as close as it seemed. One possibility is that some senators voted in favor of the waiver knowing that it would fail in order to gain favor

with the supporters of the FAIR Act, which included a number of senior members in leadership positions, including Majority Leader Frist. However, none of the interviewees for this project indicated that this was the case. To the contrary, they indicated that there was sincere support for the bill on both sides of the aisle.

34. Comments during asbestos conference in Northern California, February 10, 2004.

35. 1983 House Hearings, 45.

CHAPTER 5

1. The other four manufacturers of the polio vaccine at this time also struggled with this problem and one of them, Wyeth, produced lots that spread the disease, though on one-tenth the scale of Cutter (Offit 2005: 104).

2. Jeffrey Schwartz quoted this testimony when he testified before the U.S. House the following year in support of a new national compensation system. Testimony of Schwartz, U.S. House Subcommittee on Health and the Environment, *Vaccine Injury Compensation: Hearings on H.R. 5810*, 98th Cong., 2d sess., September 10, 1984, 81.

3. Gottsdanker eventually was able to use crutches and a brace to walk; when she reached her fifties she returned to using a wheelchair. She used some of the court award to pay for her education in college and graduate school, completed a Ph.D., and became a community college professor in California (Russell 2000).

4. *Gottsdanker v. Cutter Laboratories*, 182 Cal. App. 2d 602 (Cal. App. 1 Dist., July 12, 1960). The privity barrier for negligence claims had been knocked down in a famous earlier case, *MacPherson v. Buick Motor Co.*, 217 N.Y. 382, 111 N.E. 1050 (1916).

5. *Escola v. Coca Cola Bottling Co.*, 24 Cal.2d 453 (1944). Ms. Escola's lawyer was none other than Marvin Belli.

6. In *Stromsodt v. Parke Davis*, 257 F. Supp. 991 (1966), for example, a North Dakota family received a judgment of $500,000 for breach of warranty and failure to warn (Reitze 1985, 178).

7. *Reyes v. Wyeth*, 498 F.2d 1294 (1974), quoting *Helene Curtis Industries v. Pruitt*, 385 F.2d 862 (1968).

8. By mid-1985, more than 4,000 claims and 1500 lawsuits against the federal government had been filed. The government's payout in these claims and lawsuits was more than $83 million, nearly equaling the costs of the total cost of the swine flu vaccine program (Reitze 1985: 184–185; Levin and Sanger 2000: 59–61).

9. This is suggested by testimony from parents before the enactment of the VICP, and by the fact that after enactment, parents brought more than 4,000 claims for compensation for vaccine injuries suffered prior to 1988.

10. Testimony of Jeffrey Schwartz, *Vaccine Injury Compensation: Hearings on H.R. 5810*, September 10, 1984, 112–114.

11. Comment k provides that:

There are some products which, in the present state of human knowledge, are quite incapable of being made safe for their intended and ordinary use. These are especially common in the field of drugs. An outstanding example is the vaccine for the Pasteur treatment of rabies, which not uncommonly leads to very serious and damaging consequences when it is injected. Since the disease itself invariably leads to a dreadful death, both the marketing and use of the vaccine are fully justified, notwithstanding the unavoidable high degree of risk which they involve. Such a product, properly prepared, and accompanied by proper direction and warning, is not defective, nor is it unreasonably dangerous. The same is true of many other drugs, vaccines, and the like, many of which for this very reason cannot legally be sold except to physicians, or under the prescription of a physician. It is also true of many new or experimental drugs as to which, because of lack of time and opportunity for sufficient medical experience, there can be no assurance of safety, or perhaps even the purity of ingredients, but such experience as there is justifies the marketing and use of the drug notwithstanding a medically recognizable risk. The seller of such products, again with a qualification that they are properly prepared and marketed, and proper warning is given, when the situation calls for it, is not to be he held to strict liability for unfortunate consequences attending their use, merely because he has undertaken to supply the public with an apparently useful and desirable product, attended with a known but apparently reasonable risk. *Restatement (Second) of Torts* 402A comment k (1965).

12. *Kearl v. Lederle Laboratories*, 172 Cal. App. 3d 812, 218 Cal. Rptr. 453 (1985).

13. *Toner v. Lederle Laboratories*, 828 F.2d 510 (1987).

14. *Johnson v. American Cyanamid Co.*, 718 P.2d 1318 (1986).

15. Testimony of Douglas MacMaster, President, Merck Sharp and Dohme Division, Merck & Co., U.S. House of Representatives, Subcommittee on Select Revenue Measures, *Funding of the Childhood Vaccine Program*, March 5, 1987, 91.

16. Testimony of William H. Foege, Director, Centers for Disease Control, U.S. Senate Subcommittee on Departments Labor and Health, Education, and Welfare and Related Agencies, *Black Lung Supplemental and Oversight of HEW Positions*, May 9, 1978, 30–50.

17. A search for congressional hearings on the subject of "vaccines and vaccination" using the Proquest (formerly CIS) database found 112 between 1950 and 1984. Adding the term "liability" found 10 hearings dealing with liability issues surrounding vaccination. In these 10 hearings, no representative of families of vaccine injured children or of plaintiff lawyers suing for vaccine injuries appeared. Witnesses from the public interest group Public Citizen appeared on two occasions and at one point did discuss the need for adequate compensation.

18. *See also* Statement of Robert Johnson, President, Lederle Laboratories Division, American Cyanamid, U.S. House Subcommittee on Health and the Environment, *Vaccine Injury Compensation: Hearings on H.R. 5810*, 99th Cong., 2d sess., July 25, 1986, 233.

19. Statement of John E. Lyons, Executive Vice President, Merck and Company, U.S. House Subcommittee on Health and the Environment, *Vaccine Injury Compensation: Hearings on H.R. 1780, H.R. 4777, and H.R. 5184*, 99th Cong., 2d sess., July 25, 1986, 220–230.

20. Statement by Lederle Laboratories, U.S. House Subcommittee on Health and the Environment, *Vaccine Injury Compensation: Hearings on H.R. 5810*, 99th Cong., 2d sess., September 10, 1984, 240–247.

21. Connaught Laboratories, "Position Paper: National Childhood Vaccine Injury Compensation Act of 1986: H.R. 5184," reproduced in U.S. House Subcommittee on Health and the Environment, *Vaccine Injury Compensation: Hearings on H.R. 1780, H.R. 4777, and H.R. 5184*, 99th Cong., 2d sess., July 25, 1986, 262–263.

22. The bill, for example, contained a provision favored by Senator Hatch and the Reagan Administration that allowed drug companies to sell drugs abroad without obtaining FDA approval. Senator Howard Metzenbaum (D-OH) opposed that measure, so to placate him the bill included an Alzheimer's disease initiative he had championed. As a further gift to the Reagan Administration, the bill included a provision repealing a federal health planning law despised by conservatives.

23. John R. Bolton to James C. Miller III, October 31, 1986, HE A11 subject file, Ronald Reagan National Library.

24. Peter J. Wallison to Donald T. Regan, November 3, 1986, HE A11 subject file, Ronald Reagan National Library.

25. National Vaccine Injury Compensation Program, "Statistics Report," http://www.hrsa.gov/vaccinecompensation/statisticsreport.pdf, accessed May 14, 2014. The program also paid out nearly $200 million in attorney's fees and costs, both in cases in which claims were compensated and those in which they were denied.

26. Ibid.

27. U.S. House of Representatives Subcommittee on Criminal Justice, Drug Policy, and Human Resources, *Compensating Vaccine Injuries: Are Reforms Needed?* September 28, 1999; U.S. House of Representatives Committee on Government Reform, *The National Vaccine Injury Program: Is It Working as Congress Intended?* November 1 & December 12, 2001.

28. Barbara Loe Fisher, "The Vaccine Injury Compensation Program: A Failed Experiment in Tort Reform?," Statement to the Advisory Commission on Childhood Vaccines, November 18, 2008, available at: http://www.nvic.org/injury-compensation/vaccineinjury.aspx.

29. U.S. House of Representatives Subcommittee on Criminal Justice, Drug Policy, and Human Resources, *Compensating Vaccine Injuries: Are Reforms Needed?* September 28, 1999; U.S. House of Representatives Committee on Government Reform, *The National Vaccine Injury Program: Is It Working as Congress Intended?* November 1 & December 12, 2001.

30. Interview with Dan Burton, U.S. House of Representatives, July 21, 2011, Washington DC.

31. The 1999 GAO report observed that HHS officials interpreted the Vaccine Injury Compensation Act to recognize Table injuries only where there is a definitive link between the vaccine and the injury, but "others cite the same legislative history as directing that, until definitive information is available, the benefit of the doubt should remain with the petitioner." The report noted that HHS hadn't uniformly followed the Institute of Medicine's findings, declining to add injuries where the Institute had reported some evidence of a vaccine linkage. U.S. General Accounting Office, *Vaccine Injury Compensation*, 15–16.

32. The case of Hannah Poling, an autistic child who was awarded compensation based on the theory that thimerosal aggravated an underlying disorder, was widely cited by proponents of the vaccine-autism link (Wallis 2008).

33. Interview with Tawny Buck, former parent representative to Advisory Commission on Childhood Vaccines, representative to National Vaccine Advisory Committee, via phone, October 15, 2011.

34. *Bruesewitz v. Wyeth,* 562 U.S. ____ (2011) (Docket No. 09-152).

35. Brief for Respondent-Appellee at 21, *Bruesewitz v. Wyeth*, 562 U.S. ____ (2011), July 23, 2010.

36. The Bruesewitzes also sued Wyeth alleging that there was a defect in the manufacture of the vaccine given to Hannah, and for Wyeth's allege failure to warn them of the dangers of the DPT vaccine, but these claims were dismissed.

37. *Bruesewtiz v. Wyeth*, 526 U.S. _____ (2011), (Docket No. 09-152) (Scalia majority opinion), p. 15.

38. Ibid. (Breyer Concurrence), p. 5.

39. Ibid. (Sotomayor Dissent), p. 26.

40. In contrast, two vaccine compensation programs established during the Bush Administration, governing the smallpox and H1N1 vaccines, are purely administrative, delegating to the Health and Human Services decision-making on individual claims, and shielding them from judicial review.

41. In the 1990s the head of Merck's vaccine unit called it the "best time" for vaccine research in decades, in part because of the improved liability climate (Tanouye 1998). By 2011, Merck was making 14 of the 17 vaccines the CDC recommends for children (Timmerman, 2011). Finkelstein (2004) found the VICP was associated with an increase in the number of clinical trials but not with more fundamental pre-clinical research.

CHAPTER 6

1. We also examined briefly the Americans with Disabilities Act, an adversarial policy created by a legislature. Many adversarial policies are legislature-created, and even common law policies such as tort are subject to legislative reform.

2. Terminology here is tricky. The concept of the "welfare state" is contested and different scholars have used different terms to describe the bundle of public programs and private benefits that comprise social benefits spending. Espring-Anderson, for example, uses the term "welfare-state regime"; Hacker uses "welfare regime"; and others just the "private welfare state." We use the familiar term "welfare state," while recognizing the alternatives.

3. It remains to be seen whether the enactment of the ADA Amendments Act (2008) will result in diminished conflict.

4. Witt argues that for "mature torts," personal injury lawsuits that have become routine, like litigation over car crashes, what on the surface is an adversarial system is in fact a bureaucratic system (Witt 2006). At least in theory, if an area of litigation becomes so highly predictable that it is dominated by settlement, it should merge into bureaucratic legalism.

5. Does participation in adversarial policies, for example, lead citizens to become more active and engaged citizens? Soss observes that SSDI "does not engage clients as active decision makers" (2002: 194), echoing the concerns of disability activists that SSDI can pacify recipients. Bringing an ADA discrimination lawsuit or a vaccine injury lawsuit would seem to be more activating, while being included in a class action asbestos lawsuit in the 1990s would seem less so, though we lack data on how participation in litigation shapes political behavior at the individual claimant level.

Works Cited

Abel, Richard. 1987. "The Real Tort Crisis: Too Few Claims." *Ohio State Law Journal* 48:443–467.

Abelson, Alan. 2002. "All the Rage." *Barron's*, January 28.

Alter, Karen. 2001. *Establishing the Supremacy of European Law: The Making of an International Rule of Law in Europe.* Oxford: Oxford University Press.

Arnold, R. Douglas. 1990. *The Logic of Congressional Action.* New Haven, CT: Yale University Press.

Arrow, Kenneth. 1963. *Social Choice and Individual Values.* New Haven, CT: Yale University Press.

Atiyah, Patrick Selim, and Robert S. Summers. 1987. *Form and Substance in Anglo-American Law: A Comparative Study of Legal Reasoning, Legal Theory, and Legal Institutions.* New York: Oxford University Press.

Ausness, Richard C. 1994. "Tort Liability for Asbestos Removal." *Oregon Law Review* 73:505–550.

Austern, David. 2001. *Memorandum to Manville Trust Claimants.* Fairfax, VA: Claims Management Trust.

Autor, David H. 2011. *The Unsustainable Rise of the Disability Rolls in the United States: Causes, Consequences, and Policy Options.* No. 17697. Cambridge, MA: National Bureau of Economic Research.

Autor, David, and Mark Duggan. 2006. *The Growth in the Social Security Disability Rolls: A Fiscal Crisis Unfolding.* No. 12436. Cambridge, MA: National Bureau of Economic Research.

Autor, David H., and Mark G. Duggan. 2003. "The Rise in the Disability Rolls and the Decline in Unemployment." *The Quarterly Journal of Economics* 118(1):157–206.

Bagenstos, Samuel R. 2003. "The Americans with Disabilities Act as Welfare Reform." *William & Mary Law Review* 44: 921–1027.

Bagenstos, Samuel. 2009. *Law and the Contradictions of the Disability Rights Movement.* New Haven: Yale University Press.

Bardach, Eugene, and Robert A. Kagan. 1982. *Going by the Book: The Problem of Regulatory Unreasonableness.* Philadelphia: Temple University Press.

———. 1986. *Regulatory Justice*. New York: Basic Books.

Barnes, Jeb. 1997. "Bankrupt Bargain? Bankruptcy Reform and the Politics of Adversarial Legalism." *Journal of Law and Politics* 13(4):893–934.

———. 2004. *Overruled? Legislative Overrides, Pluralism and Contemporary Court-Congress Relations*. Palo Alto, CA: Stanford University Press.

———. 2007a. "Bringing the Courts Back In: Interbranch Perspectives on the Role of Courts in American Politics and Policy Making." *Annual Review of Political Science* 10:25–43.

———. 2007b. "Rethinking the Landscape of Tort Reform: Lessons from the Asbestos Case." *Justice Systems Journal* 28(2):157–181.

———. 2009. "In Defense of Asbestos Litigation: Rethinking Legal Process Analysis in a World of Uncertainty, Second Bests, and Shared Policy-Making Responsibility." *Law & Social Inquiry* 34(1):5–29.

———. 2011. *Dust-Up: Asbestos Litigation and the Failure of Commonsense Policy Reform*. Washington, DC: Georgetown University Press.

———. 2013. "National Interbranch Politics in the United States." In Rick Valelly (ed.), *Oxford Bibliographies in Political Science*. New York: Oxford University Press. Available at www.oxfordbibliographies.com.

Barnes, Jeb, and Thomas F. Burke. 2006. "The Diffusion of Rights: From Law on the Books to Organization Rights Practices." *Law & Society Review* 40(3):493–524.

———. 2012. "Making Way: Legal Mobilization, Organizational Response, and Wheelchair Access." *Law & Society Review* 46(1):167–198.

Baumgartner, Frank, and Bryan Jones. 2002. *Policy Dynamics*. Chicago: University of Chicago Press.

Baynes, Kenneth. 2000. "Rights as Critique and the Critique of Rights: Karl Marx, Wendy Brown, and the Social Function of Rights." *Political Theory*, 28(4):451–468.

Behrens, Mark Al., and Manuel Lopez. 2005. "Unimpaired Dockets: Are They Constitutional?" *Review of Litigation* 24:253–299.

Bell, Peter, and Jeffrey O'Connell. 1997. *Accidental Justice: The Dilemmas of Tort Law*. New Haven, CT: Yale University Press.

Bellamy, Paul B. 1997. *A History of Workmen's Compensation, 1898–1915: From Courtroom to Boardroom*. New York: Garland Publishing.

Berkowitz, Edward D. 1987. *Disabled Policy: America's Programs for the Handicapped*. New York: Cambridge University Press.

Berkowitz, Edward D., and Larry DeWitt. 2013. *The Other Welfare: Supplemental Security Income and US Social Policy*. Ithaca, NY: Cornell University Press.

Berkowitz, Edward, and Kim McQuaid, 1980. "Welfare Reform in the 1950s." *The Social Service Review* 54(1):45–58.

Berry, Jeffrey M. 1999. *The New Liberalism: The Rising Power of Citizen Groups*. Washington, DC: Brookings Institution.

Bhagavatula, Raji, Rebecca Moody, and Jason Russ. 2001. "Asbestos: A Moving Target." *Best's Review*, September 1, 85–90.

Bickel, Alexander. 1962. *The Least Dangerous Branch: The Supreme Court at the Bar of Politics*. Indianapolis, IN: Bobbs-Merrill.

Bignami, Francesca. 2011. "Cooperative Legalism and the Non-Americanization of European Regulatory Styles: The Case of Data Privacy." *American Journal of Comparative Law* 59(2):411–461.

Binder, Sarah. 1997. *Minority Rights, Majority Rule: Partisanship and the Development of Congress*. New York: Cambridge University Press.

Board of Trustees, Federal Old-Age and Survivors Insurance and Disability Insurance Trust Funds. 2005. *2005 Annual Report*. Washington DC: Government Printing Office.

Bogus, Carl T. 2001. *Why Lawsuits Are Good for America: Disciplined Democracy, Big Business, and Common Law*. New York: New York University Press.

Bowe, Frank. 1978. *Handicapping America: Barriers to Disabled People*. New York: Harper and Row.

Bowker, Michael. 2003. *Fatal Deception: The Untold Story of Asbestos: Why It Is Still Legal and Still Killing Us*. New York: Rodale.

Brodeur, Paul. 1986. *Outrageous Misconduct: The Asbestos Industry on Trial*. New York: Pantheon Books.

Brown, Wendy. 1995. *States of Injury: Power and Freedom in Late Modernity*. Princeton, NJ: Princeton University Press.

Bumiller, Kristin. 1988. *The Civil Rights Society: The Social Construction of Victims*. Baltimore, MD: Johns Hopkins University Press.

Burke, Edmund, and J. G. A. Pocock. 1987. *Reflections on the Revolution in France*. Indianapolis, IN: Hackett Pub. Co.

Burke, Thomas F. 1997. "On the Rights Track: The Americans with Disabilities Act." In Pietro Nivola (ed.), *Comparative Disadvantages? Social Regulations and the Global Economy*. Washington D.C: Brookings Institution Press, 242–318.

———. 2001. "The Rights Revolution Continues: Why New Rights are Born (and Old Rights Rarely Die)." *University of Connecticut Law Review* 33(4):1259–1274.

———. 2002. *Lawyers, Lawsuits, and Legal Rights: The Battle over Litigation in American Society*. Berkeley: University of California Press.

Burke, Thomas F., and Jeb Barnes. 2009. "Is There an Empirical Literature on Rights?" *Studies in Law, Politics, and Society* 48:69–92.

Campbell, Andrea Louise. 2003. *How Policies Make Citizens: Senior Political Activism and the American Welfare State*. Princeton, NJ: Princeton University Press.

———. 2006. "Policy Feedbacks and the Political Mobilization of Mass Publics" (unpublished manuscript on file with the authors).

———. 2012. "Policy Makes Mass Politics." *Annual Review of Political Science* 15:333–351.

Campbell, Thomas J., Daniel P. Kessler, and George B. Shepherd. 1995. *The Causes and Effects of Liability Reform: Some Empirical Evidence*. NBER Working Paper 4989. Cambridge, MA: National Bureau of Economic Research.

Carroll, Stephen J., Deborah Hensler, Jennifer Gross, Elizabeth M. Sloss, Allan Abrahamse, and J. Scott Ashwood. 2005. *Asbestos Litigation*. Santa Monica, CA: RAND Institute for Civil Justice.

Cauchon, Dennis. 1999. "The Asbestos Epidemic: An Emerging Catastrophe." *USA Today*, February 8.

Chambliss, W. J. 1964. "A Sociological Analysis of the Law of Vagrancy." *Social Problems* 12(1):67–77.

Charlton, James I. 1998. *Nothing About Us Without Us: Disability Oppression and Empowerment*. Berkeley: University of California Press.

Clemens, Elisabeth S., and James M. Cook. 1999. "Politics and Institutionalism: Explaining Durability and Change." *Annual Review of Sociology* 25:441–466.

Coffee, John C., Jr. 1995. "Class Wars: The Dilemmas of the Mass Tort Class Action." *Columbia Law Review* 95:1343–1465.

Cole, Alyson M. 2007. *The Cult of True Victimhood: From the War on Welfare to the War on Terror*. Palo Alto, CA: Stanford University Press.

Crohley, Steven. 2008. *Regulation and Public Interests: The Possibility of Good Regulatory Government*. Princeton, NJ: Princeton University Press.

CQ Almanac 1994. "Congress Updates Nanny Tax."

CQ Almanac 1999. "Determined Campaign by Advocates for the Disabled Wins Over Divided Congress."

CQ Researcher. 1956. "Social Security for the Disabled." *CQ Researcher plus Archive*. 28 March.

CQ Weekly 1974a. "Workmen's Compensation: Hearings." *CQ Weekly* 32:1441.

CQ Weekly 1974b. "Workmen's Compensation: Hearings." *CQ Weekly* 32:1696.

Damaska, Mirjan R. 1986. *The Faces of Justice and State Authority: A Comparative Approach to the Legal Process*. New Haven, CT: Yale University Press.

DeJong, Gerben. 1979. *The Movement for Independent Living: Origins, Ideology, and Implications for Disability Research*. Boston: Medical Rehabilitation Institute, Tufts-New England Medical Center.

Derthick, Martha. 1979. *Policymaking for Social Security*. Washington: Brookings Institution.

——. 1990. *Agency under Stress: The Social Security Administration in American Government*. Washington, DC: Brookings Institution.

——. 2005. *Up in Smoke: From Legislation to Litigation in Tobacco Politics* (2nd ed.). Washington, DC: Congressional Quarterly Press.

Devins, Neil. 2004. "Is Judicial Policymaking Countermajoritarian?" In Mark Miller and Jeb Barnes (eds.), *Making Policy, Making Law*. Washington, DC: Georgetown University Press, 189–201.

Elliot, Euel, and Susette Talarico. 1991. "An Analysis of Statutory Development: The Correlates of State Activity in Product Liability Legislation." *Policy Studies Review* 10(2/3):61–76.

Engel, David. 1984. "The Oven Bird's Song: Insiders, Outsiders and Personal Injuries in an American Community." *Law and Society Review* 18(4):551–582.

EPA Report. 1985. *Guidance for Controlling Asbestos-Containing Material in Buildings.* Washington, DC: Government Printing Office.

Epp, Charles R. 1998. *The Rights Revolution: Lawyers, Activists, and Supreme Courts in Comparative Perspective.* Chicago: University of Chicago Press.

———. 2009. *Making Rights Real: Activists, Bureaucrats, and the Creation of the Legalistic State.* Chicago: University of Chicago Press.

———. 2010. "Law's Allure and the Power of Path-Dependent Legal Ideas." *Law & Social Inquiry* 35(4):1041–1052.

Epstein, Richard. 1988. The Political Economy of Product Liability Reform. *American Economic Review* 78(2):311–315.

Erkulwater, Jennifer L. 2006. *Disability Rights and the American Social Safety Net.* Ithaca, NY: Cornell University Press.

Esterling, Kevin. 2004. *The Political Economy of Expertise: Information and Efficiency in American National Politics.* Ann Arbor: University of Michigan Press.

Ewick, Patricia, and Susan S. Silbey. 1998. *The Common Place of Law: Stories from Everyday Life, Language and Legal Discourse.* Chicago: University of Chicago Press.

Faler, Bryan. 2012. "Social Security Disability Trust Fund Projected to Run Out of Cash in 2016." *The Washington Post.* 30 May.

Farhang, Sean. 2008. "Public Regulation and Private Lawsuits in the American Separation of Powers System." *American Journal of Political Science* 52(4):821–839.

———. 2010. *The Litigation State: Public Regulation and Private Lawsuits in the United States.* Princeton, NJ: Princeton University Press.

Feeley, Malcolm M., and Edward Rubin. 1998. *Judicial Policy Making and the Modern State: How the Courts Reformed America's Prisons.* New York: Cambridge University Press.

Fenno, Richard F., Jr. 1982. *The United States Senate: A Bicameral Perspective.* Washington, DC: American Enterprise Institute.

Fessler, Pamela. 1984. "Senate Agrees to Limitations on Disabled Worker Reviews." *Congressional Quarterly Weekly Report* 42 (May 26):1253–1254.

Finkelstein, Amy. 2004. "Static and dynamic effects of health policy: Evidence from the vaccine industry." *The Quarterly Journal of Economics* 119(2):527–564.

Fiorina, Maurice. 1989. *Congress: Keystone of the American Establishment.* New Haven, CT: Yale University Press.

Fishback, Price Van Meter, and Shawn Everett Kantor. 2000. *A Prelude to the Welfare State: The Origins of Workers' Compensation.* Chicago: University of Chicago Press.

Fisher, Louis. 2004. "Judicial Finality or an Ongoing Colloquy?" In Mark Miller and Jeb Barnes (eds.), *Making Policy, Making Law: An Interbranch Perspective.* Washington, DC: Georgetown University Press, 153–169.

Fisher, Barbara Loe. 2008. "The Vaccine Injury Compensation Program: A Failed Experiment in Tort Reform?" Statement to the Advisory Commission on Childhood Vaccines. November 18, 2008. http://www.nvic.org/injury-compensation/vaccin-einjury.aspx.

Fitzpatrick, Lawrence. 1990. "The Center for Claims Resolution." *Law and Contemporary Problems* 53(4):13–26.

Forbath, William E. 1991. *Law and the Shaping of the American Labor Movement.* Cambridge, MA: Harvard University Press.

Ford, Richard Thompson. 2011. *Rights gone wrong: how law corrupts the struggle for equality.* New York: Farrar, Strauss & Giroux.

Freeman, Alan D. 1978. "Legitimizing Racial Discrimination through Anti-Discrimination Law." *Minnesota Law Review* 62:1049–1120.

Friedman, Barry. 1993. "Dialogue and Judicial Review." *Michigan Law Review* 91:577–682.

———. 2001. "The History of the Countermajoritarian Difficulty: The Lesson of Lochner." *New York University Law Review* 76:1383–1455.

Frymer, Paul. 2003. "Acting When Elected Officials Won't: Federal Courts and Civil Rights Enforcement in US Labor Relations, 1935–1985." *American Political Science Review* 97(3):483–499.

Fuller, Lon. 1978. "The Forms and Limits of Adjudication." *Harvard Law Review* 92:353–409.

Funk, Robert. 1987. "Disability Rights: From Caste to Class in the Context of Civil Rights." In Alan Gartner (ed.), *Images of the Disabled, Disabling Images.* Westport, CT: Praeger Publishers, 7–30.

Gabel, Peter, and Duncan Kennedy. 1984. "Roll Over Beethoven." *Stanford Law Review* 36(1/2):1–55.

Galanter, Marc. 1974. "Why the 'Haves' Come out Ahead: Speculations on the Limits of Legal Change." *Law and Society Review* 9(1):95–151.

Gash, Alison. 2013. "Under the Gaydar." The Washington Monthly (May/June), http://www.washingtonmonthly.com/mag/may_june 2013.

Gaura, Maria Alicia, and Alan Gathright. 2000. "Eastwood Wins Suit Over ADA But Jury Says Resort Needs Improvements." *The San Francisco Chronicle*, September 30.

Gerring, John. 2004. "What Is a Case Study and What Is It Good For?" *American Political Science Review* 98(2):341–354.

———. 2007. *Case Study Research: Principles and Practices.* New York: Cambridge University Press.

———. 2010. "Causal Mechanisms: Yes, But. . . " *Comparative Political Studies* 43:1499–1526.

Gifford, Donald G. 2010. *Suing the Tobacco and Lead Pigment Industries: Government Litigation as a Public Health Prescription.* Ann Arbor: University of Michigan Press.

Gillman, Howard. 2004. "Martin Shapiro and the Movement from 'Old' Institutionalism to 'New' Institutionalism in Public Law Scholarship." *Annual Review of Political Science* 7:363–382.

Ginsburg, Tom. 2003. *Judicial Review in New Democracies: Constitutional Courts in East Asia.* New York: Cambridge University Press.

Glendon, Mary Ann. 1987. *Abortion and Divorce in Western Law, The Julius Rosenthal Foundation Lectures; 1986.* Cambridge, MA: Harvard University Press.

——. 1991. *Rights Talk: The Impoverishment of Political Discourse.* New York: The Free Press.

Goldstein, Judith, ed. 2001. *Legalization and World Politics.* Cambridge, MA: MIT Press.

Goodale, Mark, and Sally Engle Merry, eds. 2007. *The Practice of Human Rights: Tracking Law between the Global and the Local.* New York: Cambridge University Press.

Gottron, Martha V. 1975. "Workers' Compensation: Federal Role Debated." *CQ Weekly*, August 30, 1975:1883–1886.

——. 1976. "Workers' Compensation: Federal Standards?" *CQ Weekly*, February 28, 1976: 485.

Graber, Mark. 1993. "The Non-Majoritarian Difficulty: Legislative Deference to the Judiciary." *Studies in American Political Development* 7:35–73.

Gusfield, J.R. 1967. "Moral Passage: The Symbolic Process in Public Designations of Deviance." *Social Problems* 15(2):175–188.

Hacker, Jacob S. 2002. *The Divided Welfare State: The Battle over Public and Private Social Benefits in the United States.* New York: Cambridge University Press.

——. 2004. "Privatizing Risk without Privatizing the Welfare State: The Hidden Politics of Social Retrenchment in the United States." *American Political Science Review* 98(2):243–260.

Hahn, Harlan. 1985. "Disability Policy and the Problem of Discrimination." *American Behavioral Scientist* 28(3): 293–318.

Haltom, William, and Michael W. McCann. 2004. *Distorting the Law: Politics, Media, and the Litigation Crisis.* Chicago: University of Chicago Press.

Hanlon, Patrick M. 2006. "An Elegy for the FAIR Act." *Connecticut Insurance Law Journal* 12:517–582.

Hartz, Louis. 1955. *The Liberal Tradition in the United States.* New York: Harcourt Brace.

Hausegger, Laurie, and Laurence Baum. 1999. "Inviting Congressional Action: A Study of Supreme Court Motivations in Statutory Interpretation." *American Journal of Political Science* 43:162–185.

Hazard, Geoffrey. 1969. "Social Justice Through Civil Justice." *University of Chicago Law Review* 36:699–712.

Hensler, Deborah. 2001. "The Role of Multi-Districting in Mass Tort Litigation: An Empirical Investigation." *Seton Hall Law Review* 31:883–906.

Hensler, Deborah R., United States. Dept. of Health and Human Services., and Institute for Civil Justice (U.S.). 1991. *Compensation for Accidental Injuries in the United States.* Santa Monica, CA: Rand, Institute for Civil Justice.

Hensler, Deborah, William L. F. Felstiner, Molly Selvin, and Patricia A. Ebener. 1985. *Asbestos in the Courts: The Challenge of Mass Toxic Torts.* Santa Monica, CA: RAND Institute for Civil Justice.

Hensler, Deborah, R. Nicholas, M. Pace, Bonita Dombey-Moore, Beth Giddens, Jennifer Gross, and Erik K. Moller. 2000. *Class Action Dilemmas; Pursuing Public Goals through Private Gain*. Santa Monica, CA: RAND Institute for Civil Justice.

Hensler, Deborah, Stephen Carroll, Michelle White, and Jennifer Gross. 2001. *Asbestos Litigation in the US: A New Look at an Old Issue*. Santa Monica, CA: RAND Institute for Civil Justice.

Hickox, Stacy A. 2010. "The Underwhelming Impact of the Americans with Disabilities Amendments Act." *University of Baltimore Law Review* 40: 419–492.

Higgins, Sean. 2005. "Senate Asbestos Bill Gains New Life with Provisions Aimed at Democrats; Asbestos Stocks Climb as Specter Sees Deal on Proposed Trust Fund." *Investor's Business Daily*, April 13.

Hirschl, Ran. 2004. *Towards Juristocracy: The Origins and Consequences of the New Constitutionalism*. Cambridge, MA: Harvard University Press.

——. 2008. "The Judicialization of Politics." In Keith Whittington, Daniel Keleman, and Gregory Caldeira (eds.), *The Oxford Handbook of Law and Politics*. New York: Oxford University Press, 119–141.

Horowitz, Donald J. 1977. *The Courts and Social Policy*. Washington, DC: Brookings Institution.

House Committee on Education and Labor, Hearings on National Workers' Compensation Act of 1975, 94th Cong., 2nd Sess., 1976 ("House Hearings 1976").

House Report. 1986. *Asbestos Hazard Emergency Response Act of 1986, H.R. Rep. No. 763, 99th Congress, 2nd Sess. 14*. Washington, DC: Government Printing Office.

Howard, Christopher. 1997. *The Hidden Welfare State: Tax Expenditures and Social Policy in the United States*. Princeton, NJ: Princeton University Press.

——. 2008. *The Welfare State Nobody Knows: Debunking Myths about U.S. Social Policy*. Princeton, NJ: Princeton University Press.

Howard, Philip K. 1995. *The Death of Common Sense: How Law Is Suffocating America*. Thorndike, ME: G. K. Hall.

Hoyer, Steny. 2002. "Not Exactly What We Intended." *The Washington Post*, January 20.

Hughes, Robert. 1994. *Culture of Complaint: The Fraying of America*. New York: Warner Books.

Ignagni, Joseph and James Meernik. 1994. "Explaining Congressional Attempts to Reverse Supreme Court Decisions." *Political Research Quarterly* 47:353–371.

Institute of Medicine (IOM). 2006. *Asbestos: Selected Cancers (Consensus Report)*. Washington, D.C.: Institution of Medicine.

Kagan, Robert A. 1991. "Adversarial Legalism and American Government." *Journal of Policy Analysis & Management*. 10(3):369–406.

——. 1994. Do Lawyers Cause Adversarial Legalism? *Law and Social Inquiry* 19(1):1–62.

——. 1997. "Should Europe Worry About Adversarial Legalism?" *Oxford Journal of Legal Studies* 17:165–183.

———. 2001. *Adversarial Legalism: The American Way of Law*. Cambridge, MA: Harvard University Press.

———. 2007. "The Americanization of European Law?" *Regulation & Governance* 1:99–120.

Kahneman, Daniel, and Amos Tversky. 1979. "Prospect Theory: An Analysis of Decision Under Risk." *Econometrica* 47:263–292.

Kakalik, James S., Michael G. Shanley, William L. F. Felstiner, and Patricia A. Ebener. 1983. *Costs of Asbestos Litigation*. Santa Monica, CA: RAND Institute for Civil Justice.

Kapiszewski, Diana, Gordon Silverstein, and Robert A. Kagan, eds. 2013. *Consequential Courts: Judicial Roles in Global Perspective*. New York: Cambridge University Press.

Katzmann, Robert A. 1986. *Institutional Disability: The Saga of Transportation Policy for the Disabled*. Washington, DC: Brookings Institution.

Keck, Thomas M. 2009. "Beyond Backlash: Assessing the Impact of Judicial Decisions of LGBT Rights." *Law & Society Review* 43(1):151–186.

Kelemen, R. Daniel. 2006. "Suing for Europe: Adversarial Legalism and European Governance." *Comparative Political Studies* 39(1): 101–127.

———. 2011. *Eurolegalism: The Transformation of Law and Regulation in the European Union*. New York: Cambridge University Press.

Kirchhoff. Sue. 1999a. "Health: Aid for Working Disabled Snags Again as Gramm Balks Over Tax Implications" *CQ Weekly*, May 29, 1270.

———. 1999b. "Social Policy: Disability Bill's Advocates Rewrite the Book on Lobbying." *CQ Weekly*, November 20, 2762.

———. 1999c. "Social Policy: House is Left to Find Offsets a Senate Passes Bill Expanding Health Benefits for Working Disabled." *CQ Weekly,* June 19, 1999, 1460.

Kingdon, John W. 1999. *America the Unusual*. Boston: St. Martin's.

———. 2011. *Agendas, Alternatives, and Public Policies (2nd Updated Ed.)*. Boston: Longman.

Klarman, Michael J. 1994. "How *Brown* Changed Race Relations: The Backlash Thesis." *The Journal of American History* 81:81–118.

———. 2004. *From Jim Crow to Civil Rights: The Supreme Court and the Struggle for Racial Equality*. New York: Oxford University Press.

———. 2012. *From the Closet to the Altar: Courts, Backlash, and the Struggle for Same-Sex Marriage*. New York: Oxford University Press.

Knight, J. 2005. "Asbestos Stocks Hostage to Fate of Legislation on Liability." *Washington Post*, July 25.

Koniak, Susan P. 1995. "Feasting While the Widow Weeps: *Georgine v. Amchem Products, Inc.*" *Cornell Law Review* 80:1045–1158.

Krent, Harold J., and Scott Morris. 2013. *Achieving Greater Consistence in Social Security Disability Adjudication: An Empirical Study and Suggested Reforms*. Washington DC: Administrative Conference of the United States, April 3, 2013.

Krieger, Linda Hamilton, ed. 2003. *Backlash Against the ADA: Reinterpreting Disability Rights.* Ann Arbor: University of Michigan Press.

Kritzer, Herbert M., and Susan S. Silbey, eds. 2003. *In Litigation: Do the Haves Still Come Out Ahead?* Palo Alto, CA: Stanford University Press.

Lando, Mordechai E., and Aaron Krute. 1976. "Disability Insurance: Program Issues and Research." *Social Security Bulletin* 39 (October):3–17.

Lang, Robert D. 1985. "Danger in the Classroom: Asbestos in American Public Schools." *Columbia Journal of Environmental Law* 11:111–130.

Leone, Robert A. 1986. *Who Profits: Winners, Losers and Government Regulation.* New York: Basic Books.

Levin, Martin A., and Mary Bryna Sanger. 2000. *After the cure: managing AIDS and other public health crises.* Lawrence, KS: University of Kansas Press.

Lilienfeld, D. E., J. S. Mandel, P. Coin, and L. M. Schuman. 1988. "Projections of Asbestos Related Diseases in the United States, 1985–2009." *British Journal of Industrial Medicine* 45:283–291.

Longmore, Paul. 2003. *Why I Burned My Book and Other Essays on Disability.* Philadelphia: Temple University Press.

Lovell, George. 2003. *Legislative Deferrals: Statutory Ambiguity, Judicial Powers, and American Democracy.* New York: Cambridge University Press.

Lowi, Theodore. 1964. "American Business, Public Policy, Case Studies and Political Theory." *World Politics* 61(4):677–715.

———. 1972. "Four Systems of Policy, Politics, and Choice." *Public Administrative Review* 32: 298–310.

Lupia, Arthur, and Matthew D. McCubbins. 1994. "Learning From Oversight: Fire Alarms and Police Patrols Reconstructed." *Journal of Institutional and Theoretical Economics* 150: 203–210.

MacIntyre, Alasdair C. 1981. *After Virtue: A Study in Moral Theory.* Notre Dame, IN: University of Notre Dame Press.

Mahoney, James, and Kathleen Thelen, eds. 2010. *Explaining Institutional Change: Ambiguity, Agency, & Power.* New York: Cambridge University Press.

Mann, Thomas E., and Norm J. Ornstein. 2012. *It's Even Worse Than It Looks: How the American Constitutional System Collided with the New Politics of Extremism.* New York: Basic Books.

Marshall, Thomas R. 1989. *Public Opinion and the Supreme Court.* Boston: Unwin Hyman.

Marx, Karl. 1978. "On the Jewish Question." In Robert C. Tucker (ed.), *The Marx Engels Reader.* New York: Norton Press, 26–52.

Mashaw, Jerry L. 1983. *Bureaucratic Justice: Managing Social Security Disability Claims.* New Haven, CT: Yale University Press.

Mashaw, Jerry L., and Virginia P. Reno. 1996. *Balancing Security and Opportunity: The Challenge of Disability Income Policy.* Washington, DC: National Academy of Social Insurance.

Mather, Lynn. 1998. "Theorizing about Trial Courts: Lawyers, Policymaking, and Tobacco Litigation." *Law & Social Inquiry* 23(4): 897–936.

Mayhew, David. 1974. *Congress: The Electoral Connection*. New Haven, CT: Yale University Press.

McCann, Michael. 1994. *Rights at Work: Pay Equity Reform and the Politics of Legal Mobilization*. Chicago: University of Chicago Press.

McCubbins, Matthew, and Thomas Schwartz. 1984. "Congressional Oversight Overlooked: Police Patrols versus Fire Alarms." *American Journal of Political Science* 28: 165–179.

McGovern, Francis. 1989. "Resolving Mature Mass Tort Litigation." *Boston Law Review* 69:659–694.

Mealey's Litigation Report: Asbestos Bankruptcy. 2005. "CRMC to Stop Accepting Reports Prepared by Silica MDL Doctors." E-Mail Bulletin, September 14.

Melnick, R. Shep. 1983. *Regulation and the Courts: The Case of the Clean Air Act*. Washington, DC: Brookings Institution Press.

———. 1994. *Between the Lines: Interpreting Welfare Rights*. Washington, DC: The Brookings Institution.

———. 1998. "Strange Bedfellows Make Normal Politics: An Essay." *Duke Environmental Law & Policy* 9:75–94.

Merry, Sally Engle. 2005. *Human Rights & Gender Violence: Translating International Law into Local Justice*. Chicago: University of Chicago Press.

Mettler, Suzanne, and Joe Soss. 2004. "The Consequences of Public Policy for Democratic Citizenship: Bridging Policy Studies and Mass Politics." *Perspectives on Politics* 2(1): 55–73.

Miller, Lisa C. 2010. "The Invisible Black Victim: How American Federalism Perpetuates Racial Inequality in Criminal Justice." *Law & Society Review* 44(3/4): 805–842.

Miller, Mark C. 1992. "Congressional Committees and the Federal Courts: A Neo-Institutional Perspective." *Western Political Quarterly* 45:949–970.

Miller, Mark C., and Jeb Barnes, eds. 2004. *Making Policy, Making Law: An Interbranch Perspective*. Washington, DC: Georgetown University Press.

Mishler, William, and Reginald Sheehan. 1993. "The Supreme Court as a Countermajoritarian Institution? The Impact of Public Opinion on the Court." *American Political Science Review* 87:87–101.

Nagareda, Richard A. 2007. *Mass Torts in an Age of Settlement*. Chicago: University of Chicago Press.

Neustadt, Richard E., and Harvey V. Fineberg. 1978. *The Swine Flu Affair: Decision-Making on a Slippery Disease*. Washington, DC: The National Academies Press.

Nicholson, W. J., G. Perkel, and I. J. Selikoff. 1982. "Occupational Exposure to Asbestos: Population at Risk and Projected Mortality 1980–2030." *American Journal of Industrial Medicine* 3:259–311.

NIOSH (National Institute for Occupational Safety and Health). 2003. *Work-Related Lung Disease Surveillance Report 2002*. Washington, DC: NIOSH.

——. 2008. *Asbestos Fibers and Other Elongated Mineral Particles: State of Science and Roadmap for Research*. Washington, DC: Centers for Disease Control and Prevention and National Institute for Occupational Safety and Health, US Department of Health and Human Services.

Nonet, Philippe. 1969. *Administrative Justice: Advocacy and Change in a Government Agency*. New York: Russell Sage Foundation.

O'Connell, Jeffrey. 1979. *The Litigaiton Lottery: Only Lawyers Win*. New York: The Free Press.

O'Day, Bonnie, and Monroe Berkowitz. 2001. "Disability Benefit Programs: Can We Improve the Return-to-Work Record?" In Gary L. Albrecht, Katherine D. Seelman, and Michael Bury (eds.), *Handbook of Disability Studies*. Thousand Oaks, CA: Sage Publications, 633–641.

Olsen, Henry, and Jon Flugstad. 2009. "The Forgotten Entitlements." *Policy Review* 153: 41–54.

Olson, Mancur. 1965. *The Logic of Collective Action: Public Goods and the Theory of Groups*. Cambridge, MA: Harvard University Press.

Orren, Karen, and Stephen Skowronek. 2004. *The Search for American Political Development*. New York: Cambridge University Press.

Paletta, Damian. 2011. "Disability-Benefits System Faces Review." *The Wall Street Journal*, December 15.

Paletta, Damian, and Dione Searcey. 2011. "Two Lawyers Strike Gold in U.S. Disability System." *The Wall Street Journal*, December 22.

Pan, Xue-lei, Howard W. Day, Wei Wang, Laurel A. Beckett, and Mark B. Schenkar. 2005. "Residential Proximity to Naturally Occurring Asbestos and Mesothelioma Cases in California." *American Journal of Respiratory and Critical Care Medicine* 172(8):1019–1025.

Patashnik, Eric M. 2000. *Putting Trust in the US budget: Federal Trust Funds and the Politics of Commitment, Theories of Institutional Design*. New York: Cambridge University Press.

Payne, James L. 1997. "Welfare Cuts?" *The American Enterprise* 8:38–40.

Peretti, Terri Jennings. 1999. *In Defense of a Political Court*. Princeton, NJ: Princeton University Press.

Peters, Gerhard. "Presidential Vetoes." *The American Presidency Project*. Ed. John T. Woolley and Gerhard Peters. Santa Barbara, CA: University of California. 1999–2013, http://www.presidency.ucsb.edu/data/vetoes.php.

Peterson, Mark A. 1990. "Giving Money Away: Comparative Comments on Claims Resolution Facilities." *Law and Contemporary Problems* 54(4):113–136.

Pierson, Paul. 1993. "When Effect Becomes Cause: Policy Feedback and Political Change." *World Politics* 45(4):595–628.

——. 1994. *Dismantling the Welfare state?: Reagan, Thatcher, and the Politics of Retrenchment*. New York: Cambridge University Press.

——. 2004. *Politics in Time: History, Institutions, and Social Analysis.* Princeton, NJ: Princeton University Press.

Pierson, Paul, and Theda Skocpol. 2002. "Historical Institutionalism in Contemporary Political Science." In Ira Katznelson and Helen V. Milner (eds.), *Political Science: State of the Discipline.* New York: Norton, 693–721.

Polsby, Nelson W. 1986. *Congress and the Presidency* (4th Ed.). Englewood Cliffs, NJ: Prentice Hall.

Powe, Lucas A., Jr. 2000. *The Warren Court and American Politics.* Cambridge, MA: Belknap Press.

Rabkin, Jeremy. 1989. *Judicial Compulsions: How Public Law Distorts Public Policy.* New York: Basic Books.

Reno, Virginia P., Elisa Walker, and Thomas N. Bethell. 2013. "Social Security Disability Insurance: Action Needed to Address Finances." *Social Security Brief* 41. Washington DC: National Academy of Social Insurance.

Resnik, Judith. 1982. "Managerial Judges." *Harvard Law Review* 96: 374–448.

——. 2000. "Trial as Error, Jurisdiction as Injury: Transforming the Meaning of Article III." *Harvard Law Review* 113:924–1036.

Reitze Jr, Arnold W. 1985. "Federal compensation for vaccination induced injuries." *Boston College Environmental Affairs Law Review* 13: 169.

Rodgers, Daniel T. 1998. *Atlantic Crossings: Social Politics in a Progressive Age.* Cambridge, MA: Harvard University Press.

Roggli, Victor L., Tim D. Oury, and Thomas A. Sporn, eds. 2004. *Pathology of Asbestos-Associated Diseases.* New York: Springer.

Rosenberg, Gerald. 1991. *The Hollow Hope: Can Courts Bring About Social Change?* Chicago: University of Chicago Press.

——. 1992. "Judicial Independence and the Reality of Political Power." *Review of Politics* 54:369–398.

Russell, Sabin. 2000. "When Polio Vaccine Backfired." *The San Francisco Chronicle,* April 25.

Sabel, Charles F., and William Simon. 2004. "Destabilization Rights: How Public Law Succeeds." *Harvard Law Review* 117:1015–1101.

Sandler, Ross, and David Schoenbrod. 2003. *Democracy by Decree: What Happens when the Courts Run Government.* New Haven, CT: Yale University Press.

Sarat, Austin. 1990. "Law Is All Over: Power, Resistance and the Legal Consciousness of the Welfare Poor." *The Yale Journal of Law and Humanities* 2(2): 343–379.

Schattschneider, E. E. 1935. *Politics, Pressures, and the Tariff: A Study of Free Private Enterprise in Pressure Politics, as Shown in the 1929–1930 Revision of the Tariff.* New York: Prentice Hall.

Sheingate, Adam. 2006. "Structure and Opportunity: Committee Jurisdiction and Issue Attention in Congress." *American Journal of Political Science* 50(4):844–859.

Scheingold, Stuart. 2004. *The Politics of Rights* (2nd Ed.) Ann Arbor: University of Michigan Press.

Schickler, Eric. 2001. *Disjointed Pluralism: Institutional Innovation and the Development of the U.S. Congress.* Princeton, NJ: Princeton University Press.

Schlozman, Kay, and John Tierney. 1986. *Organized Interests and American Democracy.* New York: Harper and Row.

Schroeder, Elinor. 1986. "Legislative and Judicial Responses to the Inadequacy of Compensation for Occupational Diseases." *Law & Contemporary Problems* 49:151–182.

Schuck, Peter H. 1986. *Agent Orange on Trial: Mass Toxic Disasters in the Courts.* Cambridge, MA: Belknap Press.

——. 1992. "The Worst Should Go First: Deferral Registries in Asbestos Litigation." *Judicature* 75:1–13.

Schur, Lisa, and Meera Adya. 2013. "Sidelined or mainstreamed? Political participation and attitudes of people with disabilities in the United States." *Social Science Quarterly* 94(3): 811–839.

Schur, Lisa A., and Douglas L. Kruse. 2000. "What Determines Voter Turnout? Lessons from Citizens with Disabilities." *Social Science Quarterly* 81(2):571–587.

Shepsle, Kenneth A. 1992. "Congress Is a 'They' Not an 'It': Legislative Intent as Oxymoron." *International Review of Law and Economics* 12: 239–256.

Shklar, Judith. 1964. *Legalism: Laws, Morals, and Political Trials.* Cambridge, MA: Harvard University Press.

Selikoff, I., J. Churg, and E. C. Hammond. 1965. "The Occurrence of Asbestos among Insulation Workers in the United States." *Annals of the New York Academy of Science* 32:139–155.

Sengupta, Ishita, Marjorie Baldwin, and Virginia Reno. 2011. *Workers' Compensation: Benefits, Coverage and Costs, 2011.* Washington, DC: National Academy of Social Insurance.

Shapiro, Martin. 1964a. "Political Jurisprudence." *Kentucky Law Journal* 52:294–345.

——. 1964b. *Law and Politics in the Supreme Court: New Approaches to Political Jurisprudence.* New York: Free Press.

——. 1966. *Freedom of Speech: The Supreme Court and Judicial Review.* Englewood Cliffs, NJ: Prentice Hall.

——. 1968. *The Supreme Court and Administrative Agencies.* New York: Free Press.

——. 1993. Public Law and Judicial Politics. In Ada W. Finifter, (ed.), *Political Science: The State of the Discipline II.* Washington, DC: American Political Science Association, 365–381.

Shapiro, Martin, and Alec Stone Sweet. 2002. *On Law, Politics and Judicialization.* New York: Oxford University Press.

Sikkink, Kathryn. 2011. *The Justice Cascade: How Human Rights Prosecutions Are Changing World Politics.* New York: W. W. Norton & Company.

Silverstein, Gordon. 2009. *Law's Allure: How Law Shapes, Constrains, Saves, and Kills Politics*. Cambridge: Cambridge University Press.

Skocpol, Theda. 1992. *Protecting Soldiers and Mothers: The Political Origins of Social Policy in the United States*. Cambridge, MA: Belknap Press.

———. 2003. *Diminished Democracy: From Membership to Management in American Civic Life*. Norman: University of Oklahoma Press.

Soss, Joe. 2002. *Unwanted Claims: The Politics of Participation in the U.S. Welfare System*. Ann Arbor: University of Michigan Press.

Soss, Joe, and Sanford F. Schram. 2007. "A Public Transformed? Welfare Reform as Policy Feedback." *American Political Science Review* 101:111–127.

Stapleton, David, Gina Livermore, Craig Thornton, Bonnie O'Day, Robert Weathers, Krista Harrison, So O'Neil, Emily Sama Martin, David Wittenburg, and Debra Wright. 2008. *Ticket to Work at the Crossroads: A Solid Foundation with an Uncertain Future*. Washington, DC: Mathematica Policy Research.

Stapleton, David C., Bonnie L. O'Day, Gina A. Livermore, and Andrew J. Imparato. 2006. "Dismantling the Poverty Trap: Disability Policy for the Twenty-first Century." *Milbank Quarterly* 84(4): 701–732.

Steinmo, Sven, and John Watts. 1995. "It's the Institutions, Stupid! Why Comprehensive National Insurance Always Fails in America." *Journal of Health Politics, Policy and Law* 20:329–423.

Stern, Seth. 2005. "Asbestos Bill Takes Big Step in Senate." *CQ Weekly*, May 27, 1448.

———. 2006a. "Asbestos Bill Set Back on Point of Order." *CQ Weekly*, February 21, 492.

———. 2006b. Difficult Sticking Points on Asbestos. *CQ Weekly*, February 13, 4.

Stern, May Elizabeth, and Lucy P. Allen. 2013. "Asbestos Payments Pulled Back Slightly in 2012, although Average Payments per Resolved Claim Remained High." *Insight in Economics* June 3, 2013 (NERA).

Stiglitz, Joseph, Jonathan Orzag, and Peter Orzag. 2002. *The Impact of Asbestos Liabilities on Workers in Bankruptcy Firms*. Sebago Associates. Available at www.instiueforlegalreform.com.

Stone, Deborah A. 1984. *The Disabled State, Health, Society, and Policy*. Philadelphia: Temple University Press.

Streeck, Wolfgang, and Kathleen Thelen. 2005. "Introduction: Institutional Change in Advanced Political Economies." In William Streeck and Kathleen Thelen (eds.), *Beyond Continuity*. New York: Oxford University Press.

Strolovitch, Dara Z. 2007. *Affirmative Advocacy: Race, Class, and Gender in Interest Group Politics*. Chicago: University of Chicago Press.

Sugarman, Steven D. 1989. *Doing Away with Personal Injury Law: New Compensation Mechanisms for Victims, Consumers, and Business*. New York: Quorum Books.

Sutton, John R., Frank Dobbin, John W. Meyer, and W. Richard Scott. 1994. "The Legalization of the Workplace." *American Journal of Sociology* 99: 944–971.

Swank, Drew. 2012. "An Argument against Administrative Acquiescence." *North Dakota Law Review* 88:1–20.

Swanson, Jeffrey, Scott Burris, Kathryn Moss and Michael Ullman. 2011. "Justice Disparities: Does the ADA Enforcement System Treat People with Psychiatric Disabilities Fairly?" *Maryland Law Review*: 66:94–139.

Sweet, Alex Stone. 1999. "Judicialization and the Construction of Governance." *Comparative Political Studies* 32(2): 147–184.

———. 2000. *Governing with Judges: Constitutional Politics of Europe*. New York: Oxford University Press.

Tanouye, Elyse. 1998. "The Vaccine Business Gets a Shot in the Arm." *The Wall Street Journal*. February 25, B1.

Tate, C. Neal, and Torbjörn Vallinder. 1995. *The Global Expansion of Judicial Power*. New York: New York University Press.

Ten Broek, Jacobus. 1966. "The right to live in the world: The disabled in the law of torts." *California Law Review* (1966): 841–919.

Teubner, Gunther. 1987. "Concepts, Aspects, Limits, Solutions." In Teubner (ed.), *Juridification of Social Spheres: A Comparative Analysis of Labour Corporate Government: Trust and Social Welfare Law*. New York: de Gruyter, 3–48.

Taylor, Charles. 1998. "The Dangers of Soft Despotism." In Amitai Etzioni (ed.), *The Essential Communitarian Reader*. Lanham, MD: Rowman & Littlefield, 47–54.

Thelen, Kathleen. 1999, "Historical Institutionalism in Comparative Politics." *Annual Review of Political Science* 2:369–404.

———. 2003. "How Institutions Evolve: Insights from Comparative Historical Research." In James Mahoney and Dietrich Rueschemeyer (eds.), *Comparative Historical Analysis in the Social Sciences*. New York: Cambridge University Press.

Timmerman, Luke. 2011. "Merck's Julie Gerberding, Former CDC Director, on the Future of Vaccines." *Xconomy*, June 24, 2011. http://www.xconomy.com/national/2011/06/24/mercks-julie-gerberding-former-cdc-director-on-the-future-of-vaccines/

Tushnet, Mark. 1984. "An Essay on Rights." *Texas Law Review* 62:1363–1403.

Tweedale, Geoffrey. 2000. *Magic Mineral to Killer Dust: Turner & Newall and the Asbestos Hazard*. New York: Oxford University Press.

Virta, Robert. 2003. *Worldwide Asbestos Supply and Consumption Trends from 1900 to 2000*. Washington DC: U.S. Geological Survey.

Vogel, Steven K. 1996. *Freer Markets, More Rules: Regulatory Reform in Advanced Industrial Countries*. NY: Cornell University Press.

Vinke, Harriet, and Ton Wilthagen. 1992. *The Non-Mobilization of Law by Asbestos Victims in the Netherlands: Social Insurance versus Tort-Based Compensation*. Amsterdam: Hugo Sinzheimer Institute, University of Amsterdam.

Waldron, Jeremy. 1987. *'Nonsense upon Stilts': Bentham, Burke, and Marx on the Rights of Man*. New York: Methuen.

Walker, Jack L., Jr. 1991. *Mobilizing Interest Groups in America: Patrons, Professions and Social Movements*. Ann Arbor: University of Michigan Press.

Walker, Alexander M., Jeanne E. Loughlin, Emily R. Friedlander, Kenneth J. Rothman, and Nancy A. Dreyer. 1983. "Projections of Asbestos-Related Diseases." *Journal of Occupational Medicine* 25:409–425.

"War Hero Regains Disability Benefit." 1983. *The New York Times.* July 13, 1983.

Weinstein, James. 1981. *The Corporate Ideal in the Liberal State, 1900–1918.* Westport, CT: Greenwood Press.

Weller, Nicholas, and Jeb Barnes. 2014. *Finding Pathways: Mixed-Methods Research for Studying Causal Mechanisms.* New York: Cambridge University Press.

White, G. Edward. 1985. *Tort Law in America: An Intellectual History.* Expanded ed. New York: Oxford University Press.

White, Michelle J. 2002. "Why the Asbestos Genie Won't Stay in the Bankruptcy Bottle." *University of Cincinnati Law Review* 70:1319–1340.

Whittington, Keith. 2001. "The Road Not Taken: Dred Scott, Judicial Authority and Political Questions." *Journal of Politics* 63(2):365–391.

Willging, Thomas E. 1985. *Asbestos Case Management: Pretrial and Trial Procedures.* Washington, DC: Government Printing Office.

Wilson, James Q. 1973. *Political Organizations.* New York: Basic Books.

——. 1989. *Bureaucracy: What Government Agencies Do and Why They Do It.* New York: Basic Books.

Witt, John Fabian. 2006. "Bureaucratic Legalism, American Style: Private Bureaucratic Legalism and the Governance of the Tort System." *DePaul Law Review* 56: 261.

——. 2004. *The Accidental Republic: Crippled Workingmen, Destitute Widows, and the Remaking of American Law.* Cambridge, MA: Harvard University Press.

Wolfe, Jeffrey S. 2013. "Civil Justice Reform in Social Security Administration." *Journal of the National Association of Administrative Law Judiciary* 33(1):137–213.

"Work or Die." 1983. *The New York Times.* May 23, 1983.

World Health Organization. 2006. Elimination of Asbestos-Related Diseases. Available at WHO/SDE/OEH/06.03.

CASES CITED

Amchem Products, Inc., et al. v. George Windsor, et al., 521 U.S. 591, 716 (1997).

Beshada v. Johns-Mansville Products Corp., 90 N.J. 191 (N.J. 1983).

Borel v. Fibreboard Paper Products Corporation, 493 F.2d 1076 (5th Cir. 1973) rehearing and rehearing en banc denied, 493 F.2d at 1109, certiorari denied 419 U.S. 869 (1974).

Brown v. Board of Education, 347 U.S. 483 (1954).

Bruesewtiz v. Wyeth, 526 U.S. _____ (2011), (Docket No. 09-152).

Buckley v. Valeo, 424 U.S. 1 (1976).

CSX Transportation, Inc. v. Williams, 608 S.E.2d 208 (Ga. 2005).

Daubert v. Merrell Dow Pharmaceuticals, Inc., 509 U.S. 579 (1993).

Elmore v. Owens-Illinois, Inc., 673 S.W.2d 434 (Mo. S. Ct. 1984).

Escola v. Coca Cola Bottling Co. (1944) 24 Cal.2d 453.

Gottsdanker v. Cutter Laboratories, 182 Cal. App. 2d 602 (Cal. App.1 Dist., July 12, 1960).

Hardy v. Johns-Manville Sales Corporation, 681 F.2d 334 (5th Cir. 1982).

Helene Curtis Industries v. Pruitt 385 F.2d 862 (1968).

Holdampf v. A.C. & S., Inc. (In the Matter of New York City Asbestos Litigation), 5 N.Y.3d 486 (Court of Appeals of New York 2005).

INA v. Forty-Eight Insulation, Inc., 633 F.2d 1212 (6th Cir. 1980).

In re Asbestos and Asbestos Material Products Liability Litigation, 431 F. Supp. 906 (JPML 1977).

In re Combustion Engineering, 391 F.3d 190 (3rd Cir. 2004).

In re Report of the Advisory Group, 1993 WL 30497 (D. Me. Feb 1, 1993).

In re USG Corp., 290 B.R. 223 (Bankr. D. Del. 2003).

Johnson v. American Cyanamid Co., 718 P.2d 1318 (1986).

Karjala v. Johns-Manville Products Corporation, 523 F.2d 155 (8th Cir. 1975).

Kearl v. Lederle Laboratories, 172 Cal. App. 3d 812, 218 Cal. Rptr. 453 (1985).

Loving v. Virginia, 388 U.S. 1 (1967).

MacPherson v. Buick Motor Co., 217 N.Y. 382, 111 N.E. 1050 (1916).

Moran v. Johns-Manville Sales Corporation, 691 F.2d 811 (6th Cir. 1982).

Norfolk & Western Railway Co. v. Ayers, 538 U.S. 135 (2003).

Olivio v. Owens-Illinois, Inc., 895 A.2d 1143 (N.J. 2006).

Ortiz et al. v. Fibreboard et al., 527 U.S. 815 (1999).

Reyes v. Wyeth, 498 F.2d 1294 (1974).

Roe v. Wade, 410 U.S. 113 (1973).

Sophia v. Owens-Corning Fiberglass, 601 N.W.2d 627 (Wis. 1999).

Stromsodt v. Parke Davis, 257 F. Supp. 991 (1966).

Sullivan v. Zebley, 493 U.S. 521 (1990).

Sutton v. United Air Lines, 527 U.S. 471 (1999).

Toner v. Lederle Laboratories, 828 F.2d 510 (1987).

United States v. Windsor, 570 U.S. _____ (2013) (Docket No. 12–307).

Subject Index